INTRODUCTION TO DIFFERENTIAL EQUATIONS

ALLYN AND BACON, INC., BOSTON, 1962

COLLEGE MATHEMATICS SERIES

INTRODUCTION TO

DIFFERENTIAL

EQUATIONS

RICHARD A. MOORE

Department of Mathematics, Carnegie Institute of Technology

PREFACE

This book is essentially a text for the one-semester undergraduate course in differential equations. As a rule, this is the introductory course taken by students of science, engineering, and mathematics who have completed the traditional calculus sequence. Indeed, the author has tested the substance of this book in just such a course.

The aim of this book is to provide more than a catalogue of explicit solution techniques. The hope is that even the beginning student will reach a point where he can say something useful about the solutions of a differential equation whether it is solvable or not. This is in direct response to the needs of scientists and mathematicians who simply cannot prosper on a knowledge that is restricted to solvable cases or even linear cases. In fact, then, this is an introduction to a theorizing technique for the discussion of differential equations. This technique depends in varying degrees on mathematical theory, geometric inferences, argument by analogy with solvable cases and, in applications, the requirements of the physical situation. It is clear from this that such a technique does not lend itself well to systematic exposition. Rather, it is presented here by illustrative examples found in Chapters 3, 6, and 7. Not all of the applications, however, are of this "unsolvable" type.

The remaining chapters form a unified discussion of explicit solutions methods, fundamental theory, and qualitative geometric arguments in preparation for the above aim. The substance of these chapters is that of a somewhat shortened, but standard, introductory course in differential equations. In order to relate the explicit methods more closely to both the theory and the applications, these methods are made to lead directly to solutions of initial-value problems rather than to general solutions. For example, the definite integral is employed to the exclusion of the indefinite integral in solving first-order initial-value problems, and the Laplace transform is consistently used for all linear equations and systems of equations with constant coefficients. The use of the Laplace transform has the additional advantage of leading in a natural way to the idea and form of integral representations of solutions even in the most general linear case. It is important to note, however, that the Laplace transform is given no independent interest here; therefore, the essential results are given without proof.

Problems of varying difficulty are given with each section. Often an alternative to the method given in the text is developed in a short sequence of problems. Two sections (on undetermined coefficients) have no text and are entirely in the form of problems. The reader is to develop this technique himself by working a sequence of problems of increasing difficulty and generality.

R. A. M.

CONTENTS

INTRODUCTION TO DIFFERENTIAL EQUATIONS

1

FIRST-ORDER EQUATIONS

▶ 1.1 INTRODUCTION

A first-order differential equation has for us the standard form

$$y' = f(x, y). \tag{1.11}$$

In some instances, an equation may be presented, or studied, in differential form,

$$M(x, y)\, dx + N(x, y)\, dy = 0,$$

or occasionally in implicit form

$$F(x, y, y') = 0,$$

but the latter forms are of less interest here, and normally are equivalent to (1.11). The obvious problem posed by (1.11) is the finding of solutions, that is, functions which satisfy the equation identically. Specifically, a *solution* of (1.11) is a function $y(x)$, defined on an interval $a < x < b$, such that

$$y'(x) \equiv f(x, y(x))$$

holds for $a < x < b$. For example, e^x is a solution of

$$y' = y$$

for $-\infty < x < +\infty$ since, for all x,

$$(e^x)' \equiv e^x.$$

Similarly, the function $\dfrac{1}{1 - x^2}$ is a solution of

$$y' = 2xy^2$$

for $-1 < x < 1$, as is easily verified.

How we obtained these solutions in these examples is a matter of certain formal solution techniques which we shall describe shortly. It is important, however, to place solution techniques of any nature in proper perspective by observing that a function is (or is not) a solution only according as is satisfies (or does not satisfy) the equation at hand. Along with this, we must remember that a function may exist while a formula for the functional values does not. This is the status of solutions of many differential equations—solutions exist, but no manipulative technique exists to display them. It is natural that purely mathematical interests should center on such equations, and it is not surprising that the most interesting and pressing modern applications rest on equations of the same intractable type.

For a truly useful knowledge of the subject, then, the obvious problem of finding solutions in the sense of displayed formulas is too narrow; this must be, at best, an introduction to and a part of the deeper problem of saying something useful about solutions in every case. For example, we are not able to "solve" the equation

$$y' = x^2y^2 + 1. \tag{1.12}$$

Nonetheless, as a consequence of a general theory, which we develop later, solutions do exist. Given any solution $y(x)$ we can see from the equation that $y'(x)$ is positive; thus, $y(x)$ is increasing. Further, we can say that $y'(x)$, that is to say, $x^2y^2(x) + 1$, is also an increasing function of x for $y(x) \geq 0$. With now only a little more information, say, the value of $y(x)$ at one point, we could produce a very plausible sketch of the graph of this solution which is a convex, increasing function. This is what is meant by useful information, and it is by no means all that can be said of (1.12).

What we have to say in the first six sections concerns solvable cases. Since here solutions can be displayed, we do not need a theorem

2

which asserts that each of a large class of differential equations has solutions. Since for a solvable equation we can show directly that there is only one solution which satisfies some side condition, a general uniqueness theorem is not necessary. The theory is a necessity for our deeper aims, and it will be stated and proved in later sections. The ideas of the theory, however, can be simply and concisely stated; moreover, they form a useful guide and principle even in routine solvable cases. It is not unnatural to give these ideas a physical meaning and, indeed, to derive them from physics. Typically, a physical experiment may be represented mathematically as a problem in differential equations; e.g., the first-order equation

$$\frac{dv}{dt} = -32,$$

together with the initial condition $v(t_0) = 50$, describes (ignoring friction among other things) the experiment of throwing a ball from the surface of the earth at time t_0 with velocity 50 ft/sec. Now, a well-posed experiment has three obvious properties:

(*i*) Something happens.

(*ii*) Only one thing happens; that is, the experiment can be repeated under the same conditions with the same results.

(*iii*) Small variations in initial state, physical components, or any other physical parameters produce only small variations in results.

These hardly need comment, but from them we infer that a mathematical problem which purports to describe a well-posed experiment must be well posed in the mathematical sense; namely,

(*i*) A solution exists.

(*ii*) The solution is unique.

(*iii*) The solution is continuous in all parameters of the problem.

It is now a simple matter to describe concisely the fundamental theory of differential equations. It is a collection of theorems which asserts that a wide class of standard problems are well posed. It is not, of course, restricted to first-order equations. Specifically, the fundamental theory takes the form of an *existence* theorem, a *uniqueness* theorem, and various theorems on *continuity* in parameters, each of substantial generality.

We see, for example, that the initial value problem

$$\frac{dv}{dt} = -32$$

$$v(t_0) = 50$$

is indeed well posed, for, by well-known results of elementary calculus, all solutions of the differential equation are given by

$$v(t) = -32t + c$$

where c is any constant. Only one of these functions satisfies the initial condition, and c is determined by

$$50 = v(t_0) = -32t_0 + c.$$

The unique solution is thus given by

$$v(t) = -32(t - t_0) + 50.$$

PROBLEMS

1. Show that xe^x is a solution of
$$y' = y + e^x.$$

2. For what constant a is e^{ax} a solution of
$$y' = 3y.$$

3. Show that
$$x^2 - xy - y^2 = c$$
defines solutions of
$$y' = \frac{2x - y}{x + 2y}.$$

4. For what n is x^n a solution of
$$y' = \frac{2y}{x}.$$

5. Exhibit a solution of
$$y' = y^2 - 1.$$

6. Exhibit a solution of
$$y' = y^2 - x^4 + 2x.$$

7. Show that $e^{x^2} \int_0^x e^{-t^2}\, dt$ is a solution of
$$y' = 2xy + 1.$$

8. Show that
$$y(x) = \begin{cases} 0, & x \le 0 \\ x^2, & x > 0 \end{cases}$$
is a solution of
$$y' = 2\sqrt{y}$$
for all x.

4

9. Find the unique solution of the initial value problem

$$\frac{dv}{dt} = -g$$

$$v(t_0) = v_0.$$

Verify that this solution is continuous in all the parameters t_0, v_0, and g.

▶ 1.2 SEPARABLE EQUATIONS

The equation

$$y' = f(x)g(y) \tag{1.21}$$

is said to be *separable*, where, unless otherwise specified, the functions $f(x)$ and $g(y)$ are assumed to be continuous in their domains. For example,

$$y' = 2x + 1 \tag{1.22}$$

is separable. All solutions of (1.22) are given by the formula

$$y(x) = x^2 + x + c \tag{1.23}$$

because $x^2 + x$ is one primitive of (1.22), and any two primitives differ by a constant; that is, (1.22) is solved by integration.

A standard problem for (1.22) and, indeed, for any first-order equation, is that of finding the solution which satisfies an initial condition

$$y(x_0) = y_0.$$

We may solve this by specializing (1.23); thus

$$y(x_0) = x_0^2 + x_0 + c,$$

from which the unique solution is

$$y(x) = x^2 + x + y_0 - x_0^2 - x_0. \tag{1.24}$$

Formula (1.23) is said to be the *general solution* of (1.22), while (1.24) defines a single *particular* solution, but if we allow x_0 and y_0 to take on all values, these two are virtually the same. The difference lies only in point of view, for (1.23) gives all possible solutions while (1.24) gives each solution possible. A general solution is usually the result of indefinite integration. It may or may not contain all solutions. It is certainly useful, but in the long run the idea of a differential equation is best revealed by going directly after the solution(s) of each possible initial value problem.

5

This would be

$$y' = f(x, y)$$
$$y(x_0) = y_0$$

(1.25)

in the general case and

$$y' = f(x)g(y)$$
$$y(x_0) = y_0$$

(1.26)

in the separable case.

The definite integral is an apt device for these purposes. Thus, our view of the problem

$$y' = f(x)$$
$$y(x_0) = y_0$$

(1.27)

is as follows. If (1.27) has a solution, then

$$\int_{x_0}^{x} y'(t) \, dt \equiv \int_{x_0}^{x} f(t) \, dt,^*$$

hence

$$y(x) \equiv y_0 + \int_{x_0}^{x} f(t) \, dt$$

(1.28)

in view of the initial condition $y(x_0) = y_0$. That is, if there is a solution, it is uniquely given by (1.28). On the other hand, this is a solution since

$$y'(x) \equiv \left(y_0 + \int_{x_0}^{x} f(t) \, dt \right)' \equiv f(x)$$

and

$$y(x_0) = y_0 + \int_{x_0}^{x_0} f(t) \, dt = y_0$$

hold.

To deal with more complicated problems we combine these simple ideas with permissible arithmetic operations. For example, if $y(x)$ is a solution of

$$y' = xy$$
$$y(x_0) = y_0,$$

(1.29)

then

$$\int_{x_0}^{x} \frac{y'(t)}{y(t)} \, dt = \int_{x_0}^{x} t \, dt$$

* Note that

$$\int_{x_0}^{x} f(x) \, dx \equiv \int_{x_0}^{x} f(t) \, dt \equiv \int_{x_0}^{x} f(\theta) \, d\theta,$$

but, of these, the first equation is obviously confusing and will be avoided.

6

provided $y(x)$ is not zero on some interval about x_0. This will be true, for example, if $y(x_0) = y_0 \neq 0$, and assuming this we have

$$\ln\left[\pm y(x)\right] - \ln\left(\pm y_0\right) = \frac{x^2}{2} - \frac{x_0{}^2}{2},$$

$\ln|y(x)| - \ln|y_0| = \frac{x^2}{2} - \frac{x_0^2}{2}$

where $+$ or $-$ apply according as $y_0 > 0$ or $y_0 < 0$. In each case the result is the same,

$$y(x) = y_0 e^{x^2/2 - x_0^2/2} \tag{1.210}$$

is the only possible solution, and the above arguments are easily reversed to show that this is a solution. Moreover, this is a solution defined for all x; the technical restriction to some interval about x_0 is, in this instance, not necessary. Solutions which are not zero at any one point x_0 are evidently never zero since the exponential function is never zero.

We must now consider the missing case, $y_0 = 0$. We cannot integrate, but once our attention is drawn to it we see a solution,

$$y(x) \equiv 0.$$

That this is the only solution is implied by the content of the last sentence of the preceding paragraph.

The need for careful procedure is illustrated by the following example,

$$y' = \sqrt{y}$$
$$y(x_0) = y_0. \tag{1.211}$$

The arithmetic operations needed to separate this equation draw our attention to two cases: $y_0 = 0$ and $y_0 > 0$ ($y_0 < 0$ is, of course, impossible). If $y_0 = 0$, we cannot integrate; however, there is a solution,

$$y(x) \equiv 0,$$

by inspection. We must see later whether this is the only solution.

If $y_0 > 0$, we integrate:

$$\int_{x_0}^{x} \frac{y'(t)}{\sqrt{y(t)}}\, dt = \int_{x_0}^{x} dt.$$

From this, the solution is uniquely given by

$$2\sqrt{y(x)} \equiv (x - x_0 + 2\sqrt{y_0})$$

as long as $y(x) > 0$; i.e., as long as $x > x_0 - 2\sqrt{y_0}$. Here, the restriction of x to some interval about x_0 in order to permit integration is, in fact, a real one, and evidently a solution is defined only on the interval

$$x_0 - 2\sqrt{y_0} < x < +\infty.$$

7

However, the fact that both $y(x)$ and $y'(x)$ go to zero as x approaches $x_0 - 2\sqrt{y_0}$ from the positive side, together with our previous knowledge of the identically vanishing solution, permit us to piece together a unique solution of (1.211) with $y_0 > 0$ which is defined for all x. Indeed, the function

$$y(x) = \begin{cases} \frac{1}{4}(x - x_0 + 2\sqrt{y_0})^2, & x > (x_0 - 2\sqrt{y_0}) \\ 0, & x \le (x_0 - 2\sqrt{y_0}) \end{cases}$$

is the desired solution (see Fig. 1.1).

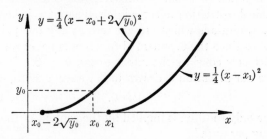

FIG. 1.1

This behavior also makes it clear that the solution of the initial value problem $y_0 = 0$ is not unique, for, as well as the solution $y(x) \equiv 0$, we have

$$y(x) = \begin{cases} \frac{1}{4}(x - x_1)^2, & x > x_1 \\ 0, & x \le x_1 \end{cases}$$

where $x_1 \ge x_0$.

These examples are indicative of what occurs in the general problem

$$y' = f(x)g(y)$$
$$y(x_0) = y_0. \tag{1.212}$$

If

$$g(y_0) = 0,$$

there is a constant solution $y(x) \equiv y_0$. If $g(y_0) \ne 0$, a solution is uniquely defined by

$$G(y(x)) - G(y_0) \equiv \int_{x_0}^{x} \frac{y'(t)}{g(y(t))}\, dt \equiv \int_{x_0}^{x} f(t)\, dt \tag{1.213}$$

on some interval about x_0, where $G(y)$ is a primitive of $[g(y)]^{-1}$. The natural domain of such a nonconstant solution will show up in this inte-

8

gration.   There are two possibilities: either such a solution meets a constant solution at a finite point in the domain of $f(x)$, or it does not.   And this is a question which must be resolved on each side of each root of $g(y) = 0$.   When no meeting is possible, all the initial value problems in (1.212) are well posed.

If the nonconstant solution for the initial point (x_0, y_0) does meet the solution $y(x) \equiv r$ at a finite point x_1 (in which case certain initial value problems are not well posed), then

$$\lim_{y \to r} \int_{y_0}^y \frac{dv}{g(v)} = \int_{x_0}^{x_1} f(t)\, dt.$$

This is to say, the improper integral

$$\int_{y_0}^r \frac{dy}{g(y)} \tag{1.214}$$

exists.   In general, the existence of this integral is also sufficient for the meeting of solutions and a corresponding lack of uniqueness, although this depends on $f(x)$.   Certainly, if (1.214) does not exist, then uniqueness prevails and, while we omit the details, the continuity of solutions in the parameters x_0 and y_0 also holds.   Recall that for (1.29),

$$\int_0^{y_0} \frac{dy}{y}$$

does not exist, but that

$$\int_0^{y_0} \frac{dy}{\sqrt{y}}.$$

for (1.211) does exist.

PROBLEMS

Find the solution of each of the following problems.

1. $y' = y^2 + 1, \quad y(0) = 1.$

2. $y' = \dfrac{x}{y+1}, \quad y(1) = 0.$

3. $y' = y^3 + y - 2, \quad y(0) = 1.$

4. $y' = \dfrac{y}{x}, \quad y(1) = 1.$

5. $y' = x(y^2 - 1), \quad y(0) = 2.$

6. $y' = x(y^2 - 1), \quad y(1) = -1.$

7. $y' = (y + 1)^2, \quad y(x_0) = y_0.$

Discuss the uniqueness of solutions in Problems 8 through 13 for all possible initial value problems.

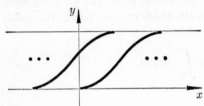

FIG. 1.2

8. $y' = y^{\frac{1}{3}}.$

9. $y' = y^a.$

10. $y' = y \log |y|.$

11. $y' = y(1 - x^2).$

12. $y' = y + x^2.$ (Consider here the equation satisfied by the difference of two solutions of the given equation.)

13. $y' = y^2 + x.$ (Employ the idea used in Problem 11.)

14. Construct a differential equation whose solutions have the appearance shown in Figure 1.2.

▶ **1.3 LINEAR EQUATIONS**

The equation

$$y' = -p(x)y,$$

as well as being separable, is *linear* in y and y', and it has become traditional to write it in the equivalent normal form

$$y' + p(x)y = 0. \tag{1.31}$$

This equation is the *homogeneous* (each term is of the same degree in y and y') linear equation; whence, if $f(x) \not\equiv 0$, we should call

$$y' + p(x)y = f(x) \tag{1.32}$$

the *nonhomogeneous* linear equation.

Equation (1.31) has a distinguishing property which is shared by all linear, homogeneous differential equations of any order, ordinary or partial. This is the principle of superposition:

If $y_1(x)$ and $y_2(x)$ are solutions of (1.31), then $c_1y_1(x) + c_2y_2(x)$ is also a solution, for any constants c_1 and c_2.

10

The proof is very simple:

$$[c_1y_1(x) + c_2y_2(x)]' + p(x)[c_1y_1(x) + c_2y_2(x)]$$
$$\equiv c_1[y_1'(x) + p(x)y_1(x)] + c_2[y_2'(x) + p_2(x)y_2(x)]$$
$$\equiv 0.$$

Since (1.31) is explicitly solvable, this result is not particularly revealing of the structure of solutions. It does assume greater importance for higher order equations.

By the results and techniques of the preceding section, the problem

$$y' + p(x)y = 0$$
$$y(x_0) = y_0$$
(1.33)

is well posed and has the solution

$$y(x) = y_0 e^{-\int_{x_0}^{x} p(t)\, dt}$$

which we obtain by integration if $y_0 \neq 0$ and by inspection if $y_0 = 0$. We may as well put both cases in the same formula. Equation (1.32) may also be separable, e.g.,

$$y' + y = 1,$$
$$y' + xy = x,$$

but in general it is not, and new techniques are necessary. Before looking for these methods of solution, we can settle the question of uniqueness. Suppose that each of $y_1(x)$ and $y_2(x)$ is a solution of the problem

$$y' + p(x)y = f(x)$$
$$y(x_0) = y_0.$$
(1.34)

Denote $u(x) = y_1(x) - y_2(x)$; then

$$u'(x) + p(x)u(x) \equiv y_1'(x) - y_2'(x) + p(x)[y_1(x) - y_2(x)]$$
$$\equiv [y_1'(x) + p(x)y_1(x)] - [y_2'(x) + p(x)y_2(x)]$$
$$\equiv f(x) - f(x) \equiv 0,$$

thus $u(x)$ is a solution of (1.31). Moreover,

$$u(x_0) = y_1(x_0) - y_2(x_0) = y_0 - y_0 = 0,$$

whence $u(x)$ is a solution of (1.33) for the initial value zero, but we know there is only one solution of this problem, the identically vanishing one. From this,

$$y_1(x) - y_2(x) \equiv u(x) \equiv 0,$$

and there cannot be two distinct solutions of (1.34).

11

In the process we have proved a result which is useful quite apart from initial value problems:

The difference of any two solutions of (1.32) is a solution of (1.31).

Equivalent to this is:

The sum of a solution of (1.31) and a solution of (1.32) is a solution of (1.32).

For example, $x - 1$ is one solution of

$$y' + y = x, \tag{1.35}$$

and e^{-x}, indeed, ce^{-x}, is a solution of the *reduced* equation

$$y' + y = 0;$$

therefore, $x - 1 + ce^{-x}$ is a solution of (1.35) for any c. We have, as a matter of fact, all solutions in this, for we see that any initial condition $y(x_0) = y_0$ for (1.35) can be satisfied by choosing c so that

$$y_0 = x_0 - 1 + ce^{-x_0},$$

namely,

$$c = (y_0 - x_0 + 1)e^{x_0}.$$

This analysis is an application of the following theorem.

Theorem 1.31. *If $y(x)$ is any nontrivial (i.e., any but the identically vanishing) solution of (1.31), and if $y_1(x)$ is any one solution of (1.32), then every solution of (1.31) is of the form*

$$cy(x),$$

and every solution of (1.32) is of the form

$$y_1(x) + cy(x).$$

We need only observe what we already know: the only solution of (1.31) which is ever zero is always zero; hence, a nontrivial solution $y(x)$ is never zero. This means that we can satisfy any initial condition for (1.31) by choosing

$$c = \frac{y_0}{y(x_0)}$$

and any initial condition for (1.32) by choosing

$$c = \frac{y_0 - y_1(x_0)}{y(x_0)}.$$

Since we can always solve (1.31), it appears then that the most efficient technique for (1.32) is that which produces any single solution. We may see a solution, as in equation (1.35) and in

12

$$y' + xy = x^2 + 1, \tag{1.36}$$

which has "by inspection" the solution $y(x) \equiv x$, but this is accidental and depends too delicately on the equation. (For example, no solution of the simple variant on (1.36)

$$y' + xy = x^2 \tag{1.37}$$

is at all evident.) There is a class of equations, of which

$$y' + 2y = x^2 - x + 1 \tag{1.38}$$

is an example, that admits to a systematic search. We argue: if $y(x)$ is a polynomial of degree two, then $y'(x) + 2y(x)$ is also a polynomial of degree two; therefore, there may be a polynomial

$$a_2 x^2 + a_1 x + a_0$$

which is a solution. We have only to try it and find that

$$(2a_2 x + a_1) + 2(a_2 x^2 + a_1 x + a_0)$$
$$\equiv 2a_2 x^2 + (2a_2 + 2a_1)x + 2a_0 \equiv x^2 - x + 1$$

if

$$2a_2 = 1$$
$$2a_2 + 2a_1 = -1$$
$$2a_0 = 1;$$

thus, $\frac{1}{2}x^2 - x + \frac{1}{2}$ is a solution. This is the method of undetermined coefficients which we return to later.

Efficiency aside, there is a method of solving (1.34) in all cases. It is based on the observation that

$$[y'(x) + p(x)y(x)]e^{\int_{x_0}^{x} p(t)\,dt} \equiv \left[e^{\int_{x_0}^{x} p(t)\,dt} y(x)\right]'.$$

By multiplying (1.32) through by the *integrating factor* $e^{\int_{x_0}^{x} p(t)\,dt}$, we have the equivalent equation

$$\left[e^{\int_{x_0}^{x} p(t)\,dt} y\right]' = f(x)e^{\int_{x_0}^{x} p(t)\,dt}. \tag{1.39}$$

Another way of putting this is: with the new variable

$$y e^{\int_{x_0}^{x} p(t)\,dt} = u,$$

(1.32) becomes the separable equation

$$u' = f(x)e^{\int_{x_0}^{x} p(t)\,dt}.$$

13

In any case, if $y(x)$ is a solution of (1.34), it satisfies (1.39), and we may integrate both sides from x_0 to x; thus,

$$e^{\int_{x_0}^{x} p(t)\, dt} y(x) \Big]_{x_0}^{x} = \int_{x_0}^{x} f(t) e^{\int_{x_0}^{t} p(s)\, ds}\, dt.$$

We finally recover $y(x)$ as

$$y(x) = \left(e^{-\int_{x_0}^{x} p(t)\, dt} \int_{x_0}^{x} f(t) e^{\int_{x_0}^{t} p(s)\, ds}\, dt \right) + \left(y_0 e^{-\int_{x_0}^{x} p(t)\, dt} \right). \quad (1.310)$$

In accordance with Theorem 1.31, the first term on the right is seen to be a particular solution of (1.32) and the second is a solution of (1.31). We note also for future reference that this first term may be written as

$$\int_{x_0}^{x} f(t) e^{-\int_{x_0}^{x} p(t)\, dt} e^{\int_{x_0}^{t} p(s)\, ds}\, dt \equiv \int_{x_0}^{x} f(t) e^{-\int_{t}^{x} p(s)\, ds}\, dt.$$

Let us call $e^{-\int_{t}^{x} p(s)\, ds} = y_1(x, t)$ and observe that it is the solution of the initial value problem

$$y' + p(x)y = 0$$
$$y(t) = 1.$$

The resulting *integral representation*

$$\int_{x_0}^{x} f(t) y_1(x, t)\, dt,$$

of a solution of (1.32) has a certain theoretical and practical importance. We solve

$$y' + y = e^{-x}$$
$$y(0) = 1$$

as follows:

$$y(x) = e^{-x} \int_{0}^{x} e^{-t} e^{t}\, dt + e^{-x}$$
$$= x e^{-x} + e^{-x}.$$

PROBLEMS

Find the solution of each of the following initial value problems.

1. $y' - xy = 0$, $y(0) = 1$.

2. $y' - x^2 y = 1$, $y(0) = 0$.

3. $y' - 3y = e^x$, $y(x_0) = y_0$.

14

4. $y' + \dfrac{y}{x} = 1, \quad y(1) = 1.$

5. $y' + y = \cos x, \quad y(0) = 1.$

6. $y' + y = \sin x, \quad y(x_0) = 0.$

7. $y' + 2y = (x + 1)e^x + 1, \quad y(0) = 0.$

8. Regard the solution of Problem 6 as a function of x and x_0, $y(x, x_0)$. Find

$$\lim_{x_0 \to -\infty} y(x, x_0) = y(x).$$

9. Find the solution of

$$y' - y = e^{ax}, \quad y(0) = 0.$$

Regard the solution as a function of x and a, $y(x, a)$, and find

$$\lim_{a \to 1} y(x, a) = y(x).$$

Of what linear equation is $y(x)$ a solution?

▶ 1.31 UNDETERMINED COEFFICIENTS

In this section a technique for solving the linear equation with constant coefficients,

$$y' + ay = f(x),$$

is developed entirely in a sequence of problems which is left to the reader. We assume throughout that $a \neq 0$.

1. If $y(x)$ is a polynomial of degree n, show that $y'(x) + ay(x)$ is also a polynomial of degree n.

2. In view of Problem 1, find a solution of

$$y' - 2y = x^3 + x.$$

3. If $y(x) = (a_2 x^2 + a_1 x + a_0)e^{kx}$, show that $y'(x) + ay(x)$ is the product of e^{kx} and a polynomial of degree one or two. When is it one, and when is it two?

4. Find a solution of

$$y' - 2y = x^2 e^x.$$

5. Find a solution of

$$y' + y = xe^{-x}.$$

6. If $y(x) = P_n(x)e^{kx}$ where $P_n(x)$ is a polynomial of degree n, what is the form of $y'(x) + ay(x)$? Note all cases.

15

7. Find a solution of
$$y' + y = e^x,$$
and find a solution of
$$y' + y = e^{-x}.$$
In view of these, find a solution of
$$y' + y = e^x - e^{-x}.$$

8. If $y(x) = b \cos \omega x + c \sin \omega x$, what is $y'(x) + ay(x)$? If $y(x) = e^{kx}(b \cos \omega x + c \sin \omega x)$, what is $y'(x) + ay(x)$?

9. Find a solution of
$$y' + 2y = \cos 2x.$$

10. Find a solution of
$$y' - y = e^x(\sin x + x).$$

11. If $y(x) = e^{kx}P_n(x)(b \cos \omega x + c \sin \omega x)$, where $P_n(x)$ is a polynomial of degree n, what is the form of $y'(x) + ay(x)$?

12. Find a solution of
$$y' + 4y = x \sin x + e^x x^2 \cos x.$$

▶ **1.32 APPLICATIONS**

Consider now the RC circuit shown in Figure 1.3, where $E(t)$ is the external applied voltage. Let v be the voltage across the capacitor and i the current; then

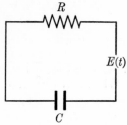

$$v(t) = v(t_0) + \frac{1}{C} \int_{t_0}^{t} i(s) \, ds,$$

or

$$\frac{dv}{dt} = \frac{i}{C}.$$

The voltage across the resistor is iR, which can be written

$$iR = RC \frac{dv}{dt}.$$

Fig. 1.3

Finally, the fact that the voltage around the circuit is zero can be written

$$RC \frac{dv}{dt} + v = E(t).$$

In standard form the circuit is described by the problem

$$\frac{dv}{dt} + \frac{c}{RC} = \frac{E(t)}{RC}$$

$$v(t_0) = v_0,$$

(1.311)

which has the solution

$$v(t) = \int_{t_0}^{t} \frac{E(s)}{RC} e^{-(t-s)/RC} \, ds + v_0 e^{-(t-t_0)/RC}.$$

(1.312)

In the language of circuitry, a term in a solution of the form $ce^{-t/RC}$ is called a *transient;* it represents the behavior of the undriven circuit (that is, $E(t) \equiv 0$). Any two possible voltages differ by a transient. Since in this dissipative case, transients go to zero, all solutions approach one another as $t \rightarrow +\infty$. What is the same, all solutions approach any one as $t \rightarrow +\infty$. This raises the question of whether there is a best choice of one solution, to which all others should be compared. For example, is there a response of the circuit which has no transients? This is the case when $E(t)$ is a constant E_0. By inspection we have the constant solution

$$v(t) = E_0,$$

which is called the *steady-state* solution. Similarly, when $E(t)$ is sinusoidal,

$$E(t) = E_0 \sin \omega t,$$

there is a sinusoidal solution, which we find by the method of undetermined coefficients,

$$E(t) = \frac{E_0}{1 + R^2 C^2 \omega^2} (\sin \omega t + RC\omega \cos \omega t)$$

$$= \frac{E_0}{\sqrt{1 + R^2 C^2 \omega^2}} \sin (\omega t - \gamma), \qquad \gamma = \tan^{-1} (RC\omega).$$

Again, we call this the steady-state solution. It is unique; no other solution is sinusoidal.

In both of these examples, there has been a unique solution which most closely reflected the nature of the driving voltage $E(t)$. This suggests a new kind of well-posed problem, that of finding the steady-state solution for a more general function $E(t)$. For example, we look for a unique periodic solution of period τ if $E(t)$ is any given periodic function of period τ, that is,

$$E(t + \tau) \equiv E(t)$$

for $-\infty < t < +\infty$. The problem is too general for us to look for this solution by the method of undetermined coefficients, and it can be very difficult (but not impossible) to work out (1.312) and drop the transient terms. On the surface, the problem is hardly an initial value problem; but, in fact, it is if we see things the right way. Although this has little physical meaning, we note that a transient is unbounded as $t \to -\infty$. The periodic solution, if any, has no transients and is bounded as $t \to -\infty$; it is therefore the solution of the symbolic initial value problem:

$$|v(-\infty)| \leq M < \infty.$$

If we do set $t_0 = -\infty$ in (1.312) and if it makes sense at all, then we must also require $v_0 = 0$. We are led to

$$v_0(t) = \int_{-\infty}^{t} \frac{E(s)}{RC} e^{-(t-s)/RC} ds. \tag{1.313}$$

We must show that this exists, is a solution, and is periodic. When it is written

$$v_0(t) = e^{-t/RC} \int_{-\infty}^{t} \frac{E(s)}{RC} e^{s/RC} ds,$$

existence is assured by the facts that $e^{s/RC}$ is integrable on $(-\infty, t)$ and $E(s)/RC$ is bounded. Moreover,

$$\frac{dv_0(t)}{dt} \equiv -\frac{1}{RC} e^{-t/RC} \int_{-\infty}^{t} \frac{E(s)}{RC} e^{s/RC} ds + e^{-t/RC} \left[\frac{E(t)}{RC} e^{t/RC} \right]$$

$$\equiv -\frac{1}{RC} v_0(t) + \frac{E(t)}{RC},$$

thus $v_0(t)$ is a solution of (1.311).

When $E(t)$ is bounded for all t, much less periodic, we can show that $v_0(t)$ defined by (1.313) is likewise bounded.

$$|v_0(t)| = e^{-t/RC} \left| \int_{-\infty}^{t} \frac{E(s)}{RC} e^{s/RC} ds \right| \leq e^{-t/RC} \int_{-\infty}^{t} \frac{|E(s)|}{RC} e^{s/RC} ds$$

$$\leq e^{-t/RC} \int_{-\infty}^{t} \frac{M}{RC} e^{s/RC} ds \equiv M.$$

In view of the presence of transients in all other solutions, this is the unique bounded solution. This uniqueness can be used to show that $v_0(t)$ is periodic when $E(t)$ is. Note that if $v(t)$ is any solution of (1.311), then

$v(t + \tau) = u(t)$ is also a solution. For let $s = t + \tau$, so that $v(s) = u(t)$, then

$$\frac{du(t)}{dt} = \frac{dv(s)}{ds}\frac{ds}{dt} = \frac{dv(s)}{ds} \cdot 1 = -\frac{v(s)}{RC} + \frac{E(s)}{RC}$$

$$\equiv -\frac{u(t)}{RC} + \frac{E(t + \tau)}{RC} \equiv -\frac{u(t)}{RC} + \frac{E(t)}{RC},$$

where the last step makes use of the periodicity of $E(t)$. Now, if $v_0(t)$ is the unique, bounded solution, then $v_0(t + \tau)$ is also a solution and is also bounded; therefore, these must be the same,

$$v_0(t) \equiv v_0(t + \tau).$$

While the evidence presented here is not exhaustive, (1.313), or something like it (see Problem 1), is to be regarded as the most characteristic solution of the linear equation. This is explored further in some of the problems.

PROBLEMS

1. Show that the "steady-state" solution of

$$y' - ay = \sin x,$$

where $a > 0$, is given by

$$y_0(x) = -\int_x^\infty (\sin t)e^{a(x-t)}\, dt.$$

2. Find

$$y_0(x) = \int_{-\infty}^x (t^2 + t - 1)e^{(t-x)}\, dt$$

and show that it is the same solution of

$$y' + y = x^2 + x - 1$$

as that which is obtained by the method of undetermined coefficients.

3. Let $E(t)$ in (1.311) be periodic of period τ and let $v_1(t)$ be *any* solution. As is known, $v_1(t + \tau)$ is also a solution, but it is not necessarily $v_1(t)$. What is $v_1(t + \tau) - v_1(t)$? If $v_1(t)$ is not already periodic, find a transient $v_2(t)$ such that $v_1(t) + v_2(t)$ is the periodic solution of (1.311).

4. Again, let $E(t)$ be periodic in (1.311). Show that the condition

$$v(t_0) = v(t_0 + \tau)$$

characterizes the periodic solution.

19

5. Let $y_1(x)$ be a solution of

$$y' + 2y = 3 \sin x,$$

such that $y_1(0) = 1$ and $y_1(2\pi) = 0$. Find, in terms of $y_1(x)$, the periodic solution of this equation.

6. If $E(t + \tau) = E(t)$ in (1.311), and if $E(t)$ has *mean a*, that is,

$$\frac{1}{\tau} \int_0^\tau E(t) \, dt = a,$$

show that

$$\frac{1}{\tau} \int_0^\tau v_0(t) \, dt = a.$$

7. If $E(t)$ is periodic of period τ, show that

$$\max v_0(t) \leq \max E(t)$$

and

$$\min v_0(t) \geq \min E(t).$$

▶ 1.4 THE LAPLACE TRANSFORM

With each member of a certain class of functions we associate the new function

$$L[f(x)] = \int_0^\infty e^{-xs} f(x) \, dx = g(s)$$

which is called the Laplace transform of $f(x)$. The domain of $f(x)$ is assumed to be at least the half axis $0 \leq x < +\infty$, and the domain of $g(s)$ consists of those values of s for which the improper integral exists. It is certainly plausible, and it is not hard to prove, that if the finite number s_1 is in the domain of $g(s)$, then all larger values of s are also in the domain. Indeed, the domain of $L[f(x)]$ is a half axis: $r < s < +\infty$, where r may be finite as in

$$\int_0^\infty e^{-xs} x \, dx = \frac{1}{s^2}, \qquad s > 0;$$

r may be $-\infty$ as in

$$\int_0^\infty e^{-xs} e^{-x^2} \, dx;$$

or r may be $+\infty$ as in

$$\int_0^\infty e^{-xs} e^{x^2} \, dx$$

(in other words, e^{x^2} has no transform).

20

We note also that if $g(s)$ has a non-empty domain, then necessarily,

$$\lim_{s \to +\infty} g(s) = 0.$$

Among all functions which have transforms are found all continuous and piecewise continuous functions whose growth is not more than exponential; i.e., for some a, $e^{-ax}f(x)$ is bounded as x goes to infinity. For such a function the domain of $L[f(x)]$ is at least $a < s < +\infty$. And, for such a function which is also differentiable, we have

$$L[f'(x)] = -f(0) + sL[f(x)] \tag{1.41}$$

for all s in the domain of $L[f(x)]$. We obtain this by integration by parts, together with the fact that

$$\lim_{x \to +\infty} f(x)e^{-xs} = 0$$

for each s in the domain of $L[f(x)]$; viz.,

$$\int_0^\infty e^{-xs}f'(x)\,dx = \left[f(x)e^{-xs}\right]_0^\infty + s\int_0^\infty e^{-xs}f(x)\,dx.$$

We note also the *linearity* property,

$$L[c_1f_1(x) + c_2f_2(x)] = c_1L[f_1(x)] + c_2L[f(x)], \tag{1.42}$$

where c_1 and c_2 are constants. That is, when all of the integrals exist,

$$\int_0^\infty e^{-xs}[c_1f_1(x) + c_2f_2(x)]\,dx = c_1\int_0^\infty e^{-xs}f_1(x)\,dx + c_2\int_0^\infty e^{-xs}f_2(x)\,dx.$$

Properties (1.41) and (1.42) give the Laplace transform special relevance to the linear equation

$$y' + ay = f(x) \tag{1.43}$$

with constant coefficients. If $f(x)$ has a transform and if a solution $y(x)$ has a transform, then

$$L[y'(x) + ay(x)] = L[f(x)].$$

By (1.42), this becomes

$$L[y'(x)] + aL[y(x)] = L[f(x)]$$

and, in turn, by (1.41), we have

$$-y(0) + sL[y(x)] + aL[y(x)] = L[f(x)].$$

After some manipulation, we arrive at

$$L[y(x)] = \frac{y(0) + L[f(x)]}{a + s} = F(s). \tag{1.44}$$

21

If $F(s)$ is a Laplace transform, then it is the transform of the solution of (1.43) which has the initial value $y(0)$. Conversely, if we know that the functional equation (1.44) has only one continuous solution $y(x)$, then it is the solution of (1.43). In other words, if the Laplace transform has a single-valued inverse, then the solution in question of (1.43) is given by

$$y(x) = L^{-1}[F(s)].^* \tag{1.45}$$

The following result settles this.

Uniqueness Theorem. *If $f_1(x)$ and $f_2(x)$ are continuous on $[0, +\infty)$ and if $L[f_1(x)] \equiv L[f_2(x)]$, then $f_1(x) \equiv f_2(x)$.*

The sense of the theorem is that the inverse of the Laplace transform is well defined. The proof, although not difficult, is omitted. Very extensive tables of Laplace transforms exist, and rather than look for a functional equation which defines the inverse, we shall invert by using the tables backward. The above theorem justifies this.

To illustrate, consider

$$\begin{aligned} y' + y &= \sin x \\ y(0) &= 1. \end{aligned} \tag{1.46}$$

According to (1.44),

$$L[y(x)] = \frac{1}{1+s} + \frac{L(\sin x)}{1+s}.$$

Either we compute

$$L(\sin x) = \frac{1}{1+s^2}$$

or we look it up; in any case,

$$L[y(x)] = \frac{1}{1+s} + \frac{1}{(1+s)(1+s^2)}.$$

Few tables, if any, have an entry whose transform is

$$\frac{1}{(1+s)(1+s^2)}.$$

However, there are certain to be such entries as

$$L(e^{ax}) = \frac{1}{s-a}$$

---

* This is true provided, of course, $F(s)$ is a transform at all.

22

and

$$L(\cos bx) = \frac{s}{b^2 + s^2}.$$

By partial fractions and a suitable table, we have

$$\frac{1}{(1 + s)(1 + s^2)} = \frac{1}{2}\left[\frac{1}{1 + s} + \frac{1}{1 + s^2} - \frac{s}{1 + s^2}\right]$$

$$= \frac{1}{2}\left[L(e^{-x}) + L(\sin x) - L(\cos x)\right].$$

Altogether,

$$L[y(x)] = L\left[\frac{3}{2}e^{-x} + \frac{1}{2}(\sin x - \cos x)\right]$$

from which the solution of (1.46) is recovered by uniqueness.

Much of the power in the idea of the Laplace transform does not see effective use when it is used only as one more solution technique. This transform is well suited to initial value problems involving $x_0 = 0$, and simple modifications adapt it to arbitrary initial points. But, on the surface, it has not brought any new ideas to the study of differential equations, nor is it a particularly efficient method of explicit solution. Later developments will show us, however, that it is a unifying technique which reduces all linear equations with constant coefficients to linear, algebraic equations. The meaning of "all" must be clarified: we include, for example, (a) differential equations of any order; (b) systems of simultaneous differential equations; (c) mixed systems of equations, some of which are differential and some algebraic; and (d) partial differential equations.

To illustrate (c), for example, the system of two equations

$$y' + y - 2u = 0$$
$$2y + u = 1^* \tag{1.47}$$

in the two unknowns y and u is equivalent to the algebraic system

$$(1 + s)L[y(x)] - 2L[u(x)] = y(0)$$
$$2L[y(x)] + L[u(x)] = \frac{1}{s}, \tag{1.48}$$

* It is also clear that we could derive at once the equation

$$y' + 5y = 2$$

from (1.47) and proceed in an obvious way.

23

where we have simply taken transforms of each given equation. Solving (1.48), we have

$$L[y(x)] = \frac{y(0) + \frac{2}{s}}{s+5}, \qquad L[u(x)] = \frac{\frac{(1+s)}{s} - 2y(0)}{s+5}.$$

Bringing these to forms which correspond to transform table entries, we have

$$L[y(x)] = \frac{y(0)}{s+5} + \frac{2}{5}\left(\frac{1}{s} - \frac{1}{s+5}\right)$$

$$= L\left(y(0)e^{-5x} + \frac{2}{5} - \frac{2}{5}e^{-5x}\right)$$

and

$$L[u(x)] = \frac{1}{5}\left(\frac{1}{s} - \frac{1}{s+5}\right) + \frac{[1 - 2y(0)]}{s+5}$$

$$= L\left(\frac{1}{5} - \frac{1}{5}e^{-5x} + [1 - 2y(0)]e^{-5x}\right).$$

It is a matter for direct verification that these two functions are solutions of (1.47).

PROBLEMS

In each of the first five problems, find the solution by taking Laplace transforms.

1. $y' + y = 2x$

$y(0) = 0.$

2. $y' + u' = 1$

$y - u = x, \quad y(0) = 1, \quad u(0) = 1.$

3. $y' - y = 2e^x$

$y(0) = 0.$

4. $y' = u$

$u' = y, \quad y(0) = 1, \quad u(0) = 0.$

5. $y' + 2u' = y - u$

$y' - u' = y + u, \quad y(0) = 1, \quad u(0) = 1.$

24

6. Show that formally

$$\frac{d}{ds}\left(L[y(x)]\right) = -L[xy(x)],$$

and hence show that if $y(x)$ is a solution of

$$y' - \frac{a}{x}y = 0, \quad a > 0$$

then the transform of $y(x)$ is a solution of

$$\frac{du}{ds} + \frac{(1+a)}{s}u = 0.$$

7. Let $f(x)$ be the function defined by

$$f(x) = \begin{cases} 1, & 0 \le x \le 1 \\ 0, & \text{otherwise.} \end{cases}$$

Show that

$$L[f(x)] = \frac{1}{s} - \frac{e^{-s}}{s}.$$

Find the transform of the solution of

$$y' + 2y = f(x)$$
$$y(0) = 0.$$

▶ 1.5 EXACT EQUATIONS

Suppose that a function $y(x)$ satisfies

$$F(x, y(x)) \equiv c \qquad (1.51)$$

for $a < x < b$. Then, if the indicated derivatives are continuous, we know that

$$\frac{\partial F}{\partial x}(x, y(x)) + \frac{\partial F}{\partial x}(x, y(x))y'(x) \equiv 0. \quad = \frac{d}{dx} F(x, y^{(n)})$$

In other words, $y(x)$ is a solution of the differential equation

$$y' = -\frac{\dfrac{\partial F}{\partial x}(x, y)}{\dfrac{\partial F}{\partial y}(x, y)} \qquad (1.52)$$

as is every solution of (1.51), for every c. In the present context, equation (1.52) is usually written in the differential form

$$\frac{\partial F}{\partial x}(x, y)\, dx + \frac{\partial F}{\partial y}(x, y)\, dy = 0, \tag{1.53}$$

and (1.53) is said to be *exact*.

From a different point of view, any given equation

$$M(x, y)\, dx + N(x, y)\, dy = 0 \tag{1.54}$$

is said to be exact in a region R if there is a function $F(x, y)$ such that

$$M(x, y) \equiv \frac{\partial F}{\partial x}(x, y), \qquad N(x, y) \equiv \frac{\partial F}{\partial y}(x, y) \tag{1.55}$$

both hold in R. A function $y(x)$ is thus a solution of (1.55) if

$$F(x, y(x)) \equiv c$$

holds for some c. For example, the equation

$$(y + x^2)\, dx + (x + y^2)\, dy = 0 \tag{1.56}$$

is exact in the whole plane, as we notice that

$$y + x^2 \equiv \frac{\partial}{\partial x}\left(\frac{x^3}{3} + xy + \frac{y^3}{3}\right), \qquad x + y^2 \equiv \frac{\partial}{\partial y}\left(\frac{x^3}{3} + xy + \frac{y^3}{3}\right).$$

Solutions of (1.56) are given implicitly by

$$\frac{x^3}{3} + xy + \frac{y^3}{3} = c.$$

It is not often easy, however, to simply see the existence, or the non-existence, of a function $F(x, y)$. The following theorem gives an easily applied test for exactness, and the proof contains a straightforward method of computing $F(x, y)$.

Theorem 1.51. *Let*

$$\frac{\partial M}{\partial y}(x, y) \quad and \quad \frac{\partial N}{\partial x}(x, y)$$

be continuous in a rectangle R, $a < x < b$, $c < y < d$. A necessary and sufficient condition that (1.54) be exact in R is that

$$\frac{\partial M}{\partial y}(x, y) \equiv \frac{\partial N}{\partial x}(x, y) \tag{1.57}$$

hold in R.

26

Proof:

If (1.54) is exact in R, then by a well-known result on mixed second derivatives,

$$\frac{\partial M}{\partial y}(x, y) \equiv \frac{\partial^2 F}{\partial x \, \partial y}(x, y) \equiv \frac{\partial^2 F}{\partial y \, \partial x}(x, y) \equiv \frac{\partial N}{\partial x}(x, y),$$

which proves the necessity of (1.57).

Assume now that (1.57) holds, and form

$$F(x, y) = \int_{x_0}^{x} M(t, y_0) \, dt + \int_{y_0}^{y} N(x, t) \, dt, \qquad (1.58)$$

where (x_0, y_0) is any convenient fixed point in R. First,

$$\frac{\partial F}{\partial y}(x, y) = \frac{\partial}{\partial y} \int_{x_0}^{x} M(t, y_0) \, dt + \frac{\partial}{\partial y} \int_{y_0}^{y} N(x, t) \, dt$$

$$= 0 + N(x, y) = N(x, y).$$

Also,

$$\frac{\partial F}{\partial x}(x, y) = \frac{\partial}{\partial x} \int_{x_0}^{x} M(t, y_0) \, dt + \frac{\partial}{\partial x} \int_{y_0}^{y} N(x, t) \, dt$$

$$= M(x, y_0) + \int_{y_0}^{y} \frac{\partial N}{\partial x}(x, t) \, dt.$$

By (1.57), this becomes

$$\frac{\partial F}{\partial x}(x, y) = M(x, y_0) + \int_{y_0}^{y} \frac{\partial M}{\partial t}(x, t) \, dt$$

$$= M(x, y_0) + M(x, y) - M(x, y_0) = M(x, y).$$

Thus, the function defined by (1.58) satisfies conditions (1.55).

Formula (1.58) gives us a method of solution. For example,

$$(y \cos xy) \, dx + (1 + x \cos xy) \, dy = 0$$

is exact since

$$\cos xy - yx \sin xy = \cos xy - xy \sin xy.$$

We form

$$F(x, y) = \int_{x_0}^{x} y_0 \cos t y_0 \, dt + \int_{y_0}^{y} (1 + x \cos xt) \, dt$$

$$= (\sin xy + y) - (\sin x_0 y_0 + y_0).$$

Thus the solution, if any, of the initial value problem $y(x_0) = y_0$ is given by

$$\sin xy + y = \sin x_0 y_0 + y_0.$$

Even if

$$M(x, y) \, dx + N(x, y) \, dy = 0$$

$$F(x, y) = \int_{x_0}^{x} M(t, y) \, dt + \int_{y_0}^{y} N(x_0, y) \, dy$$

is not exact, there is a function $I(x, y)$, called an *integrating factor*, such that

$$I(x, y)N(x, y) \, dx + I(x, y)N(x, y) \, dy = 0$$

is exact. The existence of such functions is not easy to prove, nor are there, in general, any simple, systematic means of finding integrating factors. But, for example, the linear equation (in differential form)

$$[-q(x) + p(x)y] \, dx + dy = 0$$

always has the integrating factor $e^{-\int p(x) \, dx}$. Further, an eye for simple differential combinations such as

$$d(xy) = x \, dy + y \, dx$$

and

$$d\left(\frac{y}{x}\right) = \frac{x \, dy - y \, dx}{x^2}$$

will often help in finding possible integrating factors. For example, given

$$(y - xy^2) \, dx + x \, dy = 0,$$

we rearrange it to

$$y \, dx + x \, dy - xy^2 \, dx = d(xy) - xy^2 \, dx,$$

in order to isolate $d(xy)$. The integrating factor $1/x^2y^2$ is perhaps not obvious, but we see the idea and the effect:

$$\frac{d(xy)}{x^2y^2} - \frac{dx}{x} = 0,$$

which is exact by inspection. Indeed, solutions are given by

$$-\frac{1}{xy} - \log x = c.$$

If equation (1.54) is exact, then any solution of the initial value problem

$$M(x, y) \, dx + N(x, y) \, dy = 0$$
$$y(x_0) = y_0 \tag{1.59}$$

is a solution of the problem

$$F(x, y) = F(x_0, y_0)$$
$$y(x_0) = y_0 \tag{1.510}$$

and conversely. The existence of a unique solution of (1.510) is the conclusion of the Implicit Function Theorem (cf. any text on advanced calculus). Briefly, if $\partial F(x, y)/\partial x$ and $\partial F(x, y)/\partial y$—i.e., $M(x, y)$ and $N(x, y)$—are continuous in a neighborhood of (x_0, y_0), and if

$$\frac{\partial F}{\partial y}(x_0, y_0) = N(x_0, y_0) \neq 0, \qquad (1.511)$$

then there is a unique, differentiable solution of (1.510) on some interval about x_0. Thus, under the hypotheses of Theorem 1.51 and the condition (1.511), the problem (1.59) is well posed.

PROBLEMS

Test each of the following for exactness, and solve.

1. $(e^x \cos y - 1)\, dx - e^x \sin y \, dy = 0.$

2. $\left(\dfrac{1}{x^2 y} + 2y\right) dx + \left(\dfrac{1}{xy^2} + 2x\right) dy = 0.$

3. $\left(\tan^{-1}\dfrac{y}{x} - \dfrac{y}{x^2 + y^2}\right) dx + \dfrac{x}{x^2 + y^2} \, dy = 0.$

4. $(x^3 - y)\, dx + (x + x^2 y)\, dy = 0.$

5. $y \, dx - (xy + x)\, dy = 0.$

6. Show that $\qquad F(x,y) = \int_{x_0}^{x} M(t,y)\,dt + \int_{y_0}^{y} N(x_0, y)\,dt$

$$F(x, y) = \int_{y_0}^{y} M(x_0, t)\, dt + \int_{x_0}^{x} N(t, y)\, dt \qquad (1.512)$$

also satisfies (1.55) if equation (1.54) is exact. *Note:* The reader who is familiar with the notion of a line integral should observe that the right-hand sides of both (1.58) and (1.512) are of the form

$$\int_C M(x, y)\, dx + N(x, y)\, dy$$

where C is one of two particular contours. Conditions (1.57) imply that this line integral is independent of path in a simply-connected domain; hence,

$$F(x, y) = \int_{(x, y_0)}^{(x, y)} M(x, y)\, dx + N(x, y)\, dy$$

will satisfy (1.55) if the integral is taken over any path in R from (x_0, y_0) to (x, y).

29

▶ 1.6 TRANSFORMATIONS

Some equations, while neither separable, linear, nor exact, are equivalent to a "solvable" equation under a simple change of variable. For example,

$$y' = (y + x)^2 + 1 \qquad (1.61)$$

is in this category. The *substitution*, or *change of variable*,

$$u = y + x$$

transforms (1.61) into the separable equation

$$u' = u^2 + 2 \qquad (1.62)$$

as follows:

$$u' = y' + 1 = (y + x)^2 + 1 + 1 = u^2 + 2.$$

In other words, if $y(x)$ is a solution of (1.61), then $y(x) + x$ is a solution of (1.62); conversely, if $u(x)$ is a solution of (1.62), then $u(x) - x$ is the solution of (1.61). We note also that well-posed problems are preserved under this transformation.

Another example is

$$y' = e^y + x. \qquad (1.63)$$

Certainly, since no other technique is available to us, a change of variable should be tried, and $u = e^y$ is an obvious choice. We have

$$u' = e^y y' = uy' = u(u + x),$$

where we must keep in mind that $u > 0$. While

$$u' = u^2 + ux \qquad (1.64)$$

is, in appearance, much simpler than (1.63), it is still not in one of our solvable classes. It would, perhaps, be some time before we saw that $u = e^{-y}$ transforms (1.63) into a linear equation (cf. Problems 7 and 8).

Success with the obvious—or near obvious— is not always assured. Neither $u = xy$ nor $u = xy + 1$, for example, transforms

$$y' = (xy + 1)^3 \qquad (1.65)$$

into what we would call a solvable equation (Problem 1). In fact, no explicit methods are available for this equation. However, a success of some importance is achieved for

$$y' = f\left(\frac{y}{x}\right). \qquad (1.66)$$

30

Here $u = y/x$ (or what is the same, $y = ux$) separates the equation as follows:

$$y' = u'x + u = f(u)$$

or

$$u' = \frac{f(u) - u}{x}.\qquad(1.67)$$

PROBLEMS

1. Carry through each of the indicated substitutions for equation (1.65).

2. Transform the separable equation

$$y' = f(x)g(y)$$

by means of $u = y/x$. Infer from the result what general type of equation is transformed into a separable equation by means of the substitution $u = yx$.

3. While the equation

$$y' = \frac{y + x}{y - x}\qquad(1.68)$$

is not of form of (1.66), its equivalent

$$y' = \frac{\dfrac{y}{x} + 1}{\dfrac{y}{x} - 1}$$

is. Find the general solution of this equation. (Note, too, that a transformation is not really necessary to the solution of (1.68), as in differential form it is exact.)

4. Transform

$$y' + y = x$$

by $y = e^{-x}u$.

5. Discuss the equation

$$y' = f(ax + by).$$

6. Show that

$$y' + p(x)y = f(x)$$

becomes

$$u' + \frac{p(x)}{n}u = \frac{f(x)}{n}u^{1-n}$$

under $y = u^n$.

7. In view of the result of Problem 6, exhibit a change of variable which transforms the *Bernoulli equation*

$$y' + p(x)y = f(x)y^n$$

into a linear equation.

8. Apply the result of Problem 7 to equation (1.64). Exhibit then the general solution of (1.63).

9. Problems 2, 6, and 7 illustrate a process of deriving rules for specific cases, namely: start with a solvable case, change variable, and then change variable so as to recover the original equation. Give an example which is neither separable nor linear but is separated by means of $y = ux^2$.

▶ 1.61 TRANSFORMATIONS (Continued)

In the preceding section we viewed changes of variable as a means of solving certain classes of differential equations. Here our view is more general. Changing variables may result in the reduction of an equation to solvable form, but it is more likely to result merely in the description of some property of solutions. We shall admit more general transformations, namely, those which are described by the pair of functions

$$u = u(x, y)$$
$$v = v(x, y). \tag{1.69}$$

Whether we regard this as a change of coordinates or a mapping of the xy plane into the uv plane does not matter. We do require, though, that the transformation be one-to-one, that is, that we be able to solve (1.69) for x and y,

$$x = x(u, v)$$
$$y = y(u, v) \tag{1.610}$$

in the domain involved. We also require that all of the functions involved in (1.69) and (1.610) have continuous first partial derivatives.

To illustrate, consider the transformation of

$$y' = f(x, y) \tag{1.611}$$

under

$$u = ax$$

$$v = by.$$

Formally,

$$dy = \frac{1}{b} dv$$

$$dx = \frac{1}{a} du,$$

whence

$$\frac{dv}{du} = \frac{b}{a} \frac{du}{dx} = \frac{b}{a} f\left(\frac{u}{a}, \frac{v}{b}\right) \tag{1.612}$$

is the result. What this means is that if $y(x)$ is a solution of (1.611), then the equations

$$u = ax$$

$$v = by(x)$$

define a function

$$v(u) = by\left(\frac{u}{a}\right),$$

which is a solution of (1.612). Conversely, by the same argument, when $v(u)$ is a solution of (1.612), then $(1/b)v(ax)$ is a solution of (1.611).

Consider

$$y' = f\left(\frac{y}{x}\right). \tag{1.613}$$

While this is separable by means of $u = y/x$, the end result is usually a general solution of the form

$$F\left(\frac{y}{x}, x\right) = c,$$

which can be very difficult to analyze. We observe, though, that under

$$u = ax$$

$$v = ay,$$

which is a *dilation* of the xy plane, (1.613) transforms into

$$\frac{dv}{du} = \frac{a}{a} f\left(\frac{v/a}{u/a}\right) = f\left(\frac{v}{u}\right),$$

i.e., into itself. To know that (1.613) is *invariant* under dilations is to know that dilations of solution curves are again solution curves. (Analytically, if $y(x)$ is a solution of (1.513), then $(1/a)y(ax)$ is also a solution.) If we can sketch one solution curve (other than a linear one $y = mx$), we can by this dilation property at once sketch many others (see Fig. 1.4).

33

The transformation of (1.611) under the most general transformation (1.610) is best carried out in differential form,

$$dx = \frac{\partial x}{\partial u}(u, v)\, du + \frac{\partial x}{\partial v}(u, v)\, dv$$

$$dy = \frac{\partial y}{\partial u}(u, v)\, du + \frac{\partial y}{\partial v}(u, v)\, dv,$$

whence

$$dy = f(x, y)\, dx$$

becomes

$$y_u(u, v)\, du + y_v(u, v)\, dv = f[x(u, v), y(u, v)][x_u(u, v)\, du + x_v(u, v)\, dv].$$

This in turn is separable into the form

$$\frac{dv}{du} = g(u, v) \quad \left(= \frac{fx_u - y_u}{y_v - fx_v} \right). \tag{1.614}$$

The idea of invariance under a transformation as illustrated by (1.613) is an important one. Let us consider other examples. Of the simplest variety is

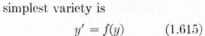

$$y' = f(y) \tag{1.615}$$

which is invariant under translations $x = u + c,\ y = v$. Similarly,

$$y' = f(x) \tag{1.616}$$

is invariant under the translation $x = u,\ y = v + c$. The linear equation

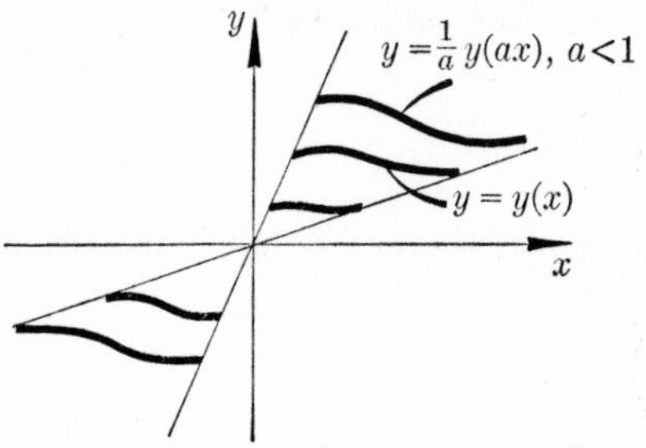

$$y' + p(x)y = 0 \tag{1.617}$$

is invariant under $x = u,\ y = cu$.

A symmetry property of an equation may suggest an invariant property. Thus, since

$$y' = 1 - xy \tag{1.618}$$

has the symmetry

$$1 - (-x)(-y) \equiv 1 - xy,$$

this equation may be invariant under $x = -u,\ y = -v$. It is, in fact (see Problem 2). Note the analytic result: if $y(x)$ is a solution of (1.618), then $-y(-x)$ is also a solution.

Fig. 1.4

34

If $f(x, y)$ is periodic in x, as is often the case in applications,

$$f(x + \tau, y) \equiv f(x, y),$$

then

$$y' = f(x, y)$$

is invariant under $x = u + \tau$, $y = v$. Indeed, we have already noticed this for certain linear equations.

PROBLEMS

1. Verify the indicated invariant properties of (1.615), (1.616), and (1.617).

2. Show that (1.618) is invariant under $x = -u$, $y = -v$.

3. Transform

$$y' = \frac{y - x}{y + x}$$

by the polar transformation $x = v \cos u$, $y = v \sin u$.

4. Transform

$$y' = \frac{y + x}{y - x + 1}$$

by means of $y = v + \frac{1}{2}$, $x = v - \frac{1}{2}$, and solve the resulting equation.

5. Discuss, in view of Problem 4, a solution method for

$$y' = f\left(\frac{a_1 x + b_1 y + c_1}{a_2 x + b_2 y + c_2}\right).$$

6. Give an example of an equation which is invariant under $x = -u$, $y = v$. Describe the most general equation

$$y' = f(x, y)$$

which is invariant under this transformation.

7. If $p(x + \tau) \equiv p(x)$, then show that

$$y' + p(x)y = 0$$

is invariant under the translation $x = t + \tau$.

8. We now know that if $y(x)$ is a solution of (1.616), then $y(x + \tau)$ is also a solution. Show, in view of the structure of solutions of (1.617) (cf. Theorem 1.31), that either all nontrivial solutions of (1.617) are periodic or none is.

9. Assume that $p(x + \tau) \equiv p(x)$ and $f(x + \tau) \equiv f(x)$. Then

$$y' + p(x)y = f(x) \tag{1.620}$$

35

is clearly invariant under $x = t + \tau$. Show that (1.620) has a unique periodic solution if and only if (1.617) has no nontrivial periodic solution.

10. Show that the equation

$$\frac{dv}{dt} + \frac{v}{RC} = \frac{E(t)}{RC}$$

becomes

$$\frac{dv}{ds} + v = E(RCs)$$

under $s = t/RC$. (Physically, s is dimensionless time since RC, which is referred to as the *time constant* of an RC circuit, has the dimension of time.)

▶ 1.7 GEOMETRIC ANALYSIS

Until now we have relied entirely on analytic arguments aimed largely at the explicit solution of certain equations. We have not yet used the geometric content of the first-order equation. The equation

$$y' = f(x, y) \tag{1.71}$$

defines a slope at each point in the domain of $f(x, y)$, the slope, in fact, of the solution curve—or curves—through each point. We say then that

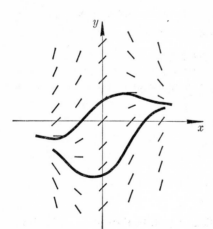

(1.71) defines a *slope field*, which can be represented graphically by sketching in a short lineal element of slope $f(x, y)$ at each of a large number of points. Even when this is done crudely, we may obtain a clear impression of the "flow" and behavior of solution curves. For example, the slope field of the linear equation

$$y' = 1 - xy \tag{1.72}$$

is indicated in Figure 1.5.

To turn this into a sketch of solution curves we have only to sketch in smooth curves which reasonably match the slope elements.

FIG. 1.5

Often enough this gives a more accurate description of solutions than all but the most careful direct analysis of the general solution—if, indeed, the general solution is available. (Recall that for curve-sketching problems in the elementary calculus we differentiated to find the slope of the curve. Here, we have much the same problem from a different point of view.)

For the present we shall use the ideas of a slope field in an intuitive and qualitative way, often simply to find results which can then be proved directly. The ideas can be refined, however, and as such are the basis of digital methods of approximating solutions. We should also not proceed without mentioning limitations. A purely geometric view can miss entirely the point of an equation. To illustrate, the slope fields of the equations

(i) $y' = y$

(ii) $y' = \sqrt{y}$

(iii) $y' = y^2$

are entirely similar in the upper half plane $(y \geq 0)$. In this case they are too similar; even careful geometric analysis does not bring out the substantial differences in behavior of the corresponding solutions, with which we are already familiar. By solving, we see that the solution curves of (iii) have vertical asymptotes but do not meet the x axis, those of (ii) have no vertical asymptotes but do meet the x axis at finite points, while those of (i) have no vertical asymptotes nor do they meet the x axis. Here we are saved from misinterpretation by the explicit solutions available, but this only makes clear the need for great care when solutions are not available.

As clear an illustration of geometrical arguments as any will emerge from a relatively complete discussion of one equation, (1.72). We note first that the general solution can be exhibited:

$$y(x) = e^{-x^2/2} \int_0^x e^{t^2/2} \, dt + c e^{-x^2/2}$$

is one form of it. Properties of the function $e^{-x^2/2}$ are well known; however, the function $\int_0^x e^{t^2/2} \, dt$ is not an elementary function. Difficulties, then, in discussing any solution of (1.72) are concentrated in the one solution

$$y(x) = e^{-x^2/2} \int_0^x e^{t^2/2} \, dt, \tag{1.73}$$

and we look at it.

Let us also note—and use—a systematic representation of slope fields which is somewhat different from the obvious one of placing lineal

37

elements at closely spaced lattice points. This is the method of *isoclines* or loci of equal slopes. Thus, the isocline of zero slope for (1.72) is the hyperbola

$$f(x, y) = 1 - xy = 0,$$

while the locus of all slopes 1 consists of the coordinate axes,

$$xy = 0$$

(see Fig. 1.6). For many descriptive purposes it is sufficient to look at the uncluttered sketch incorporating only the isocline of zero slope and, with

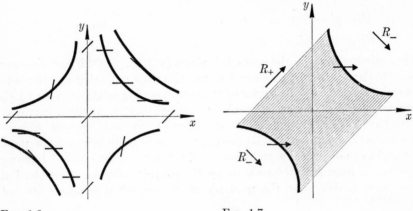

Fig. 1.6   Fig. 1.7

it, the regions of slopes all positive or all negative into which this locus divides the plane. This is shown in Figure 1.7, and in this context we give a running account of the course of the solution curve of (1.72) through $(0, 0)$. This solution is given by (1.73). Initially, the curve has slope 1 and $y(x)$ increases as x increases. It will continue to increase as long as $y'(x)$ remains positive, i.e., as long as the curve remains in R_+. With this, $xy(x)$ is increasing, and hence $1 - xy(x) = y'(x)$ is decreasing. Geometrically speaking, the curve is concave at least as long as it remains in R_+. In view of these geometric considerations, the curve must reach the zero isocline, $y = 1/x$, at some finite point x_0. Since a concave curve lies beneath any tangent and since $y = x$ is the tangent line at the origin, we also see that $x_0 > 1$ (see Fig. 1.8). At x_0, $y(x)$ has a relative maximum. *Note:* This is clear but, for example, we might also argue that $y(x_0) = 1/x_0$, thus

38

$$y''(x_0) = -x_0 y'(x_0) - y(x_0)$$
$$= -x_0[1 - x_0 y(x_0)] - y(x_0) = -\frac{1}{x_0} < 0.$$

Continuing, beyond x_0, $y(x)$ decreases, either for all x while $y(x)$ remains greater than $1/x$ or until the curve again intersects $y = 1/x$ at a finite point x_1.   The latter is impossible, for $y(x)$ would also have to have a relative maximum at x_1, and $y(x)$ could not decrease to a maximum.

Since the former holds, we infer that the curve has a horizontal asymptote $y = y_0$, or, what is the same,

$$\lim_{x \to +\infty} e^{-x^2/2} \int_0^x e^{t^2/2}\, dt = y_0.$$

We can check that this limit exists and evaluate y_0 by applying l'Hospital's rule:

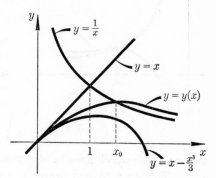

Fig. 1.8

$$\lim_{x \to \infty} \frac{\int_0^x e^{t^2/2}\, dt}{e^{x^2/2}} = \lim_{x \to +\infty} \frac{e^{x^2/2}}{x e^{x^2/2}} = 0.$$

With this, it is still true that $y(x) > 1/x$ for large x; therefore, we are led to compare $y(x)$ and $1/x$.   We do this by the change of variable

$$u = y - \frac{1}{x}.$$

Equation (1.72) becomes

$$u' = \frac{1}{x^2} - xu. \tag{1.74}$$

In particular, we are interested in the solution which satisfies

$$u(x_0) = y(x_0) - \frac{1}{x_0} = 0.$$

We may apply slope field methods to (1.74) to obtain the sketch shown in Figure 1.9.   We can also exhibit the desired solution

$$u(x) = e^{-x^2/2} \int_{x_0}^x \frac{e^{t^2/2}}{t^2}\, dt$$

39

since (1.74) is linear. The evidence of Figure 1.9 is that $u(x)$ is comparable to $1/x^3$, and we may check this by computing

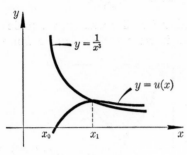

$$\lim_{x \to +\infty} x^3 u(x) = 1$$

(Problem 8). All of this means that

$$y(x) = \frac{1}{x} + \frac{1}{x^3}$$

with an error which goes to zero more rapidly than $1/x^3$ as $x \to +\infty$. A different approach might have been to transform (1.74) by $w = u - (1/x^3)$, to find in the end that

FIG. 1.9

$$y(x) = \frac{1}{x} + \frac{1}{x^3} + \frac{3}{x^5}$$

with an error which goes to zero more rapidly than $1/x^5$, etc.

To return to $y(x)$ nearer $x = 0$, we have from Figure 1.8 that

$$y(x) \le x$$

for $x \ge 0$. Since this is the case,

$$y'(x) = 1 - xy(x) \ge 1 - x^2, \qquad x \ge 0.$$

We may integrate this inequality, obtaining

$$y(x) - y(0) = \int_0^x y'(t)\, dt \ge \int_0^x (1 - t^2)\, dt = x - \frac{x^3}{3},$$

or, since $y(0) = 0$,

$$y(x) \ge x - \frac{x^3}{3}, \qquad x \ge 0 \tag{1.75}$$

(see Fig. 1.8). We draw a simple conclusion from this, that the maximum of $y(x)$, which is $y(x_0) = 1/x_0$, is greater than the maximum of $x - (x^3/3)$, which is $2/3$; that is, $1/x_0 > 2/3$ or

$$x_0 < 3/2.$$

Employing (1.75) again, we have

$$y'(x) = 1 - xy(x) \le 1 - x\left(x - \frac{x^3}{3}\right) = 1 - x^2 + \frac{x^4}{3}.$$

which on integration yields the inequality,

$$y(x) \le x - \frac{x^3}{3} + \frac{x^5}{3 \cdot 5}, \qquad x \ge 0. \tag{1.76}$$

40

Together, (1.75) and (1.76) imply that

$$y(x) = x - \frac{x^3}{3}$$

with error less than $x^5/3 \cdot 5$. Indeed, by continuing the process it is not hard to show that

$$y(x) = x - \frac{x^3}{3} + \frac{x^5}{3 \cdot 5} - \cdots + \frac{(-1)^n x^{2n+1}}{3 \cdot 5 \cdot 7 \cdots (2n+1)} \tag{1.77}$$

with error less than

$$\frac{x^{2n+3}}{3 \cdot 5 \cdots (2n+3)}.$$

Clearly, the above is simply another means to the Taylor's series of $y(x)$ which could be calculated from (1.73) by standard methods. The estimate of the error, however, is not so easily obtained. Note also that the alternating sequence of inequalities on $y(x)$ depend on $-y$ appearing in the equation. No such sequence of inequalities can be simply obtained in discussing

$$y' = 1 + xy, \tag{1.78}$$

while, on the other hand, they could be obtained by repeated integration for the equation

$$y' = 1 - xy^3. \tag{1.79}$$

It is clearly a somewhat special device.

Although it did not enter directly into the preceding example, the notion of a well-posed problem has a role in geometric arguments. *If the problem*

$$y' = f(x, y)$$

$$y(x_0) = y_0$$

is well posed for each point (x_0, y_0) in the domain of $f(x, y)$, then this domain is covered by nonintersecting solution curves.

While a first-order equation always has a slope field as geometric content, there is no single method of using this field which applies to all cases. The following general outline may help, however.

(1) Sketch an uncluttered slope with just a few isoclines of the equation, including the isocline $y' = 0$ if it exists. If this is found unproductive in the following steps, then only an accurate slope field with lineal elements at closely spaced lattice points will be useful.

(2) Examine the slope field for suggestions of such properties as

41

boundedness of solutions or asymptotes or symmetries. In the process, sketch a few sample solution curves.

(3) If feasible, note convexity properties by computing y'' from the given equation. The locus $y'' = 0$ divides the plane into regions in which y'' is of one sign. All solution curves are convex where $y'' < 0$, etc.

(4) There may be some reason for concentrating on a particular solution. Much of the success of geometric methods depends on whether a particular solution curve can be sketched in essentially one and only one way.

PROBLEMS

The first seven problems form a unit.

1. Sketch the slope field of equation (1.78).

2. Note that most solutions of (1.78) appear to be unbounded as $x \to +\infty$. In particular, show that any solution which satisfies $y(x_0) = 0$ is unbounded.

3. Sketch the course of a solution curve of (1.78) which intersects the isocline $y = -1/x$ at any point $(x_0, -1/x_0)$.

4. Denote the solution in Problem 3 by $y(x, x_0)$. Let $x_0 > 0$. What is the behavior of the value $y(0, x_0)$ as a function of x_0?

5. Show, in fact, that
$$\lim_{x_0 \to +\infty} y(0, x_0) = y_0$$
is finite.

6. Give geometric reasons for the conjecture that the solution of (1.78) satisfying $y(0) = y_0$ is bounded as $x \to +\infty$.

7. Show, analytically, that there is at most one solution of (1.78) which is bounded as $x \to +\infty$. Show that there is a bounded solution by picking it from the general solution
$$e^{x^2/2} \int_{x_0}^{x} e^{-t^2/2} \, dt + y_0 e^{x^2/2 - x_0^2/2}.$$

8. Show that
$$\lim_{x \to +\infty} x^3 u(x) = 1,$$
where $u(x)$ is the solution of (1.74) previously under discussion.

9. Carry out the transformation of (1.74) by $w = u - (1/x^3)$. Sketch the slope field of the resulting equation. What is indicated as the asymptotic behavior of a solution as $x \to +\infty$?

42

10. Show that

$$\lim_{x \to +\infty} x^5 w(x) = 3$$

for a solution of the above equation.

Problems 11 through 16 form a single unit.

11. Suppose that in a region of the xy plane $f_1(x, y) > f_2(x, y)$ holds. How would a solution $y_1(x)$ of

$$y' = f_1(x, y) \tag{1.710}$$

and a solution $y_2(x)$ of

$$y' = f_2(x, y) \tag{1.711}$$

compare if at some point $y_1(x_0) = y_2(x_0)$? Make this clear with a sketch. We could say that the slope field of (1.710) is *steeper* than that of (1.711).

12. The differential equation

$$y' = y^2 + x \tag{1.712}$$

is not solvable by any elementary methods; nevertheless, let us assume that it has a unique solution which satisfies $y(0) = 1$. By slope field methods, sketch this solution curve for $x < 0$. What appears to be the asymptotic behavior as $x \to -\infty$?

13. Sketch the solution curve of Problem 12 for $x > 0$. Show that

$$y(x) \geq 1 + x, \qquad x \geq 0.$$

Employ this inequality to show that

$$y(x) \geq 1 + x + \frac{3}{2}x^2 + \frac{x^3}{3}, \qquad x \geq 0.$$

14. The slope field of

$$y' = y^2 \tag{1.713}$$

is less steep than that of (1.712). By solving (1.713) show that

$$y(x) \geq \frac{1}{1 - x}, \qquad x \geq 0$$

holds, where $y(x)$ is the solution of (1.712) under discussion.

15. As a consequence of the above, argue that $y(x)$ has a vertical asymptote at x_1, $0 < x_1 < 1$.

16. By comparing (1.712) with

$$y' = y^2 + 1$$

for $0 \leq x \leq 1$, show that $\pi/4 < x_1$, where x_1 is described in Problem 15.

17. Assume that the problem

$$y' = -y^3 + \sin x$$
$$y(x_0) = y_0$$

is well posed. Sketch the slope field and show from it that if $-1 \le y(x_0) \le 1$, then $-1 \le y(x) \le 1$ for $x \ge x_0$.

18. Sketch solution curves of

$$y' = \frac{x - y}{x + y}$$

by slope field methods. (Here the isocline of infinite slope may be useful; recall also the dilation property of this equation.)

19. Sketch solution curves of

$$y' = \frac{x - y}{y}.$$

20. Consider

$$y' = -\sqrt{1 - e^y}. \tag{1.714}$$

First discuss the uniqueness of solutions for all possible initial value problems. Show that if $y(x)$ is a solution, then $y(x + c)$ is also a solution.

21. Note any convexity properties of solutions of (1.714) and sketch the graphs of representative solutions.

22. Show that every solution of (1.714) except the constant solution tends to $-\infty$ as $x \to +\infty$. Show that for such solutions

$$\lim_{x \to +\infty} y'(x) = -1.$$

23. The above limiting property for $y'(x)$ does not, in general, imply that the solution curve $y = y(x)$ has an asymptote of the form $y = -x + c$, but we may conjecture that this is true. One possibility for checking this conjecture is to transform (1.714) by the change of variable $u = y + x$. (Show that this yields $u' = 1 - \sqrt{1 - e^{u-x}}$.) $\tag{1.715}$

We should like to show that every solution of (1.715) which corresponds to a *nonconstant* solution of (1.714), i.e., every one except the solution $u(x) \equiv x$, has a finite limit c as $x \to +\infty$. Show that in the domain $u < x$, (1.715) has a less steep slope field than

$$u' = e^{u-x}. \tag{1.716}$$

24. Show that every solution of (1.716) in the domain $u < x$ has the property that $\lim_{x \to +\infty} u(x)$ exists and is finite. Hence, retrace all steps to show that the original conjecture (of Problem 23) is true.

44

2

APPROXIMATE SOLUTIONS
AND FUNDAMENTAL THEORY

▶ 2.1 INTRODUCTION

These two topics are essentially the same, differing only in point of view. To be precise, an *approximate solution* of

$$y' = f(x, y)$$
$$y(x_0) = y_0 \tag{2.11}$$

is any one of a sequence of functions $\{y_n(x)\}$ which is formed in some manner relevant to (2.11) and which is known to converge to a solution. On the other hand, it is the substance of an existence theorem for (2.11) that a promising sequence of functions does indeed converge, and that the limit function is a solution. Fundamental theory is concerned as well with the uniqueness of solutions and their dependence on parameters, but the deepest and most difficult part of it is the proof of the existence of a solution of (2.11).

We mention three methods of generating a sequence of approximate solutions, in order of increasing generality; that is, each is applicable to a broader class of first-order equations than its predecessor in the list:

(a)   Power series
(b)   Repeated approximations
(c)   Slope field polygons.

From the point of view of theory, each yields an existence theorem; however, for simplicity we shall base our discussion of theory on (b).   Power series (Taylor's series) will be considered more as a formal technique than as a subject for rigorous investigation.   Slope field methods, or digital methods, will be touched on briefly.

▶ 2.2   REPEATED APPROXIMATIONS

We have anticipated the idea of repeated approximations by successive integrations in connection with equation (1.72).   In a much simpler form the idea is present in Newton's method for solving the equation

$$f(x) = 0. \tag{2.21}$$

Stripped of its elegant geometric content, the analytic idea is to solve the equation

$$x = x - \frac{f(x)}{f'(x)} = g(x), \tag{2.22}$$

which is equivalent to (2.21), by the following scheme.   Let x_1 be some reasonable estimate of a solution; form

$$x_2 = g(x_1)$$

(with, of course, the expectation that x_2 is a better estimate than x_1); from this form

$$x_3 = g(x_2).$$

Indeed, we form the sequence $\{x_n\}$ from x_1 by the rule

$$x_n = g(x_{n-1}), \qquad n = 2, 3, \ldots.$$

If now this sequence converges to a number a in the domain of $g(x)$, and if $g(x)$ is continuous at a, then

$$a = \lim_{n \to \infty} x_n = \lim_{n \to \infty} g(x_{n-1}) = g(\lim_{n \to \infty} x_{n-1}) = g(a).$$

46

That is, the sequence of repeated approximations converges to a solution of (2.22), and as a consequence,

$$f(a) = 0.$$

The fact that this process has a very appealing geometric description, shown in Figure 2.1, does not relieve us of necessary technical details. It must first be shown that for a reasonable range of choices for x_1, the sequence $\{x_n\}$ exists; that is, it must not happen that some approximant x_n is not in the domain of $g(x)$, in which case we could not compute x_{n+1}. Having settled this, we must be able to show that $\{x_n\}$ converges to a number also in the domain of $g(x)$, and finally, $g(x)$ must be shown to be continuous at this point.

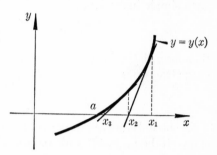

FIG. 2.1

Briefly, as this applies to, say, the solution of

$$x^2 - 2 = 0,$$

we show that there is an interval $[a, b]$ such that when x_1 is in $[a, b]$,

$$x_2 = x_1 - \frac{(x_1{}^2 - 2)}{2x_1}$$

is also in $[a, b]$. A little computation shows that $[1, 2]$ is satisfactory; thus, $\{x_n\}$ exists and each element satisfies $1 \le x_n \le 2$, provided we choose $1 \le x_1 \le 2$.

A standard technique for showing convergence of $\{x_n\}$ is to show the equivalent, the convergence of the infinite series

$$x_1 + \sum_{n=1}^{\infty} (x_{n+1} - x_n).$$

In turn, the convergence of

$$\sum_{n=1}^{\infty} |x_{n+1} - x_n| \tag{2.23}$$

is sufficient, since an absolutely convergent series is convergent. Now a computation shows that

$$|x_{n+1} - x_n| = \left| \frac{1}{2} - \frac{1}{x_n x_{n-1}} \right| |x_n - x_{n-1}|, \qquad n = 2, 3, \ldots .$$

47

Since $1 \leq x_n \leq 2$ for all n,

$$-\frac{1}{2} \leq \frac{1}{2} - \frac{1}{x_n x_{n-1}} \leq \frac{1}{4};$$

thus

$$|x_{n+1} - x_n| \leq \tfrac{1}{2}|x_n - x_{n-1}|.$$

By a simple induction,

$$|x_{n+1} - x_n| \leq \frac{1}{2^{n-1}}|x_2 - x_1|, \qquad n = 2, 3, \ldots;$$

therefore, the series (2.23) is majorized, term by term, by the convergent geometric series

$$\sum_{n=0}^{\infty} \frac{|x_2 - x_1|}{2^n}.$$

This not only proves convergence of $\{x_n\}$ to some number a (a is easily shown to be in $[0, 1]$), but we have also the estimate

$$|x_m - a| = \left| \sum_{n=m}^{\infty} (x_{n+1} - x_n) \right| \leq |x_2 - x_1| \sum_{n=m}^{\infty} \frac{1}{2^{n-1}} = \frac{|x_2 - x_1|}{2^{m-2}},$$

of the error at each step.

In order to apply these ideas to (2.11), we want first an equivalent form of this problem which admits the formation of successive approximations. It is

$$y(x) = y_0 + \int_{x_0}^{x} f(t, y(t))\, dt = F(y), \tag{2.24}$$

for if $y(x)$ is a solution of (2.24), then we have $y(x_0) = y_0$ and, on differentiating,

$$y'(x) = f(x, y(x));$$

thus $y(x)$ is a solution of (2.11). Conversely, (2.24) is obtained from (2.11) by an integration. The formation of the sequence of repeated approximations $\{y_n(x)\}$ by

$$y_{n+1}(x) = F(y_n) = y_0 + \int_{x_0}^{x} f(t, y_n(t))\, dt, \qquad n = 1, 2, \ldots$$

is the means to the following theorem.

Theorem 2.21. *Let (x_0, y_0) be in an interior point of a closed rectangle R, $a \leq x \leq b$, $c \leq y \leq d$, in which $f(x, y)$ is continuous. Let $f(x, y)$ satisfy the Lipschitz condition,*

$$|f(x, y_1) - f(x, y_2)| \leq K|y_1 - y_2|,$$

for all possible (x, y_1) *and* (x, y_2) *in R and some fixed constant K.* Then (2.11),

$$y' = f(x, y)$$
$$y(x_0) = y_0,$$

has a unique solution.

Some remarks are in order before we proceed with a proof. The Lipschitz condition states simply that the difference quotient $\Delta f / \Delta y$ is uniformly bounded. It is implied by the condition: $\partial f(x, y)/\partial y$ exists and is bounded in R; i.e.,

$$\left| \frac{\partial f}{\partial y} (x, y) \right| \leq K,$$

at each point of R. An application of the Mean Value Theorem shows this. For fixed x, we have by the Mean Value Theorem

$$f(x, y_1) - f(x, y_2) = \frac{\partial f}{\partial y} (x, \bar{y})(y_1 - y_2),$$

where $\bar{y}$ is between y_1 and y_2. Taking absolute values of both sides, we have the Lipschitz condition after observing that

$$\left| \frac{\partial f}{\partial y} (x, \bar{y}) \right| \leq K.$$

The Lipschitz condition is not assumed in place of differentiability for the sake of greater generality, but rather because it, and only it, is explicitly used in the proof.

In the proof of the theorem—indeed, in all of the succeeding sections devoted to the theory—the analysis is carried out in a cone-shaped sub-region of R determined as follows. Since $f(x, y)$ is continuous in the closed, bounded set R, it is bounded there:

$$|f(x, y)| \leq M.$$

If, therefore, a solution $y(x)$ of (2.11) exists, then

$$-M \leq y'(x) \leq M.$$

Integrating this from x_0 to x, we have

$$-M(x - x_0) \leq y(x) - y_0 \leq M(x - x_0),$$

if $x \geq x_0$, and

$$-M(x - x_0) \geq y(x) - y_0 \geq M(x - x_0),$$

49

if $x \leq x_0$. In all, any solution is constrained by the inequality

$$|y(x) - y_0| \leq M|x - x_0|. \tag{2.25}$$

Geometrically speaking, a solution curve must be in the cone determined by the lines

$$y = y_0 \pm M(x - x_0).$$

We therefore restrict our search for a solution to this cone. Further, a solution curve through (x_0, y_0) must remain in R. The only possibility of reaching a boundary point of R—and thus presumably leaving R—is at a point outside of the minimal interval, $\alpha \leq x \leq \beta$, determined by the four intersections of the above lines with the boundary of R (see Fig. 2.2). In the details of the proof we restrict ourselves to the class of functions which are continuous on $[\alpha, \beta]$ and which satisfy (2.25), where α and β are determined by the geometry of (x_0, y_0), M, and R (see Fig. 2.2). We denote this class by $C_M[\alpha, \beta]$.

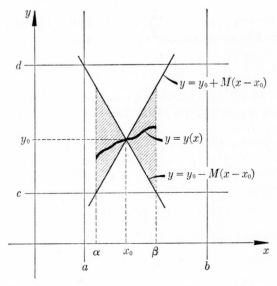

Fig. 2.2

In order now to prove Theorem 2.21 by the method of repeated approximations, we must first be assured that we can form a sequence $\{y_n(x)\}$.

Lemma 2.22. *If $y_1(x)$ is in $C_M[\alpha, \beta]$, then*

$$y_2(x) = y_0 + \int_{x_0}^{x} f(t, y_1(t))\, dt$$

is also in $C_M[\alpha, \beta]$.

By the properties of $y_1(t)$ and geometry, the point $(t, y_1(t))$ is in R for $\alpha \leq t \leq \beta$; $f(t, y_1(t))$ is continuous for $\alpha \leq t \leq \beta$; therefore, $y_2(x)$ is defined and continuous for $\alpha \leq x \leq \beta$. Further,

$$|y_2(x) - y_0| = \left| \int_{x_0}^{x} f(t, y_1(t))\, dt \right| \leq \left| \int_{x_0}^{x} |f(t, y_1(t))|\, dt \right|$$

$$\leq M \left| \int_{x_0}^{x} dt \right| = M|x - x_0|;$$

i.e., $y_2(x)$ satisfies (2.25). $y_2(x)$ is in $C_M[\alpha, \beta]$, as was to be shown.

By induction, the functions

$$y_n(x) = y_0 + \int_{x_0}^{x} f(t, y_{n-1}(t))\, dt, \qquad n = 2, 3, \ldots \qquad (2.26)$$

are all in $C_M[\alpha, \beta]$; thus, a sequence of approximants $\{y_n(x)\}$ exists provided $y_1(x)$ is in $C_M[\alpha, \beta]$.

The convergence of this sequence is shown by the standard device of showing the absolute convergence of the infinite series

$$y_1(x) + \sum_{n=2}^{\infty} [y_n(x) - y_{n-1}(x)] \qquad (2.27)$$

whose sequence of partial sums is precisely $\{y_n(x)\}$.

Since the first term $y_1(x)$ of (2.27) does not affect the convergence, we estimate the terms $y_n(x) - y_{n-1}(x)$ beginning with $n = 2$:

$$|y_2(x) - y_1(x)| = |(y_2(x) - y_0) - (y_1(x) - y_0)|$$

$$\leq |y_2(x) - y_0| + |y_1(x) - y_0|$$

$$\leq 2M|x - x_0|.$$

Further, by (2.26),

$$|y_3(x) - y_2(x)| \leq \left| \int_{x_0}^{x} |f(t, y_2(t)) - f(t, y_1(t))|\, dt \right|,$$

and, in view of the Lipschitz condition, the term on the right is not greater than

$$\left| \int_{x_0}^{x} K|y_2(t) - y_1(t)|\, dt \right|.$$

Combining this with the inequality on $|y_2(x) - y_1(x)|$, we have

51

Taking limits of both sides of this inequality, we have

$$\lim_{n \to \infty} |y_n(x) - y_0| = |y(x) - y_0| \leq \lim_{n \to \infty} M|x - x_0| = M|x - x_0|.$$

This completes the proof of (2).

Since $y(x)$ is in $C_M[\alpha, \beta]$, $f[t, y(t)]$ is defined and continuous on $[\alpha, \beta]$ and hence integrable there. We wish to show that

$$y(x) = \lim_{n \to \infty} y_n(x) = y_0 + \lim_{n \to \infty} \int_{x_0}^{x} f(t, y_{n-1}(t)) \, dt = y_0 + \int_{x_0}^{x} f(t, y(t)) \, dt,$$

which is to say that $y(x)$ is a solution of (2.24). Now, given $\epsilon > 0$, there is an integer n_1 such that

$$\left| \int_{x_0}^{x} f(t, y_{n-1}(t)) \, dt - \int_{x_0}^{x} f(t, y(t)) \, dt \right| \leq \left| \int_{x_0}^{x} |f(t, y_{n-1}(t)) \, dt - f(t, y(t))| \, dt \right|$$

$$\leq K \left| \int_{x_0}^{x} |y_{n-1}(t) - y(t)| \, dt \right|$$

$$\leq K|x - x_0|\epsilon$$

provided $n - 1 \geq n_1$; therefore, ϵ being arbitrary,

$$\lim_{n \to \infty} \int_{x_0}^{x} f(t, y_{n-1}(t)) \, dt = \int_{x_0}^{x} f(t, y(t)) \, dt.$$

This finishes the existence portion of the theorem; now, suppose that there are two solutions $y(x)$ and $v(x)$ of (2.11), identical or not. From this,

$$y(x) - v(x) = \int_{x_0}^{x} [f(t, y(t)) - f(t, v(t))] \, dt.$$

Each of these solutions is in $C_M[\alpha, \beta]$; therefore, by geometry,

$$|y(x) - v(x)| \leq 2M|x - x_0|.$$

By the Lipschitz condition,

$$|y(x) - v(x)| \leq K \left| \int_{x_0}^{x} |y(t) - v(t)| \, dt \right|$$

$$\leq 2MK \left| \int_{x_0}^{x} |t - x_0| \, dt \right| = 2MK \frac{|x - x_0|^2}{2!};$$

indeed, by induction,

$$\left| y(x) - v(x) \right| \leq 2MK^n \frac{|x - x_0|^{n+1}}{(n+1)!}$$

for every n. But the expression on the right tends to zero for every finite x as n increases to infinity, whence

$$|y(x) - v(x)| \equiv 0.$$

This shows that $y(x)$ and $v(x)$ are identical on $[\alpha, \beta]$, and the proof is complete.

Theorem 2.21 will be referred to as the *Fundamental Existence and Uniqueness Theorem*. As could be shown, it is not the "best" theorem of its kind, but its hypotheses are easily verified in a particular instance. The ideas—if not the technical details—of the proof are quite simple, and in practice $\{y_n(x)\}$ is a *rapidly* converging sequence. The practical disadvantages of this procedure as a means of obtaining approximate solutions are clear. In order to find $y_n(x)$ we must also find $y_k(x)$, $k \leq n$; and the types of integrations involved may themselves have to be approximated. Finally, the method is suited for analog (continuous) computers, whereas most available computers are of the digital type.

In proving Theorem 2.21 we exhibited the solution $y(x)$ of (2.11) on the interval $[\alpha, \beta]$. This interval is a technical necessity of the proof and is not in general the natural domain of this solution. In fact, if the endpoint $[\alpha, y(\alpha)]$ is still in the interior of R, there is, according to the theorem, a unique extension of $y(x)$ past α: namely, the solution of (2.11) for the initial values $x_0 = \alpha$, $y_0 = y(\alpha)$. Similarly, we can extend the solution past β if $[\beta, y(\beta)]$ is in the interior of R. We omit the details of further proof and give the end result of the above continuation process in the following theorem.

Theorem 2.23. *Under the hypotheses of Theorem 2.21 the solution of (2.11) can be continued in one and only one way until we reach a boundary point or R.*

Even the rectangle R is something of a technical device. Normally, both $f(x, y)$ and $\partial f(x, y)/\partial y$ are defined and continuous in large, geometrically simple domains such as the whole plane, half plane, etc. Every interior point (x_0, y_0) of such an extended, natural domain D of $f(x, y)$ is in a rectangle R for which the hypotheses of the above theorems hold. We extend the solution to the right and left of x_0 until we reach the boundary of R. If such a boundary point is still inside D we can surround it with another rectangle R' and proceed; the constants M and K change, of course, but the ideas do not. Indeed, this process stops only when the unique solution curve through (x_0, y_0) leaves D. For example, in the linear case, D is the entire xy plane, and solution curves leave D only as x goes to infinity—i.e., solutions are defined for all x. For the equation

$$y' = y^2$$

where again D is the entire plane, all solutions except the identically vanishing one leave along vertical asymptotes.

PROBLEMS

1. Employ, formally, the method of repeated approximations to solve

$$y' = y + x$$
$$y(0) = 0.$$

Compare the results of choosing $y_0(x) \equiv 0$ and $y_0(x) \equiv x^2/2$.

2. For

$$y' = y^2 + x$$
$$y(0) = 0$$

let R be $|x| \leq 1$, $|y| \leq 1$. Find M, K, α, and β. If $y_0(x) \equiv 0$, estimate $y(x) - y_3(x)$ on $[\alpha, \beta]$.

3. Although the hypotheses of Theorem 2.21 are not satisfied for

$$y' = \sqrt{y}$$
$$y(0) = 0$$

show that $y_n(x)$ generated by $y_0(x) = x$ and repeated approximations, converges to a solution for $x \geq 0$.

4. Show that the sequence of repeated approximations of

$$y' = \begin{cases} -\sqrt{y}, & y \geq 0 \\ \sqrt{-y}, & y \leq 0 \end{cases}$$
$$y(0) = 0$$

generated by $y_0(x) = x^2/4$ does not converge.

5. Show that the wildly inaccurate estimate $y_0(x) = \sin x$ still generates a sequence of approximants which converge to the solution of

$$y' = y$$
$$y(0) = 1.$$

▶ 2.3 CONTINUITY OF SOLUTIONS

The problem is to describe the dependence of the solution of (2.11) on the parameters x_0 and y_0 and on the function $f(x, y)$ itself. We shall, in other words, take up the continuity property of the well-posed problem (see Section 1.1). The principal idea is a geometric one of slope field comparison with certain simple, linear equations.

Suppose, under the hypotheses of Theorem 2.21, that $y_1(x)$ is the solution of (2.10) and $y_2(x)$ the solution of

$$y' = f(x, y)$$
$$y(x_0) = y_1.$$
(2.31)

Both $y_1(x)$ and $y_2(x)$ are defined over some common interval in $[a, b]$, and we compare them there. We have

$$|y_1'(x) - y_2'(x)| = |f(x, y_1(x)) - f(x, y_2(x))| \leq K|y_1(x) - y_2(x)|;$$

that is, $y_1(x) - y_2(x) = u(x)$ is a solution of the *differential inequality*

$$|u'| \leq K|u|.$$
(2.32)

A purely geometric discussion of (2.32) follows by comparison with the linear equations

$$y' = Ky$$
(2.33)

and

$$y' = -Ky.$$
(2.34)

Through a point in the upper half plane, any solution curve of (2.32) is rising not more steeply than the solution curve of (2.33) and not less steeply than the solution curve of (2.34) (see Fig. 2.3). In the lower half

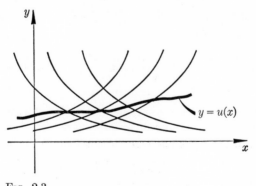

$$y = u(x)$$

FIG. 2.3

plane the reverse situation prevails (Fig. 2.4). These facts may be regarded as a geometric proof of the following: *if* $u(x)$ *satisfies (2.32) and* $u(x_0) = u_0$, *then*

$$|u(x)| \leq |u_0|e^{K|x-x_0|}.$$
(2.35)

57

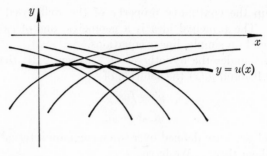

FIG. 2.4

Here we are simply recognizing that the solution curve of (2.33) through (x_0, u_0) is $y = u_0 e^{K(x - x_0)}$, and that that of (2.34) is $y = u_0 e^{-K(x - x_0)}$. Then, for example, if $u_0 > 0$ and $x \geq x_0$,

$$u_0 e^{-K(x - x_0)} \leq u(x) \leq u_0 e^{K(x - x_0)}.$$

This, and all the other cases, reduce to (2.35).

In particular, for $u(x) = y_1(x) - y_2(x)$, we have

$$|y_1(x) - y_2(x)| \leq |y_0 - y_1| e^{K|x - x_0|}.$$

On any finite interval $y_1(x) - y_2(x)$ is arbitrarily small if only $y_0 - y_1$ is small. We have proved the following result.

Theorem 2.31. *Under the hypotheses of Theorem (2.21), the solution of (2.11) is a continuous function of y_0.*

The comparison of the solution $y_1(x)$ of (2.11) with the solution $y_2(x)$ of

$$y' = f(x, y)$$
$$y(x_1) = y_0 \tag{2.36}$$

can be reduced to the preceding comparison. Since the condition

$$|f(x, y)| \leq M$$

is a bound for the slope of $y = y_2(x)$, it follows that

$$|y_2(x_0) - y_0| \leq M|x_1 - x_0|$$

(see Fig. 2.5). Thus, by (2.35),

$$|y_1(x) - y_2(x)| \leq |y_2(x_0) - y_0| e^{K|x - x_0|} \leq M|x_1 - x_0| e^{K|x - x_0|}.$$

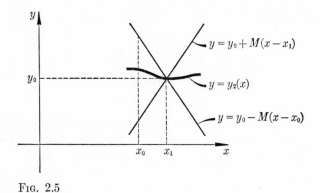

Fig. 2.5

Theorem 2.32. *Under the hypotheses of Theorem 2.21, the solution of (2.11) is a continuous function of x_0.*

We could sum all of this up by saying that if $y_1(x)$ is the solution of (2.11), and $y_2(x)$ the solution of

$$y' = f(x, y)$$
$$y(x_1) = y_1, \tag{2.37}$$

then

$$|y_1(x) - y_2(x)| \leq \{ |y_0 - y_1| + M|x_0 - x_1| \} e^{K|x - x_0|}$$

on their common domain.

Now we compare the solution of (2.11) with a solution of

$$y' = g(x, y)$$
$$y(x_0) = y_0. \tag{2.38}$$

We assume that (2.38) has a solution and that

$$|f(x, y) - g(x, y)| \leq d$$

in R.   Let $y_1(x)$ be the solution of (2.11) and $y_2(x)$ a solution of (2.38); then

$$|y_1'(x) - y_2'(x)| = |f(x, y_1(x)) - g(x, y_2(x))|$$
$$= |f(x, y_1(x)) - f(x, y_2(x)) + f(x, y_2(x)) - g(x, y_2(x))|$$
$$\leq |f(x, y_1(x)) - f(x, y_2(x))| + |f(x, y_2(x)) - g(x, y_2(x))|$$
$$\leq K|y_1(x) - y_2(x)| + d.$$

We conclude that $y_1(x) - y_2(x) = u(x)$ is a solution of the differential inequality

$$|u'| \leq K|u| + d, \tag{2.39}$$

59

which is comparable to the four nonhomogeneous linear equations

$$y' = Ky + d$$
$$y' = -Ky - d$$
$$y' = Ky - d$$
$$y' = -Ky + d.$$

Specifically, (2.39) is comparable to the first two equations on the upper half plane and the second two in the lower half plane; that is, for $u \geq 0$,

$$-Ku - d = -K|u| - d \leq u' \leq K|u| + d = Ku + d$$

and for $u \leq 0$,

$$Ku - d = -K|u| - d \leq u' \leq K|u| + d = -Ku + d.$$

Since $u(x_0) = y_1(x_0) - y_2(x_0) = y_0 - y_0 = 0$, the appropriate comparison solutions of these four equations are, in order,

$$\frac{d}{K} \left(e^{K(x-x_0)} - 1 \right), \quad \frac{d}{K} \left(e^{-K(x-x_0)} - 1 \right),$$

$$-\frac{d}{K} \left(e^{K(x-x_0)} - 1 \right), \quad \text{and} \quad -\frac{d}{K} \left(e^{-K(x-x_0)} - 1 \right),$$

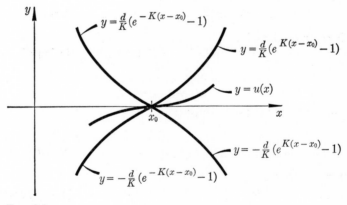

FIG. 2.6

which satisfy the same initial conditions. By an argument on slopes, we have that

$$|y_1(x) - y_2(x)| \leq \frac{d}{K} \left(e^{K|x-x_0|} - 1 \right). \tag{2.310}$$

Theorem 2.33. *If $f(x, y)$ satisfies the hypotheses of Theorem 2.21, then the solution of (2.11) is a continuous function of $f(x, y)$.*

This follows from (2.310), where we mean that $|y_1(x) - y_2(x)|$ is arbitrarily small on any finite interval if only $|f(x, y) - g(x, y)|$ is sufficiently small everywhere in R.

A special case of Theorem 2.33 which is perhaps a little more meaningful is: *if $f(x, y, \lambda)$ is continuous in the parameter λ and satisfies the conditions of Theorem 2.21 as well, then the solution of*

$$y' = f(x, y, \lambda)$$

$$y(x_0) = y_0$$

is continuous in λ.

To summarize the results of these last two sections: essentially, if $f(x, y)$ satisfies the Lipschitz condition, then (2.11) is well posed. A unique solution exists (Theorem 2.21) in the large (Theorem 2.23), and this solution is continuous in all parameters (Theorems 2.31, 2.32, 2.33, and 2.34). To be sure, stronger results are known, but these are generally useful ones.

▶ 2.4 POWER SERIES

We shall assume in this section a knowledge of the calculus of convergent power series. We shall, for example, without elaboration or explanation carry out such proper operations on convergent power series as forming the product of two series or differentiating a series term by term, etc.

The existence of a convergent power series solution—an *analytic* solution—of the initial value problem

$$y' = f(x, y)$$
$$y(x_0) = y_0, \tag{2.41}$$

presents a new kind of approximate solution. Namely, if $\sum_{n=0}^{\infty} a_n(x - x_0)^n$ is such a solution, then clearly the partial sums $\sum_{n=0}^{N} a_n(x - x_0)^n$ are approximate solutions. In practice, these are useful or not according as we can or cannot closely estimate the remainders, $\sum_{n=N+1}^{\infty} a_n(x - x_0)^n$, on some fixed, useful interval about x_0. Thus there are two problems here, the theoretical problem of the existence of such solutions and the problem of numerical details, i.e., computing the a_n, finding the radius of convergence, and estimating remainders.

The ideal situation is perhaps illustrated by the solution of the problem

$$y' = 1 - xy$$
$$y(0) = 0. \tag{2.42}$$

In Section 1.7 we proved, in effect, that (2.42) has a series solution convergent for all x, and we also had a simple bound for the remainder after any number of terms. As noted, the special techniques used for (2.42) are closely related to repeated approximations, and it is often the case that straightforward use of repeated approximations also yields the power series solution. For example, if we solve

$$y' = y$$
$$y(0) = 1 \tag{2.43}$$

in this manner with $y_1(x) \equiv 1$, then the nth approximant is exactly the nth partial sum of the well-known series solution

$$e^x \equiv \sum_{n=0}^{\infty} \frac{x^n}{n!}.$$

Something less simple occurs when we solve

$$y' = y^2$$
$$y(0) = 1 \tag{2.44}$$

by repeated approximations. Let $y_1(x) \equiv 1$; then a computation gives

$$y_2(x) = 1 + x$$

$$y_3(x) = 1 + x + x^2 + \frac{x^3}{3},$$

and so forth. The computation of a few more approximants suggests (and it can be proved, if necessary) that the nth approximant "contains" the nth partial sum of the analytic solution

$$\frac{1}{1 - x} \equiv \sum_{n=0}^{\infty} x^n.$$

We could go on, in fact, and prove that the sequence of approximants does converge to this analytic solution. Indeed, this is the idea of one proof of the following results.

62

Theorem 2.41. *The initial value problem (2.41) has an analytic solution provided $f(x, y)$ is analytic at (x_0, y_0); that is, if*

$$f(x, y) \equiv \sum_{n,m=0}^{\infty} a_{nm}(x - x_0)^n(y - y_0)^m \equiv a_{00} + a_{10}(x + x_0) + a_{01}(y - y_0)$$

$$+ a_{20}(x - x_0)^2 + a_{11}(x - x_0)(y - y_0) + a_{02}(y - y_0)^2 + \ldots$$

for $|x - x_0| < a$, $|y - y_0| < b$.

We note for reference that the analyticity of $f(x, y)$ has a number of consequences. For example, all partial derivatives of $f(x, y)$ are analytic in the rectangle R, $|x - x_0| < a$, $|y - y_0| < b$, and they are given by the appropriate differentiation of the above series, term by term. In particular,

$$\frac{\partial^{n+m}}{\partial x^n \partial y^m} f(x_0, y_0) = n!m!a_{nm},$$

so that an analytic function is its own Taylor's series. Both $f(x, y)$ and $\partial f(x, y)/\partial y$ are continuous in R; thus, in any closed subrectangle R',

$$|x - x_0| \leq \alpha < a, \qquad |y - y_0| \leq \beta < b,$$

the hypotheses of Theorem 2.21 are satisfied. If M is the maximum of $f(x, y)$ in R', then, as we know, a sequence generated by repeated approximations converges on

$$|x - x_0| \leq r_1 = \min \{\alpha, \beta/M\}$$

to the unique solution of (2.41). With some results from the theory of functions of a complex variable it can be shown that a sequence of analytic approximants can always be formed, and that a sequence converges to an analytic function—to a solution. This would prove Theorem 2.41, but it does not show that the series solution of (2.41) converges on $|x - x_0| \leq r_1$; it need not. In fact, this proof does not involve the series solution of (2.41) at all.

We turn instead to a more elementary proof which deals directly and arithmetically with the series solution. If

$$y(x) \equiv \sum_{n=0}^{\infty} a_n(x - x_0)^n$$

is a series solution of (2.41) which converges for $|x - x_0| < r$, then

$$y(x) = a_0 = y_0,$$

63

and

$$\sum_{n=1}^{\infty} a_n n(x - x_0)^{n-1}$$

$$\equiv f[x, y(x)] \equiv \sum_{n,m=0}^{\infty} a_{nm}(x - x_0)^n \left(\sum_{p=0}^{\infty} a_p(x - x_0)^p - y_0 \right)^m$$

$$\equiv \sum_{n,m=0}^{\infty} a_{nm}(x - x_0)^n \left(\sum_{p=1}^{\infty} a_p(x - x_0)^p \right)^m \equiv \sum_{n=0}^{\infty} c_n(x - x_0)^n,$$

for $|x - x_0| < r$. The c_n are generated by carrying out the indicated operations in $f(x, y(x))$ and collecting terms. Thus,

$$c_0 = a_{00}$$

$$c_1 = a_{10} + a_{01}a_1$$

$$c_2 = a_{01}a_2 + a_{20} + a_{11}a_1 + a_{02}a_1{}^2$$

.
.
.

$$c_n = f_n(a_1, a_2, \ldots a_n, a_{\nu\mu}), \qquad \nu + \mu \leq n$$

.
.
.

where $f_n(a_1, a_2, \ldots a_n, a_{\nu\mu})$ is a polynomial in $a_1, a_2, \ldots a_n$ and in the $a_{\nu\mu}$ for which $\nu + \mu \leq n$. (It is important to note that the polynomial form f_n is the same for all differential equations and contains only plus signs.) Since two series are identically equal on $|x - x_0| < r$ if, and only if, the coefficients of like powers of $(x - x_0)$ are equal, the equations

$$a_1 = a_{00}$$

$$2a_2 = a_{10} + a_{01}a_1$$

.
.
. $\hspace{8cm}$ (2.45)

$$na_n = f_{n-1}(a_1, \ldots a_{n-1}, a_{\nu\mu}), \qquad \nu + \mu \leq n - 1$$

.
.
.

must hold.

Conversely, if the coefficients of $\sum_{n=0}^{\infty} a_n(x - x_0)^n$ satisfy $a_0 = y_0$ and equations (2.45), and if this series is known to converge on $|x - x_0| < r \leq a$, then the series is the solution of (2.41). In other words, the derivation of (2.45) is reversible if the series defined by (2.45) can be shown to converge, and, note, the condition $a_0 = y_0$ and the equations (2.45) always define a unique series, convergent or not.

In many instances, we can derive at once from (2.45) a simple formula for the nth term

$$a_n = g(n),$$

from which convergence may be shown by one of the standard tests. In the general case we must proceed indirectly to prove that the series defined by (2.45) does converge on some computable interval. We pose a simpler problem,

$$y' = g(x, y)$$
$$y(x_0) = y_0,$$

whose analytic solution $\sum_{n=0}^{\infty} b_n(x - x_0)^n$ can be displayed, independently of Theorem 2.41, along with its radius of convergence r_0. Moreover, we can find a function $g(x, y)$ which *majorizes* $f(x, y)$ in the sense that

$$|a_n| \le b_n, \qquad n = 1, 2, \ldots,$$

where the a_n satisfy (2.45). By this reasoning, $\sum_{n=0}^{\infty} a_n(x - x_0)^n$ is certain to converge for $|x - x_0| < r_0$ (r_0 is nearly always an underestimate of the radius of convergence) and the proof is complete.

To introduce the idea, if not the exact details, of the proof, we consider first the example

$$y' = y^2 + x^2$$
$$y(0) = 0. \tag{2.46}$$

$\sum_{n=0}^{\infty} a_n x^n$ is the solution if and only if it converges, we have $a_0 = 0$, and

$$a_1 = 0$$
$$2a_2 = 0$$
$$3a_3 = a_1{}^2 + 1$$
$$4a_4 = a_1 a_2 + a_2 a_1$$

.
.
.

$$n a_n = \sum_{p=1}^{n-2} a_p a_{(n-1-p)}$$

.
.
.

65

(In practice, we should stop and consider these equations for immediate results. It is true that we cannot exhibit the nth term here, but it is easy to prove by induction that

$$0 \leq a_n < 1$$

for all n, which shows that $\sum_{n=0}^{\infty} a_n x^n$ converges for $|x| < 1$.) The problem

$$
\begin{aligned}
y' &= (y + x)^2 \\
y(0) &= 0
\end{aligned}
\tag{2.47}
$$

majorizes (2.46). We chose it for the following reasons: (i) each coefficient in the series expansion of $(x + y)^2 \equiv x^2 + 2xy + y^2$ about $(0, 0)$ is non-negative; (ii) each coefficient in the expansion of $y^2 + x^2$ is less than or equal to, in absolute value, the corresponding coefficient in $(x + y)^2$; and (iii), (2.47) is solvable and has an analytic solution,

$$y(x) = \tan x - x \equiv \sum_{n=0}^{\infty} b_n x^n$$

which, as we know, converges for $|x| < \pi/2$.

Properties (i) and (ii) are sufficient to prove that

$$|a_n| \leq b_n, \qquad n = 1, 2, \ldots$$

from which it follows that $\sum_{n=0}^{\infty} a_n x^n$ converges for $|x| < \pi/2$. Rather than prove this directly, however, we return to our general discussion, which will prove the assertion.

Lemma 2.42. *Assume that*

$$g(x,y) \equiv \sum_{n,m=0}^{\infty} b_{nm}(x - x_0)^n (y - y_0)^m,$$

for $|x - x_0| < \alpha$ and $|y - y_0| < \beta$, and that

$$|a_{nm}| \leq b_{nm} \tag{2.48}$$

for all n and m. If the b_n, $n = 1, 2, \ldots$ satisfy the equations

$$
\begin{aligned}
nb_n &= f_{n-1}(b_1, \ldots, b_{n-1}, b_{\nu\mu}), \qquad \nu + \mu \leq n - 1 \\
& \hspace{4.5cm} n = 1, 2, \ldots
\end{aligned}
$$

and if the a_n, $n = 1, 2, \ldots$ satisfy (4.5), then

$$|a_n| \leq b_n, \qquad n = 1, 2, \ldots.$$

This follows from the fact that f_n has only plus signs; thus,

$$|na_n| \leq f_{n-1}(|a_1|, |a_2|, \ldots |a_{n-1}|, |a_{\nu\mu}|), \qquad \nu + \mu \leq n - 1,$$

66

is immediate. Then, in view of the assumption (2.48), we have

$$|na_n| \leq f_{n-1}(|a_1|, |a_2|, \ldots |a_{n-1}|, b_{\nu\mu}), \qquad \nu + \mu \leq n - 1.$$

Finally, since

$$|a_1| = |a_{00}| \leq b_{00} = b_1,$$

we can prove the result by induction; for assume that

$$|a_k| \leq b_k, \qquad k = 1, 2 \ldots (n - 1);$$

then,

$$|na_n| \leq f_{n-1}(|a_1|, \ldots |a_{n-1}|, b_{\nu\mu}), \qquad \nu + \mu \leq n - 1$$
$$\leq f_{n-1}(b_1, b_2, \ldots b_{n-1}, b_{\nu\mu}), \qquad \nu + \mu \leq n - 1$$
$$= nb_n,$$

or

$$|a_n| \leq b_n.$$

We now exhibit a function $g(x, y)$ which satisfies the inequalities (2.48). Let $0 < \alpha < a$ and $0 < \beta < b$; then

$$\sum_{n,m=0}^{\infty} a_{nm}\alpha^n\beta^m = M.$$

Each term, therefore, satisfies

$$|a_{nm}|\alpha^n\beta^m \leq M$$

or

$$|a_{nm}| \leq \frac{M}{\alpha^n\beta^m}.$$

We define

$$g(x, y) \equiv \sum_{n,m=0}^{\infty} \frac{M}{\alpha^n\beta^m} (x - x_0)^n(y - y_0)^m$$

and observe that (2.48) is satisfied. This series converges for $|x - x_0| < \alpha$ and $|y - y_0| < \beta$; moreover,

$$g(x, y) \equiv M \left[\sum_{n=0}^{\infty} \left(\frac{x - x_0}{\alpha} \right)^n \right] \left[\sum_{n=0}^{\infty} \left(\frac{y - y_0}{\beta} \right)^m \right]$$

$$\equiv \frac{M}{\left[1 - \left(\frac{x - x_0}{\alpha} \right) \right] \left[1 - \left(\frac{y - y_0}{\beta} \right) \right]}.$$

Hence, the equation

$$y' = g(x, y)$$

67

is separable, and by standard methods,

$$y(x) = y_0 + \beta\left(1 - \left\{1 + \frac{2M\alpha}{\beta}\log\left[1 - \left(\frac{x - x_0}{\alpha}\right)\right]\right\}^{1/2}\right)$$

is the solution which satisfies $y(x_0) = y_0$. This is an analytic function

$$f(t) = y_0 + \beta[1 - (1 + t)^{1/2}]$$

of an analytic function

$$t(x) = \frac{2M\alpha}{\beta}\log\left[1 - \left(\frac{x - x_0}{\alpha}\right)\right]$$

and, hence, is analytic. Specifically, since

$$(1 + t)^{1/2} \equiv 1 + \frac{1}{2}t - \frac{1}{2^2 2!}t^2 + \frac{1\cdot 3}{2^3 3!}t^3 - \frac{1\cdot 3\cdot 5}{2^4 4!}t^4 + \cdots$$

converges for $|t| < 1$, the expansion of $y(x)$ in powers of $(x - x_0)$ will converge if

$$-1 < \frac{2M\alpha}{\beta}\log\left[1 - \left(\frac{x - x_0}{\beta}\right)\right] < 1,$$

or if

$$|x - x_0| < \alpha(1 - e^{-\beta/2M\alpha}) = r_0.$$

This completes the proof of the theorem, for, in view of the lemma, $\sum_{n=0}^{\infty} a_n(x - x_0)^n$ converges for $|x - x_0| < r_0$.

Other details can be obtained. We note that

$$|y(x)| \le |y_0| + \beta,$$

for $|x - x_0| < r_0$. In particular, then,

$$\sum_{n=0}^{\infty} b_n r_1^n \le |y_0| + \beta$$

for any $r_1 < r_0$; thus

$$b_n \le \frac{|y_0| + \beta}{r_1^n}.$$

As this holds for each $r_1 < r_0$, it must hold for $r_1 = r_0$. This yields the estimate

$$|a_n| \le b_n \le \frac{|y_0| + \beta}{r_0^n},$$

from which we infer that

$$\left|\sum_{n=N+1}^{\infty} a_n(x - x_0)^n\right| \le (|y_0| + \beta)\sum_{n=N+1}^{\infty}\left|\frac{x - x_0}{\beta}\right|^n = \frac{|y_0| + \beta}{1 - \left|\frac{x - x_0}{\beta}\right|}\left|\frac{x - x_0}{\beta}\right|^{N+1}.$$

Note that this very general method gives away a great deal in the way of sharp results. For example, should we consider (2.46) from this point of view, we would have $a = b = +\infty$. We can choose α and β as any finite positive numbers; then

$$M = \alpha^2 + \beta^2$$

and

$$r_0 = \alpha(1 - e^{-\beta/2\alpha(\alpha^2+\beta^2)}).$$

However, even crude estimates show that $r_0 < \frac{1}{2}$ for every choice of α and β.

We finally note that a convergent series $y(x) \equiv \sum_{n=0}^{\infty} a_n(x - x_0)^n$ is its own Taylor's series, i.e.,

$$a_n = \frac{y^{(n)}(x_0)}{n!},$$

so that a computation of the values $y^{(n)}(x_0)$ is equivalent to finding the a_n. With Theorem 2.41 established, we may find the solution of

$$y' = f(x, y)$$
$$y(x_0) = y_0$$

as follows. First $y(x_0) = y_0$ is given, then the differential equation determines $y'(x_0)$,

$$y'(x_0) = f(x_0, y_0),$$

and, in succession,

$$y''(x_0) = \frac{\partial f}{\partial x}(x_0, y_0) + \frac{\partial f}{\partial y}(x_0, y_0)y'(x_0)$$
$$(= a_{10} + a_{01}a_1),$$
$$y'''(x_0) = \frac{\partial^2 f}{\partial x^2}(x_0, y_0) + 2\frac{\partial^2 f}{\partial x \partial y}(x_0, y_0)y'(x_0) + \frac{\partial^2 f}{\partial y^2}(x_0, y_0)[y'(x_0)]^2$$
$$+ \frac{\partial f}{\partial y}(x_0, y_0)y''(x_0),$$

and so forth. In practice, this is often a simpler procedure than to use (2.45).

PROBLEMS

In each of the first six problems, the nth term of the series solution can be exhibited. Find it, and also find the radius of convergence of the series solution.

1. $y' = xy$
    $y(0) = 1.$

2. $y' = \dfrac{1}{y}$

$y(0) = 1.$

3. $y' = y^3$

$y(0) = 1.$

4. $y' + \dfrac{1}{x} y = \dfrac{1}{x}$

$y(1) = 0.$

5. $y' = \dfrac{x}{y - 1}$

$y(0) = 0.$

6. $y' = \dfrac{y^2}{(1 - x)^2}$

$y(0) = 1.$

7. Show that

$$y' = (y + 1)^2$$
$$y(0) = 0$$

majorizes

$$y' = y^2 + 1$$
$$y(0) = 0.$$

By solving the majorant problem, find a bound for the coefficients in the series expansion of tan x.

8. Find a majorant for

$$y' = y^3 + 1$$
$$y(0) = 0,$$

and find r_0.

9. Show that

$$y' = y^3 + xy + x^2 + 2x + y$$
$$y(0) = y_0$$

is majorized by

$$y' = (y + x + 1)^3$$
$$y(x_0) = y_0.$$

10. Show that

$$y' = p_n(x, y)$$
$$y(x_0) = y_0,$$

70

where $p_n(x, y)$ is a polynomial of degree n in x and y, is majorized by

$$y' = K(x + y + 1)^n$$
$$y(x_0) = y_0,$$

where K is a suitable constant.

11. Show that

$$y' = e^{xy}$$
$$y(0) = 0$$

is majorized by

$$y' = \frac{e^x}{1 - y}$$
$$y(0) = 0.$$

12. Show that

$$y' = e^{xy}$$
$$y(0) = 0$$

is also majorized by

$$y' = \frac{e^y}{1 - x}$$
$$y(0) = 0.$$

13. Of the two majorants in Problems 11 and 12, which is the more effective?

14. Show that the series expansion of the solution of

$$y' = y^2 + x$$
$$y(0) = 0$$

converges for $|x| < 1$.

15. For the preceding problem show that, in fact,

$$a_n = 0$$

for $n = 3k$ or $n = 3k + 1$. Show from this that

$$|a_n| \leq \frac{1}{3^n}.$$

16. In the linear equation

$$y' + p(x)y = 0$$
$$y(x_0) = y_0,$$

suppose that

$$p(x) \equiv \sum_{n=0}^{\infty} p_n(x - x_0)^n \quad \text{for} \quad |x - x_0| < a.$$

71

Show that a majorant for this problem is

$$y' = \left(\frac{M}{1 - \dfrac{x - x_0}{\alpha}} \right) y$$

$$y(x_0) = y_0,$$

where $0 < \alpha < a$ and M is an appropriate constant. Infer that any series solution of the linear, homogeneous equation about x_0 has at least the same radius of convergence as the expansion of $p(x)$ about x_0.

▶ 2.5 POLYGONAL APPROXIMATIONS

The idea of polygonal approximations to the solution of

$$y' = f(x, y)$$
$$y(x_0) = y_0 \tag{2.51}$$

is both the means to proofs of more powerful existence theorems for this problem and the key to digital computer techniques.

By such an approximation we mean one which is pieced together of slope field elements in the following way. Working to the right of x_0, we follow from (x_0, y_0) a straight line of slope $f(x_0, y_0)$ until we reach (x_1, y_1). (We shall use the notation $x_1 - x_0 = \Delta x_1$, $y_1 - y_0 = \Delta y_1$.) From (x_1, y_1) we follow a line of slope $f(x_1, y_1)$ to (x_2, y_2), and so on as long as we can compute the values $f(x_i, y_i)$. The function generated by a choice of the points x_i, $i = 1, 2, \ldots$, is seen to be continuous and piecewise linear. It is our approximate solution. Given (x_0, y_0) we are, of course, free to choose the points x_i or, what is the same, the *mesh* $\Delta x_i = x_i - x_{i-1}$, $i = 1, 2, \ldots$. The values y_i, $i = 1, 2, \ldots$ are then determined in succession from the *difference equation*

$$\frac{\Delta y_i}{\Delta x_i} = f(x_{i-1}, y_{i-1}), \qquad i = 1, 2, \ldots, \tag{2.52}$$

where $\Delta y_i = y_i - y_{i-1}$, $i = 1, 2, \ldots$. In a sense then, the idea is the simple one of replacing a derivative by a difference quotient. In principle, the finer the mesh the better the approximation.

Up to now, and in all that follows, we work only to the right of x_0. Both the ideas and computations are entirely similar if we wish approximations which are defined to the left of x_0, and they are omitted. Let us assume that $f(x, y)$ is bounded in R, $a \leq x \leq b$, $c \leq y \leq d$:

$$|f(x, y)| \leq M;$$

for example, if $f(x, y)$ is continuous in R, this is true. It then follows that polygonal approximations can be constructed on the interval $0 \leq x - x_0 \leq \alpha$ (see Fig. 2.7). That is, we observe that no linear segment of an approximation curve can have slope greater in magnitude than M; therefore, such a curve cannot, for $0 \leq x - x_0 \leq \alpha$, cross the lines $y = y_0 \pm M(x - x_0)$, much less the boundary of R. Indeed, there is a function

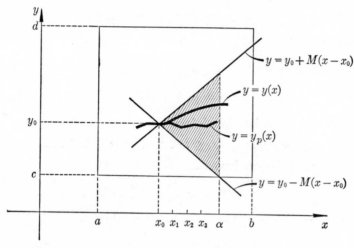

FIG. 2.7

$y_p(x)$ on $[x_0, \alpha]$ generated by each *partition* P: $x_0 < x_1 < x_2 < \ldots < x_n = \alpha$, and $y_p(x)$ must satisfy

$$|y_p(x) - y_0| \leq M|x - x_0|$$

for $0 \leq x - x_0 \leq \alpha$. (By geometric arguments it is also easily established that $y_p(x)$ satisfies the Lipschitz condition

$$|y_p(\bar{x}) - y_p(\bar{\bar{x}})| \leq M|\bar{x} - \bar{\bar{x}}|,$$

although $y_p(x)$ is not, in general, differentiable.)

In order to call $y_p(x)$ an approximate solution, we must show that as the *norm* $||P||$ of the partition P,

$$||P|| = \max \{\Delta x_{ij}\}, \qquad i = 1, 2, \ldots n$$

goes to zero, then $y_p(x)$ converges to a solution of (2.51). In fact, with only the assumption that $f(x, y)$ is continuous in R, a solution of (2.51) can be exhibited as the limit of a carefully chosen sequence of polygonal approximations. This yields a much stronger existence theorem than Theorem (2.21), but uniqueness is not assured, nor will, in general, $\lim_{||P|| \to 0} y_p(x)$ exist for a given sequence of partitions. Computationally, the following is the more useful result.

Theorem 2.51. *Assume the hypotheses of Theorem 2.21. Then, given $\epsilon > 0$, there exists $\delta > 0$ such that if $||P|| < \delta$,*

$$|y(x) - y_p(x)| \leq \epsilon(e^{K(x - x_0)} - 1)$$

for $0 \leq x - x_0 \leq \alpha$. Here, $y(x)$ is the solution of (2.51).

To prove this, we must have the representation

$$y_p(x) = y_0 + \int_{x_0}^{x} f_p(t) \, dt,$$

where $f_p(t)$ is the step function defined by

$$f_p(t) = f(x_i, y_i), \quad x_i \leq t < x_{i+1}, \quad i = 0, 1, 2, \ldots.$$

To compare with this, we have

$$y(x) = y_0 + \int_{x_0}^{x} f(t, y(t)) \, dt,$$

and if we form $u(x) = y(x) - y_p(x)$, it follows that

$$u(x) = \int_{x_0}^{x} [f(t, y(t)) - f_p(t)] \, dt.$$

We now add and subtract, $f(t, y_p(t))$ in the integrand; thus,

$$u(x) = \int_{x_0}^{x} \{[f(t, y(t)) - f(t, y_p(t))] + [f(t, y_p(t)) - f_p(t)]\} \, dt.$$

The first bracketed term in the integrand is easily estimated by means of the Lipschitz condition; in fact,

$$|f(t, y(t)) - f(t, y_p(t))| \leq K|u(t)|.$$

The second is less simple. We must argue that, for $x_i \leq t < x_{i+1}$,

$$f_p(t) = f(x_i, y_i) = f(x_i, y_p(x_i)).$$

Hence, the term is

$$f(t, y_p(t)) - f(x_i, y_p(x_i))$$

for $x_i \leq t < x_{i+1}$, $i = 0, 1, \ldots, n - 1$. But $t - x_i \leq ||P||$ and

$$|y_p(t) - y_p(x_i)| \leq M|t - x_i| \leq M||P||;$$

74

therefore, by the continuity of $f(x, y)$ in R and hence by the uniform continuity, given ϵ, there is a δ such that

$$|f(t, y_p(t)) - f_p(t)| < K\epsilon$$

for all t on $[x_0, \alpha]$ if $||P|| < \delta$. We conclude that for $x \geq x_0$, the inequality

$$|u(x)| \leq \int_{x_0}^{x} (K|u(t)| + K\epsilon)\, dt \tag{2.53}$$

holds. To exploit (2.53), we note that from Figure 2.7 that

$$|u(x)| \leq 2M(x - x_0);$$

therefore, from substituting in (2.53) and integrating, we have

$$|u(x)| \leq 2KM \frac{(x - x_0)^2}{2} + K\epsilon(x - x_0).$$

Substituting the latter inequality in (2.53) and integrating, we find

$$|u(x)| \leq 2K^2M \frac{(x - x_0)^3}{3!} + K^2\epsilon \frac{(x - x_0)^2}{2!} + K\epsilon(x - x_0).$$

Indeed, by induction it is easy to show that for each n,

$$|u(x)| \leq K\epsilon(x - x_0) + K^2\epsilon \frac{(x - x_0)^2}{2!} + \cdots$$

$$+ K^n\epsilon \frac{(x - x_0)^n}{n!} + 2K^nM \frac{(x - x_0)^{n+1}}{(n + 1)!};$$

hence, taking limits, we have

$$|u(x)| \leq \epsilon(e^{K(x - x_0)} - 1),$$

which is the conclusion of the theorem. (Also cf. Section 2.3, for we could argue in place of (2.53) that

$$|u'| \leq K|u| + K\epsilon$$

holds. Thus, the geometric techniques of Section 2.3 could be used here to obtain the result, and, of course, the analytic techniques of the above proof could have been used in Section 2.3.)

Theorem 2.51 justifies the use of equation (2.52) as an approximation to (2.51), and writing (2.52) in the form

$$y_{i+1} = y_i + f(x_i, y_i)(x_{i+1} - x_i),$$

we see clearly the applicability of digital computers to its solution. Given (x_0, y_0), a reasonable function $f(x, y)$, and a partition $\{x_i\}$, we program the computer to keep returning the computed value y_i to the computation of

y_{i+1}. The operations are the same at each step. In this simple scheme, the error is essentially a linear function of $||P||$ (cf. Problem 4), and with high-speed computers satisfactory results are often obtained. It is a very poor hand method compared to other more sophisticated and very rapidly convergent schemes, e.g. the Runge-Kutta method; however, we shall not go beyond the introductory ideas and techniques given here.

PROBLEMS

1. Prove that $y_p(x)$ does satisfy a Lipschitz condition.

2. Assume a uniform mesh, i.e., $\Delta x_i = h$, $i = 1, 2, \ldots$, and find y_n for

$$y' = y$$
$$y(0) = 1. \qquad (2.54)$$

Show, independently of Theorem 2.51, that $y_p(x)$ in this case converges to the solution of (2.54) on any finite interval.

3. For

$$y' = y^2 + 1$$
$$y(0) = 0,$$

let R be $|y| \leq 1$, $|x| \leq 1$. Find M, K, and α. With a uniform mesh $\Delta x_i = h$ estimate the error on $[0, \alpha]$ as an explicit function of h.

4. Show that if $f(x, y)$ also satisfies a Lipschitz condition with respect to x,

$$|f(y, x) - f(y, x')| \leq K|x - x'|$$

in R, then we may choose $\delta = K^2(M + 1)\epsilon$ in the proof of Theorem 2.51.

76

3

APPLICATIONS OF
FÍRST-ORDER EQUATIONS

We are concerned chiefly with applications to certain problems of nature whose plausible mathematical descriptions are in the form of first-order differential equations. In addition, we shall take up briefly some purely mathematical applications from geometry and analysis.

▶ 3.1 GEOMETRIC AND ANALYTIC APPLICATIONS

A simple and often significant problem of geometry is that of finding the *orthogonal trajectories* of a given one-parameter family of curves. These are the curves which meet the members of the given family at right angles. (This problem is not without physical significance. For example, if the given family of curves are equipotentials, then the orthogonal trajectories are the lines of force.) The mathematical procedure is straightforward. Let the family be given by

$$F(x, y) = c; \tag{3.11}$$

then they are solution curves of the (exact) equation

$$\frac{\partial f}{\partial x}(x, y) + \frac{\partial f}{\partial y}(x, y)y' = 0. \tag{3.12}$$

An orthogonal trajectory through the point (x, y) must have there a slope which is the negative reciprocal of that of the member of (3.11) through the same point. We argue, therefore, that

$$y' \frac{\partial f}{\partial x}(x, y) - \frac{\partial f}{\partial y}(x, y) = 0 \tag{3.13}$$

is the differential equation of the orthogonal trajectories. We have derived (3.13) from (3.12) by replacing y', the slope, by $-1/y'$.

For example, the differential equation of the concentric circles

$$x^2 + y^2 = c^2$$

is

$$x + yy' = 0$$

while that of the corresponding orthogonal trajectories is

$$xy' = y.$$

This is separable and easily solved, and the solution curves are the lines

$$y = kx.$$

The relations between a geometric problem and a differential equation are clear because of the correspondence of the slope and y'. Applications to analysis are much less obvious and, indeed, they can seldom be anticipated. Known applications range in difficulty—e.g., from the evaluation of certain definite integrals to a proof of the Implicit Function Theorem.

Let us evaluate the integral

$$u(x, t) = \int_{-\infty}^{\infty} e^{-ts^2} \cos sx \, ds$$

which is of importance in the study of one-dimensional heat flow. Here t is a fixed, positive parameter; thus, as a function of x alone $u(x, t)$ satisfies

$$\frac{du}{dx}(x, t) = \int_{-\infty}^{\infty} e^{-ts^2}(-s) \sin sx \, ds.$$

We integrate this by parts:

$$\frac{du}{dx}(x, t) = (\sin sx) \left.\frac{e^{-ts^2}}{2t}\right|_{-\infty}^{\infty} - \frac{x}{2t}\int_{-\infty}^{\infty} e^{-ts^2}\cos sx\, dx$$

$$= -\frac{x}{2t}\, u(x, t).$$

That is, $u(x, t)$ is a solution of the linear differential equation

$$y' = -\frac{x}{2t}\, y;$$

moreover, at $x = 0$

$$u(0, t) = \int_{-\infty}^{\infty} e^{-ts^2}\, ds = \sqrt{\frac{\pi}{t}}.^*$$

Therefore,

$$u(x, t) = \sqrt{\frac{\pi}{t}}\, e^{-x^2/4t}.$$

PROBLEMS

1. Find the orthogonal trajectories of the family of parabolas
$$y = cx^2.$$

2. Find the orthogonal trajectories of the family of confocal ellipses
$$\frac{x^2}{c^2 + 1} + \frac{y^2}{c^2} = 1.$$

3. Show that the tangent line to the curve $y = y(x)$ at (x, y) has y intercept $(y - xy')$ and x intercept $x - (y/y')$. What is the geometric interpretation of the solutions of
$$y - xy' = 2y?$$
What are the solutions?

4. If
$$y' = f(x, y)$$
is the differential equation of a family of curves, show that the equation of the *oblique trajectories* (these which intersect the given family at the constant angle θ) is

*This follows from the well-known result
$$\int_{-\infty}^{\infty} e^{-x^2}\, dx = \sqrt{\pi}.$$

$$\frac{y' + \tan\theta}{1 - \tan\theta y'} = f(x, y), \qquad 0 < \theta < \frac{\pi}{2}.$$

5. Show that the oblique trajectories $(0 < \theta < \pi/2)$ of the concentric circles

$$x^2 + y^2 = c^2$$

are logarithmic spirals.

6. Show that

$$y(x) = \int_0^\infty e^{-xt} \frac{\sin t}{t} \, dt$$

is the solution of

$$y' = -\frac{1}{1 + x^2}$$

$$y(+\infty) = 0.$$

Find this solution and evaluate $y(0)$.

7. Let $y(x)$ be the solution of the second-order problem

$$y'' + xy = 0$$

$$y(0) = 1, \quad y'(0) = 0.$$

From $L[y(x)] = u(s)$, show that

$$u'(s) = L[(y''(x)] = -y'(0) - sy(0) + s^2 L[y(x)].$$

In other words, show that $u(s)$ is a solution of

$$u' - s^2 u = -s.$$

Show that there is only one bounded solution, as $s \to +\infty$, for this equation, and hence this solution must be $u(s)$. Exhibit this solution.

▶ **3.2 DISCRETE PROCESSES**

Many physical and biological phenomena, such as radioactive decay, population growth, and chemical reactions, have the following general description. Of a large number $N(t)$ of possible identical occurrences at time t, a characteristic proportion of them will occur per unit time during the interval $[t, t + \Delta t]$. Thus, the average behavior is given by the difference equation

$$\frac{M(t + \Delta t) - M(t)}{\Delta t} = kN(t), \tag{3.21}$$

where $M(t)$ is the number of actual occurrences up to time t as measured from some initial state. By averaging behavior in (3.21) we implicitly drop the assumption that $M(t)$ and $N(t)$ are necessarily integer-valued functions. Indeed, since (3.21) is homogeneous in "number of occurrences," we might as well replace both $M(t)$ and $N(t)$ by variables which are effectively continuous such as mass, mole fraction, extent, etc., but which measure occurrences. This change involves only constants of proportionality which may be absorbed into k. We further idealize the description by replacing the difference quotient in (3.21) by the derivative; thus, we assume that the differential equation

$$\frac{dM}{dt} = kN \tag{3.22}$$

governs these phenomena.

This equation has too many unknowns. Wherever it applies we must be able to express both M and N in terms of some single variable. Suppose, for example, that we have present a large number of atoms of radium measured, say, in terms of the mass, $m(t)$. An occurrence is the decay of an atom of radium into an atom of radon, and we assume that each atom of radium present is equally likely to decay. The group behavior of a large number of atoms fits the description which led to (3.21). Here, $N(t)$ is the number of radium atoms present,

$$N(t) = k_1 m(t),$$

and $M(t)$ is the number of decays that have occurred since t_0,

$$M(t) = k_1[m_0 - m(t)], \qquad t \geq t_0.$$

In these, k_1 converts mass to number of atoms, and m_0 is the mass at t_0. Substituting these in (3.22) we find that the linear initial value problem

$$\frac{dm}{dt} = -km$$
$$m(t_0) = m_0 \tag{3.23}$$

describes the phenomenon. We can easily solve this,

$$m(t) = m_0 e^{-k(t-t_0)},$$

and we speak of this behavior as *exponential decay*. k is called the decay constant of radium, and may be determined in the following way. After a period of time τ, it is observed that there is rm_0 radium left; hence

$$rm_0 = m_0 e^{-k\tau}$$

or

$$k = \frac{1}{\tau} \log\left(\frac{1}{r}\right).$$

The τ for which $r = \frac{1}{2}$ is commonly called the half life of radium.

As an example of exponential growth, consider a colony of one-celled organisms which multiply by division. An occurrence is the creation of one additional organism when an old one divides, and we suppose for simplicity that all organisms present at time t are equally likely to divide. This again fits our general description. If $m(t)$ is a convenient measure of the number present, then

$$N(t) = k_1 m(t)$$

and $M(t)$ is the net increase in population since t_0,

$$M(t) = k_1[m(t) - m_0], \qquad t \geq t_0.$$

From (3.22) the problem governing this is

$$\frac{dm}{dt} = km \tag{3.24}$$

$$m(t_0) = m_0.$$

The solution,

$$m(t) = m_0 e^{k(t-t_0)}$$

gives us the term *exponential growth*.

Equation (3.22) is not always linear, as is shown by the law of *mass action* in chemical reactions. A typical reversible reaction is represented by

$$nA + mB \rightleftarrows pC,$$

where A, B, and C are molecular symbols and n, m, and p are the smallest integers which balance the equation, as in

$$2H_2 + O_2 \rightleftarrows 2H_2O.$$

We assume that A, B, and C are in perfectly mixed, gaseous form in a closed vessel of constant volume and temperature. An occurrence is a single reaction to the right resulting in the formation of p molecules of C. Such an occurrence is possible when, in the course of the random motion of molecules, n or more molecules of A and m or more molecules of B are all present simultaneously inside a small element of volume Δv which is characteristic of the reaction. Now, the probability p_1 of finding one molecule of A in a given Δv at time t is proportional to Δv and to the molecular density of A, $y(t)$; thus

$$p_1 = ay(t)\Delta v.$$

Since the molecules are independent, the probability of finding n molecules in Δv at time t is therefore p_1^n. Extending the argument to B, whose molecular density is $u(t)$, we argue that the probability of finding exactly n molecules of A and m molecules of B in Δv at time t is

$$q = k_1 y^n(t) u^m(t).$$

We assume that the arrival in Δv of any surplus of A or B over n and m is so unlikely by comparison that we may ignore it as a reaction possibility. Therefore, the number of reaction possibilities is proportional to q:

$$N(t) = k_2 y^n(t) u^m(t).$$

The number of reactions since t_0 is

$$M(t) = k_3[v(t) - v(t_0)] + R(t),$$

where $v(t)$ is the molecular density of C, k_3 converts molecular density to units of p molecules, and $R(t)$ is the number of reverse reactions since t_0. From (3.22) we have

$$k_3 \frac{dv}{dt}(t) + \frac{dR}{dt}(t) = k[k_2 y^n(t) u^m(t)]. \tag{3.25}$$

To analyze $R(t)$, we argue that the number of possibilities for the reverse reaction is

$$k_4 v^p(t);$$

whence,

$$\frac{dR}{dt}(t) = \bar{k} v^p(t).$$

where $\bar{k}$ is a lumped constant. Finally, we observe that

$$p[y(t) - y(t_0)] = -m[v(t) - v(t_0)]$$

and

$$p[u(t) - u(t_0)] = -n[v(t) - v(t_0)]$$

must hold, in view of the conservation of matter. We can then write (3.25) in terms of $v(t)$ alone and say that the concentration of C is determined by

$$\frac{dv}{dt} = \alpha(\beta - v)^n(\gamma - v)^m - \delta v^p$$

$$v(t_0) = v_0. \tag{3.26}$$

In this, α and δ are lumped non-negative* constants characteristic of the reaction, and

$$\beta = \frac{p}{n} y(t_0) + v_0,$$

$$\gamma = \frac{p}{m} u(t_0) + v_0.$$

It is clear that $0 \le v_0 \le \beta$ and $0 \le v_0 \le \gamma$ necessarily hold.

PROBLEMS

1. For a radioactive element decaying with a half life of 1 year, give the amount present at any time.

2. For a colony of bacteria observed to double in size in 5 hours, describe the growth of the colony at any time.

3. Radium decays into radon with decay constant k_1, but radon in turn decays into polonium with decay constant k_2. Argue that if $n(t)$ and $m(t)$ are measures of the number of radon and radium atoms present, then

$$\frac{dn}{dt} + \frac{dm}{dt} = -k_2 n.$$

In this analysis, assume that an occurrence is the decay of a radon atom. Since $\frac{dm}{dt} = -k_1 m$, find $n(t)$ if $n(t_0) = n_0$ and $m(t_0) = m_0$.

4. In the growth of bacteria a certain number $D(t)$ will have died since time t_0. If $M(t)$ is the population, show that

$$\frac{dM}{dt} + \frac{dD}{dt} = kM.$$

In particular, assume that $dD/dt = k'M^2$, $k' > 0$, and discuss the population growth for various initial populations. Discuss any possible constant populations.

5. For $n = m = p = 1$, sketch the slope field of the equation in (3.26). Exhibit the constant, equilibrium solution.

6. In the general case, show that there is exactly one constant solution of (3.26), $v(t) = v_0$, in the range $0 \le v \le \min(\beta, \gamma)$, and show that all other solutions approach it as $t \to \infty$.

* $\delta = 0$ holds if there is no reverse reaction, and $\alpha = 0$ holds if there is only a reverse reaction.

7. If $f(y_0) = 0$ and $f'(y_0) = k < 0$, argue that solutions of
$$y' = f(y)$$
near y_0 should behave like $y_0 + \varepsilon e^{kx}$. In other words, give reasons why we might *linearize* the above equation near y_0. Apply this idea to estimate the approach of solutions of

$$\frac{dv}{dt} = 2(2 - v)(1 - v) - 4v^2$$

to the equilibrium solution as $t \to \infty$.

▶ 3.3 THE POISSON DISTRIBUTION

In the preceding, to achieve mathematical simplicity, we idealized discrete processes to continuous functions. Here we look again at a discrete process, radioactive decay, but back toward the individual decays. We ask this question: what is the probability that, of a large number of atoms, exactly n will decay in an interval of duration t? Essential to this is that t shall be very short relative to the half life of the element, so that the depletion by n of the total number present can be disregarded.

As we know, the number of atoms present at time s is

$$N(s) = N_0 e^{-ks}.$$

If ks is very small, we may assume that $N(s)$ is essentially constant at N_0. The number of decays expected during the interval $(s, s + t)$ is

$$N(s) - N(s + t) = N_0 e^{-ks}(1 - e^{-kt}),$$

and if both ks and kt are small, this can be approximated by

$$N_0 kt = \lambda t.$$

It is quite plausible to assume that if we divide the interval t into a sufficiently large number m of equal subintervals of length Δt, then two or more of the expected decays will not (or will almost never) occur in the same subinterval. We also assume that each subinterval is equally likely to have one decay. We can then say that the probability of having one decay in any interval of derivation Δt is $\lambda t/m$; or

$$p_1(\Delta t) = \lambda \Delta t. \tag{3.31}$$

In view of our assumption of never finding two or more decays in such a short interval, we are certain to find one or none. Thus, the probability of finding none, $p_0(\Delta t)$, satisfies

$$p_1(\Delta t) + p_0(\Delta t) = 1,$$

85

or

$$p_0(\Delta t) = 1 - \lambda \Delta t. \tag{3.32}$$

We ask now for the probability $p_0(t)$ that no decays occur in an interval of duration t. During an interval of duration $t + \Delta t$ none occur only if none occur during t and none in the following interval Δt. As these events are independent, $p_0(t + \Delta t)$ is the product of $p_0(t)$ and $p_0(\Delta t)$:

$$p_0(t + \Delta t) = p_0(t)(1 - \lambda \Delta t).$$

On rearrangement we have

$$\frac{p_0(t + \Delta t) - p_0(t)}{\Delta t} = -\lambda p_0(t),$$

and it is inescapable that we *define* $p_0(t)$ as a solution of the linear equation

$$\frac{dp}{dt} = -\lambda p. \tag{3.33}$$

In view of (3.32), we should impose the initial condition $p_0(0) = 1$; hence

$$p_0(t) = e^{-\lambda t}.$$

Similar reasoning yields a definition of $p_1(t)$, the probability of exactly one decay in an interval of duration t. The event of one decay during $t + \Delta t$ can occur in two mutually exclusive ways: one during t and none during Δt with probability $p_1(t)p_0(\Delta t)$, or none during t and one during Δt with probability $p_0(t)p_1(\Delta t)$. In view of (3.31) and (3.32), we find that

$$p_1(t + \Delta t) = p_1(t)(1 - \lambda \Delta t) + p_0(t)\lambda \Delta t.$$

On rearrangement, this becomes

$$\frac{p_1(t + \Delta t) - p_1(t)}{\Delta t} = -\lambda p_1(t) + \lambda p_0(t).$$

We now define $p_1(t)$ to be the solution of the problem

$$\frac{dp}{dt} = -\lambda p + \lambda e^{-\lambda t}$$
$$p(0) = 0, \tag{3.34}$$

where the initial condition is a natural consequence of (3.31). Thus,

$$p_1(t) = \lambda t e^{-\lambda t}.$$

Consider now the probability $p_n(t)$ that n decays occur during t. We argue that n decays can occur in time $t + \Delta t$ in two mutually exclusive ways: n in t and none in Δt with probability $p_n(t)p_0(\Delta t)$, or $n - 1$ in t and one in Δt with probability $p_{n-1}(t)p_1(t)$. Thus

$$p_n(t + \Delta t) = p_n(t)(1 - \lambda \Delta t) + p_{n-1}(t)\lambda \Delta t,$$

and we conclude in short order that $p_n(t)$ is the solution of

$$\frac{dp}{dt} = -\lambda p + \lambda p_{n-1}(t)$$

(3.35)

$$p(0) = 0.$$

For example,

$$p_2(t) = \frac{(\lambda t)^2}{2} e^{-\lambda t}$$

and by induction

$$p_n(t) = \frac{(\lambda t)^n}{n!} e^{-\lambda t}.$$

Such a distribution is called a *Poisson* distribution. Experimentally, it has been found that it fits very well phenomena which are evenly but randomly distributed in time, such as radioactive decays and telephone calls.

PROBLEMS

1. Solve (3.34).

2. Solve (3.35) for $n = 2$.

3. Prove by induction that, as given, $p_n(t)$ is the solution of (3.35).

4. Show that

$$\sum_{n=0}^{\infty} p_n(t) \equiv 1.$$

5. Show that $p_n(t)$ has the maximum value $\dfrac{n^n}{n!} e^{-n}$ at $t = \dfrac{n}{\lambda}$.

6. Show that the functions

$$r_n(t, s) = p_0(t)p_n(s) + p_1(t)p_{n-1}(s) + \ldots + p_n(t)p_0(s)$$

satisfy the equations

$$\frac{dr_n}{dt} = -\lambda r_n + \lambda r_{n-1}, \qquad n = 1, 2, \ldots$$

$$r_n(0) = p_n(s)$$

$$\frac{dr_0}{dt} = -\lambda r_0$$

$$r_0(0) = p_0(s).$$

87

Hence, prove that $r_n(t, s) \equiv p_n(s + t)$.

7. Argue that $r_n(t, s) = p_n(s + t)$ on probabilistic grounds.

8. Show algebraically that $r_n(t, s) = p_n(s + t)$.

9. Show that

$$s_n(t, s) = p_1(t)p_{n-1}(s) + p_2(t)p_{n-2}(s) + \ldots + p_n(t)p_0(s)$$

is the solution of

$$\frac{ds_n}{dt} = -\lambda s_n + \lambda r_{n-1}(s, t)$$

$$s_n(0) = 0, \qquad n \geq 1.$$

Show that the solution of these equations agrees with the results of the elementary computation

$$s_n(t, s) = r_n(t, s) - p_0(t)p_n(s) = \lambda^n e^{-\lambda(s+t)}\left[\frac{(s+t)^n - s^n}{n!}\right].$$

10. Argue on probabilistic grounds that $s_n(t, s)$ is the probability that n decays occur in the interval $(0, s + t)$ in such a way that the last decay is in the subinterval $(s, s + t)$.

▶ 3.4 DISCONTINUITIES

In many instances, the physics or mathematics of a situation forces upon us a differential equation

$$y' = f(x, y) \tag{3.41}$$

where $f(x, y)$ has discontinuities in its domain. Moreover, we are required to continue solutions through these discontinuities. An example is the RC circuit shown in Figure 3.1, in which the driving voltage $E(t)$ has ordinary jump discontinuities, say, $E(t)$ is a pulse:

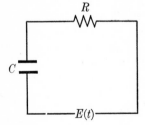

$$E(t) = \begin{cases} 0, & t < 0 \\ 1, & 0 \leq t \leq 1 \\ 0, & t > 0. \end{cases}$$

The question is, what are solutions of the linear equation of the circuit,

FIG. 3.1

$$RC\frac{de_c}{dt} + e_c = E(t), \tag{3.42}$$

which are defined for all t? In all such cases, we shall agree that a function on an interval is a solution if it satisfies the equation except at points of

88

discontinuity of $f(x, y)$, and is continuous at all points. In other words, solutions are continuous with piecewise-continuous derivatives.

To solve (3.42) we must piece together solutions of

$$RC \frac{de_c}{dt} + e_c = 0, \qquad -\infty < t \leq 0 \tag{3.43}$$

$$RC \frac{de_c}{dt} + e_c = 1, \qquad 0 \leq t \leq 1 \tag{3.44}$$

and

$$RC \frac{de_c}{dt} + e_c = 0, \qquad 1 \leq t < +\infty, \tag{3.45}$$

to form a continuous function on $(-\infty, +\infty)$. In particular, the initial value problem $e_c(-1) = 0$ for this circuit is handled as follows. The solution $e_c(t)$ satisfies

$$RC \frac{de_c}{dt} + e_c = 0$$

$$e_c(-1) = 0$$

on $(-\infty, 0)$; hence $e_c(t) \equiv 0$. From this, $e_c(0) = 0$, which generates an initial value problem on $[0, 1]$ for (3.44),

$$RC \frac{de_c}{dt} + e_c = 1$$

$$e_c(0) = 0.$$

By standard methods we find

$$e_c(t) = 1 - e^{-t/RC}, \qquad 0 \leq t \leq 1.$$

This, in turn, generates the initial value problem

$$e_c(1) = 1 - e^{-1/RC}$$

on $[1, +\infty)$ for (3.45),

$$RC \frac{de_c}{dt} + e_c = 0$$

$$e_c(1) = 1 - e^{-1/RC}.$$

Again, by routine technique,

$$e_c(t) = (1 - e^{-1/RC})e^{-(t-1)/RC}.$$

The graph of the solution is sketched in Figure 3.2. Note that the reduced equation has no discontinuities; hence all other solutions differ from this one by a transient $e_0 e^{-t/RC}$ for some e_0. One such solution is shown.

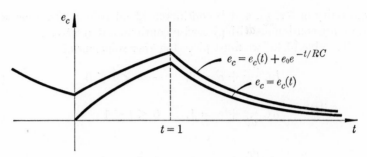

FIG. 3.2

Only somewhat more complicated is the situation where $E(t)$ is the periodic square-wave voltage of period 2:

$$E(t) = \begin{cases} 1, & 0 < t \leq 1 \\ 0, & 1 < t \leq 2 \end{cases}$$

$$E(t + 2) \equiv E(t), \quad \text{for all } t.$$

The same equations are involved but we restrict attention for the moment to the period $[0, 2]$. Several solutions are sketched with their continuations in Figure 3.3. In general, solutions have the form $k_1 e^{-t/RC}$ on

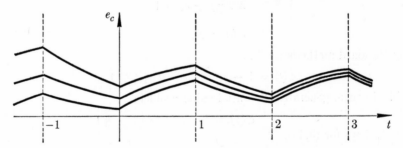

FIG. 3.3

$[-1, 0]$, $[1, 2]$, . . . and $1 + k_2 e^{-t/RC}$ on $[0, 1]$, $[2, 3]$, . . . , and they must be continuous at each integer point. It appears from this sketch that there may be a solution $e_0(t)$ such that $e_0(0) = e_0(2)$, in which case we can clearly assert that

$$e_0(t + 2) \equiv e_0(t)$$

for all t. No other solution can be thus periodic, since any two solutions differ by a nonperiodic transient. To exhibit $e_0(t)$, we argue that

90

$$e_0(t) = \begin{cases} 1 - k_1 e^{-t/RC}, & 0 < t \leq 1 \\ k_2 e^{-t/RC}, & 1 < t \leq 2. \end{cases}$$

We require that $e_0(t)$ be continuous at $t = 1$ and that $e_0(0) = e_0(2)$; i.e.,

$$1 + k_1 e^{-1/RC} = k_2 e^{-1/RC}$$

$$1 + k_1 = k_2 e^{-2/RC}.$$

The solution of this pair of equations is easily found.

A simple example of a discontinuity in the dependent variable is afforded by Coulomb friction (see Fig. 3.4). A block sliding down a plane is subject to the force $-mg \sin \theta$ due to gravity, and to a frictional force. The simplest assumptions we can make about the frictional force when

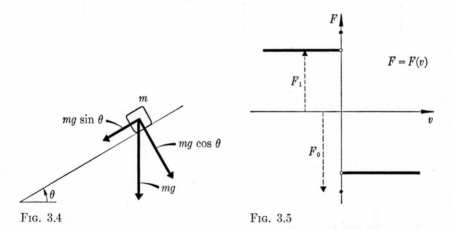

FIG. 3.4   FIG. 3.5

the block is in motion are that it is proportional to the normal force, $mg \cos \theta$, constant in magnitude over the range of velocities considered, and opposite in sign to the velocity. When $v = 0$, the block is not (or is) in equilibrium according as $mg \sin \theta$ is greater than or less than (or equal to) the static friction $F_0 mg \cos \theta$, the latter being somewhat larger than the dynamic friction. (See Fig. 3.5 for these characteristics.) The equation of motion is

$$\frac{dv}{dt} = -g \sin \theta + F(v) \cos \theta, \qquad v \neq 0.$$

If

$$g \sin \theta > F_0 \cos \theta,$$

91

so that $v = 0$ is not an equilibrum state, solutions can be continued across $v = 0$. A typical solution is shown in Figure 3.6 (a). If

$$F_0 \cos \theta \geq g \sin \theta > F_1 \cos \theta,$$

then solution curves have the appearance shown in Figure 3.6 (b). Note

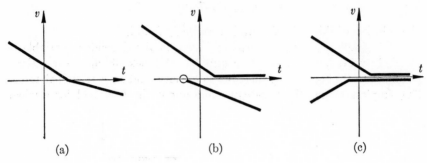

(a)   (b)   (c)

FIG. 3.6

that the solution curve in the lower half plane does not meet the t axis; $v = 0$ is an unstable equilibrium. Finally, if

$$g \sin \theta < F_1 \cos \theta,$$

then solutions are pieced together as shown in Figure 3.6 (c). In other words, the equation of motion is

$$\frac{dv}{dt} = \begin{cases} -g \sin \theta - F_1 \cos \theta, & v > 0 \\ 0, & v = 0 \end{cases}$$

in the upper half plane, and

$$\frac{dv}{dt} = \begin{cases} -g \sin \theta + F_1 \cos \theta, & v < 0 \\ 0, & v = 0 \end{cases}$$

in the lower half plane.

PROBLEMS

1. Find the solution of

$$y' = \begin{cases} y, & x \geq 0 \\ -y, & x < 0 \end{cases}$$

$$y(1) = 1,$$

and show that there is only one solution.

2. Describe all solutions of

$$y' = \begin{cases} y + 1, & y > 0 \\ 0, & y \le 0. \end{cases}$$

3. Find the response of the circuit in Figure 3.1 to the saw-tooth pulse

$$E(t) = \begin{cases} 0, & t < 0 \\ t, & 0 \le t \le 1 \\ 0, & t > 1. \end{cases}$$

4. Let $RC = 1$ in (3.42) and let $E(t)$ be the periodic saw-tooth voltage of period 1,

$$E(t) = t, \qquad 0 \le t \le 1$$
$$E(t + 1) = t, \quad \text{for all } t.$$

Find the periodic solution of equation (3.42).

5. Work out

$$y(x) = \int_{-\infty}^{t} \frac{E(s)}{RC} e^{-(t-s)/RC} ds$$

[cf. formula (1.313)] and show that it yields a solution of Problem 3 for the saw-tooth voltage given.

6. Show that the integral representation

$$y(x) = \int_{x_0}^{x} f(t) y_1(x, t) dt$$

(cf. Section 1.3) yields a continuous solution of

$$y' + p(x)y = f(x)$$

when $f(x)$ is piecewise continuous. *Note:* Here $y_1(x, t)$ is the solution of

$$y' + p(x)y = 0$$
$$y(t) = 1.$$

▶ 3.5 NONLINEAR INDUCTANCE

Current flowing in an iron-core coil produces a saturation effect. The flux $\Lambda(i)$ is a function of current which, if hysteresis is disregarded, has the general appearance shown in Figure 3.7. Mathematically speaking, $\Lambda(i)$ is an odd function which increases monotonely for all i, being nearly linear with slope L_2 for small i and linear with slope $L_1 < L_2$ for i past the "knee" at i_s.

Consider such an inductor in the circuit of Figure 3.8. By Faraday's law the voltage across L is

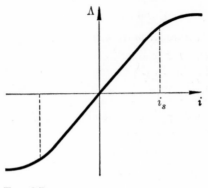

FIG. 3.7   FIG. 3.8

$$\frac{d}{dt}\Lambda(i) = \Lambda'(i)\frac{di}{dt};$$

therefore, the equation of the circuit is

$$\Lambda'(i)\frac{di}{dt} + Ri = E_0 \sin \omega t. \qquad (3.51)$$

We note an equivalent equation with the flux ϕ as the unknown,

$$\frac{d\phi}{dt} + R\Lambda^{-1}(\phi) = E_0 \sin \omega t. \qquad (3.52)$$

Indeed, many arguments are much more easily carried through with (3.52), and we can always recover the current from $i = \Lambda^{-1}[\phi(t)]$.

If we assume that $0 < L_1 \leq \Lambda'(i) \leq L_2$ for all i, then

$$\frac{1}{L_2} \leq (\Lambda^{-1})'(\phi) \leq \frac{1}{L_1}.$$

From this, it follows that the hypotheses of Theorem 2.21 are satisfied for (3.52), and thus a unique solution exists for every possible initial value problem. By the indicated relation of (3.52) to (3.51), the same is true of (3.51).

The linear case, in which $\Lambda'(i) \equiv L$ for all i, differs from that of the

94

RC circuit of Section 3.4 only in physical meaning of variables and parameters. We can exhibit the unique, periodic, steady-state solution

$$i_0(t) = \frac{E_0}{Z} \sin(\omega t - \gamma),$$

where $Z^2 = R^2 + L^2\omega^2$, and $\gamma = \tan^{-1}(\omega L/R)$. All other solutions approach this solution exponentially as $t \to +\infty$. The question then is, in what respects is the behavior of the nonlinear circuit similar to this? Is there a unique periodic response, and if so, is it stable in the sense that all other solutions approach it as $t \to \infty$?

From Figure 3.9, a sketch of the slope field of (3.51), we get the general characteristics. Above the isocline $i = (E_0/R) \sin \omega t$ all slopes

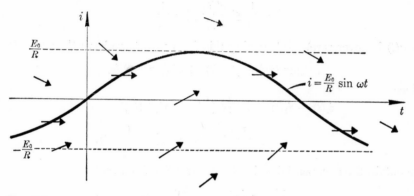

Fig. 3.9

are negative; below, they are positive. Evidently, once a solution curve is within the strip $|i| \leq E_0/R$ it stays there as $t \to \infty$. It is also true that no solution can stay outside of this strip for all t; if not, we should have the asymptotic behavior

$$\lim_{t \to \infty} i(t) = i_0, \qquad \lim_{t \to \infty} \frac{di}{dt}(t) = 0,$$

which contradicts the differential equation (3.51). We infer that all solutions are bounded as $t \to \infty$, which certainly makes sense physically.

In the linear case, a transient $ke^{-t/RC}$ is both the difference of any two solutions of the nonhomogeneous equation and a solution of the reduced equation. In the nonlinear case, the "reduced" equation ($E_0 = 0$) has no relevance, and we must look at the difference between two solutions

95

of (3.51) or of (3.52). Indeed, let $\phi_1(t)$ and $\phi_2(t)$ be distinct solutions of (3.52) on $[t_0, \infty)$. Since they are distinct and uniqueness holds, we may assume that $\phi_1(t) < \phi_2(t)$. Let $u(t) = \phi_2(t) - \phi_1(t)$; then

$$u'(t) = -R[\Lambda^{-1}(\phi_2(t)) - \Lambda^{-1}(\phi_1(t))].$$

Now,

$$\frac{1}{L_2}(\phi_2 - \phi_1) \leq \Lambda^{-1}(\phi_2) - \Lambda^{-1}(\phi_1) \leq \frac{1}{L_1}(\phi_2 - \phi_1),$$

whence, we have the inequality

$$-\frac{1}{L_1}u(t) \leq u'(t) \leq -\frac{1}{L_2}u(t),$$

or

$$-\frac{1}{L_1} \leq \frac{u'(t)}{u(t)} \leq -\frac{1}{L_2}$$

as $u(t)$ is never zero. Integrating this from t_0 to t, we have the estimate

$$u(t_0)e^{-(t-t_0)/L_1} \leq u(t) \leq u(t_0)e^{-(t-t_0)/L_2}.$$

Since

$$i_2(t) - i_1(t) = \Lambda^{-1}[\phi_2(t)] - \Lambda^{-1}[\phi_1(t)]$$

$$\leq \frac{1}{L_1}[\phi_2(t) - \phi_1(t)] = \frac{1}{L_1}u(t),$$

we obtain the exponential estimate on "transient" currents,

$$i_2(t) - i_1(t) \leq k_1 e^{-(t-t_0)/L_2}.$$

This estimate establishes the uniqueness result: *There is at most one periodic solution of (3.51)*, since the difference of two periodic solutions could not go to zero as $t \to +\infty$.

We show the existence of a periodic solution by what is known as a *fixed-point* argument. Consider a solution of (3.51) which satisfies an initial condition of the type

$$-\frac{E_0}{R} \leq i(0) = i_0 \leq \frac{E_0}{R}.$$

We have already argued that such a solution is bounded in absolute value by E_0/R for all $t \geq 0$. In particular, one period later, we have

$$-\frac{E_0}{R} \leq i\left(\frac{2\pi}{\omega}\right) \leq \frac{E_0}{R}.$$

96

In other words, as i_0 varies from $-E_0/R$ to E_0/R, $i(2\pi/\omega)$ varies from i_1 to i_2 where

$$-\frac{E_0}{R} \le i_1 < i_2 \le \frac{E_0}{R}$$

(see Fig. 3.10). By continuity of solutions in initial values, $i(2\pi/\omega)$ is a

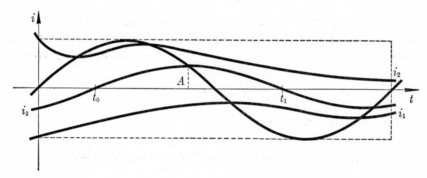

FIG. 3.10

continuous function of i_0. The continuous function $f(i_0) = i_0 - i(2\pi/\omega)$ has the properties that

$$f\left(\frac{E_0}{R}\right) \ge 0$$

and

$$f\left(-\frac{E_0}{R}\right) \le 0;$$

therefore, there exists i_3, $-E_0/R \le i_3 E_0/R$, such that $f(i_3) = 0$. The solution which satisfies $i(0) = i_3$ is periodic, for

$$i(t) \quad \text{and} \quad i\left(t + \frac{2\pi}{\omega}\right)$$

are each solutions which satisfy the same initial condition at $t = 0$.

The close description of this periodic solution, $i_0(t)$, is somewhat more difficult. First, $i_0(t)$ has a mean value zero; i.e., $\int_0^{2\pi/\omega} i_0(t)\, dt = 0$. To see this, we have

$$\Lambda'(i_0(t))\frac{di_0(t)}{dt} + Ri_0(t) \equiv E_0 \sin \omega t.$$

Integrating this from 0 to $2\pi\omega$, we find

$$\Lambda\left(i_0\left(\frac{2\pi}{\omega}\right)\right) - \Lambda(i_0(0)) + R\int_0^{2\pi/\omega} i_0(t)\,dt = E_0\int_0^{2\pi/\omega} \sin\omega t\,dt,$$

or

$$0 + R\int_0^{2\pi/\omega} i_0(t)\,dt = 0.$$

Having mean zero, $i_0(t)$ has zeros. By geometric reasoning on slopes, $i_0(t)$ can only have two zeros in a period. These are indicated in Figure 3.10. Further, we can show that $t_1 - t_0 = \pi/\omega$, or, more precisely,

$$-i_0\left(t + \frac{\pi}{\omega}\right) \equiv i_0(t).$$

First, $i(t) = -i_0\left(t + \frac{\pi}{\omega}\right) = -i_0(s)$; thus,

$$\Lambda'(i(t))\frac{di}{dt}(t) = \Lambda'(-i_0(s))\left[-\frac{di_0}{ds}(s)\right] = -\Lambda(i_0(s))\frac{di_0}{ds}(s).$$

The reasoning here is that $\Lambda(i)$ is an odd function, whence $\Lambda'(i)$ is an even function. Then,

$$\Lambda'(i(t))\frac{di}{dt}(t) = -[-Ri_0(s) + E_0\sin\omega s]$$

$$= -R[-i_0(s)] - E_0\sin\omega\left(t + \frac{\pi}{\omega}\right)$$

$$= -Ri(t) + E_0\sin\omega t,$$

that is, $i(t)$ is a solution of (3.51). As it is periodic, $i(t) \equiv i_0(t)$ must follow. As well as implying that $t_1 - t_0 = \pi/\omega$, the above also shows that the positive maximum and the negative minimum occur $\Delta t = \pi/\omega$ apart and are equal in absolute value.

We are entitled to speak of phase t_0 and amplitude A of $i_0(t)$. It is clear that $A \leq E_0/R$. Less obvious (although, physically, it must be so) is the following comparison with the linear equations

$$L_2\frac{di}{dt} + Ri = E_0\sin\omega t \tag{3.53}$$

and

$$L_1\frac{di}{dt} + Ri = E_0\sin\omega t. \tag{3.54}$$

98

Equations (3.53) and (3.54) have the periodic solutions

$$\frac{E_0}{Z_1} \sin \omega(t - \gamma_1) \quad \text{and} \quad \frac{E_0}{Z_2} \sin \omega(t - \gamma_2),$$

respectively, where

$$Z_i = L_i^2 \omega^2 + R^2, \qquad \gamma_i = \frac{1}{\omega} \tan^{-1}\left(\frac{L_i \omega}{R}\right), \quad i = 1, 2.$$

Proposition.

$$\frac{E_0}{Z_2} \le A \le \frac{E_0}{Z_1} \quad \text{and} \quad \gamma_1 \le t_0 \le \gamma_2.$$

This amounts to saying that the nonlinear circuit behaves with some sort of average inductance. Essential to the argument is the behavior of solu-

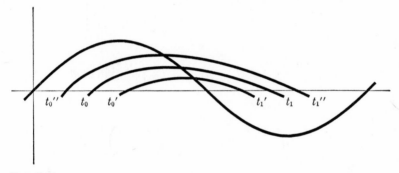

Fig. 3.11

tions of (3.51) illustrated in Figure 3.11. A solution of (3.51) which is zero at t_0'', $0 \le t_0'' < t_0$, is zero again, if at all, at $t_1'' > t_1$ (solution curves cannot intersect). Similarly, if $t_0' > t_1$, then $t_1' < t_1$. With this idea we can locate $i_0(t)$ with respect to solutions with zeros which are greater than, or less than, π/ω apart.

In particular, consider

$$\frac{E_0}{Z_1} \sin \omega(t - \gamma_1).$$

The solution of (3.51), $i_1(t)$, which satisfies $i(\gamma_1) = 0$ behaves as shown in Figure 3.12 until it achieves a positive maximum A_1. The reason for this

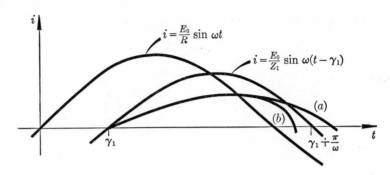

FIG. 3.12

behavior is that the slope field of (3.51) is less steep, in this region, than that of (3.54). We must now decide whether curve (a) or (b) describes the behavior beyond the maximum. If (b), then

$$i_1(t) \leq \frac{E_0}{Z_1} \sin \omega(t - \gamma_1) \quad \text{on} \quad \left[\gamma_1, \gamma_1 + \frac{\pi}{\omega} \right]$$

but

$$R \int_{\gamma_1}^{\gamma_1 + \frac{\pi}{\omega}} \frac{E_0}{Z_1} \sin \omega(t - \gamma_1) \, dt = E_0 \int_{\gamma_1}^{\gamma_1 + \frac{\pi}{\omega}} \sin \omega t \, dt$$

and

$$R \int_{\gamma_1}^{\gamma_1 + \frac{\pi}{\omega}} i_1(t) \, dt = E_0 \int_{\gamma_1}^{\gamma_1 + \frac{\pi}{\omega}} \left\{ \sin \omega t - \Lambda \left[i_1 \left(\gamma_1 + \frac{\pi}{\omega} \right) \right] \right\} dt$$

$$> E_0 \int_{\gamma_1}^{\gamma_1 + \frac{\pi}{\omega}} \sin \omega t \, dt.$$

We obtain these simply by integrating the differential equations involved. The contradiction is clear, and hence (a) must be the case.

We conclude, then, that $t_0 > \gamma_1$ and also, $A < A_1 < E_0/Z_1$. Discussion of the inequalities $t_0 < \gamma_2$, $A > E_0/Z_2$ is left for the problems.

PROBLEMS

1. Referring to Figure 3.13, why is not (a') instead of (a) a possibility, in the comparison of $(E_0/Z_1) \sin \omega(t - \gamma_1)$ and $i_1(t)$?

100

(a')

FIG. 3.13

2. Prove that $t_0 < \gamma_2$ and $A > E_0/Z_2$.

3. Often in practice the function $\Lambda(i)$ is assumed to be strictly piecewise linear; i.e., $\Lambda'(i) \equiv L_2$ for $|i| \leq i_s$ and $\Lambda'(i) \equiv L_1$ for $|i| > i_s$. The equation (3.51) then falls into the class of discontinuous cases,

$$L_2 \frac{di}{dt} + Ri = E_0 \sin \omega t, \qquad |i| \leq i_s$$

$$L_1 \frac{di}{dt} + Ri = E_0 \sin \omega t, \qquad |i| > i_s.$$

Sketch typical solution curves for the two cases $i_s > E_0/R$ and $i_s < E_0/R$. What about periodic solutions?

4. Explain in the piecewise-linear case why saturation is certain to affect the periodic solution only if $i_s < E_0/Z_2$.

5. Again assume that Λ is piecewise linear and $i_s < E_0/Z_2$. Sketch in reasonable estimates of the periodic solutions for values of $L_1 \to 0$. What is the limiting case for $L_1 = 0$?

4

HIGHER-ORDER EQUATIONS AND SYSTEMS

▶ 4.1 INTRODUCTION

The single nth-order equation

$$y^{(n)} = f(x, y, y', \ldots y^{(n-1)}) \tag{4.11}$$

can always be viewed as a special case of a system of n first-order equations

$$
\begin{aligned}
y_1' &= f_1(x, y_1, \ldots y_n) \\
y_2' &= f_2(x, y_1, \ldots y_n) \\
&\ \ \vdots \\
y_n' &= f_n(x, y_1, \ldots y_n)
\end{aligned}
\tag{4.12}
$$

in n unknowns. To illustrate, equation (4.11) is equivalent to the system

$$y_1' = y_2$$
$$y_2' = y_3$$
$$\cdot$$
$$\cdot \qquad\qquad (4.13)$$
$$\cdot$$
$$y_{n-1}' = y_n$$
$$y_n' = f(x, y_1, \ldots y_n)$$

in the following sense. If $(y_1(x), y_2(x), \ldots y_n(x))$ is any solution of (4.13), then the first component $y_1(x)$ is certainly a solution of (4.11). Conversely, if $y(x)$ is a solution of (4.11), then $(y(x),$ $y'(x), \ldots y^{n-1}(x))$ is a solution of (4.13).

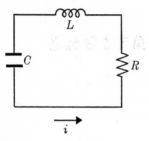

Given any nth-order equation, we may elect to study it as is or as an equivalent system, or in both ways. The same alternatives are often (but not always) available for a given system; that is, we can sometimes find a single nth-order equation with which to replace a system. To illustrate, consider the problem of the LCR circuit shown in Figure 4.1. Assuming linearity of the circuit elements, we have the system of four equations

FIG. 4.1

$$e_L = L\frac{di}{dt}$$

$$e_R = iR$$

$$\frac{de_c}{dt} = \frac{i}{C} \quad \left(\text{or} \quad e_c = \frac{1}{C}\int_{t_0}^{t} i\,dt\right) \qquad (4.14)$$

$$e_R + e_c + e_L = 0$$

in four unknowns as the representation of the circuit. First, we could make use of a method of reducing this mixed system to four algebraic linear equations, a method which in more complicated examples is a very valuable technique, and which involves use of the Laplace transform. Second, by some obvious substitution we could bring this to the system of two first-order equations

104

$$L\frac{di}{dt} = -e_c - iR$$

$$\frac{de_c}{dt} = \frac{i}{C}$$

(4.15)

in two unknowns. Finally, if we wished, we could derive from (4.15) the second-order equation

$$\frac{d^2e_c}{dt^2} = \frac{1}{C}\frac{di}{dt} = \frac{1}{LC}\left(-e_c - RC\frac{de_c}{dt}\right).$$

(4.16)

Notice that (4.15) can be recovered from (4.16), since they are equivalent.

While we should not be bound by hard and fast rules, the following reflect both tradition and present usefulness as guides to deciding which point of view to take. Knowledge of the *second-order linear* equation

$$y'' + p(x)y' + q(x)y = f(x)$$

(4.17)

is so well developed for the equation as is, that we seldom view (4.17) as an equivalent system. If a system of two first-order equations can be brought to this form it is usually preferable to do so; e.g., we would probably prefer (4.16) over (4.15). Of higher-order linear equations, we can say that the higher the order, the more likely we are to prefer a system of n first-order equations instead.

For the nonlinear case, we shall always use systems of first-order equations. The only exception to this is in problems on boundary values, which is a linear notion but has meaning for some nonlinear equations.

PROBLEMS

1. Show that the system

$$y' = y + v$$
$$v' = y - v$$

is equivalent to the second-order equation

$$y'' + 2y = 0;$$

i.e., show that a solution of one is in some sense a solution of the other.

2. Show that any second-order equation derived from the system

$$y' = y$$
$$v' = v$$

has solutions which are in no sense solutions of this system.

3. As in Problem 2, show that the system

$$y' = y + v$$
$$v' = v$$

is not equivalent to any single second-order equation.

4. Write a single third-order equation which is equivalent to

$$y' = v$$
$$v' = y + w$$
$$w' = v + y.$$

5. The definition of particle momentum is a first-order equation, as is Newton's second law. Write a system of first-order equations governing the one-dimensional motion of a particle. Write a system of first-order equations governing the motion of two particles, each constrained to one dimension.

6. Show that the system

$$y' = v$$
$$v' = y$$

is equivalent to the system

$$u' = u$$
$$w' = -w$$

and hence find all solutions of these systems.

7. Show that

$$y' = v$$
$$v' = -2y + 3v$$

is equivalent to

$$u' = u$$
$$y' = 2y - u$$

where $u = 2y - v$; hence solve these systems.

8. Find the unique solution of

$$y'' = y'$$
$$y(0) = 1, \quad y'(0) = 1.$$

9. Under what conditions does

$$y'' = f(y')$$
$$y(x_0) = y_0, \quad y'(x_0) = y_0$$

have a unique solution?

10. In what sense is the implicit first-order equation

$$y'^2 + y^2 = c^2$$

equivalent to the second-order equation

$$y'' + y = 0?$$

▶ **4.2 THEORY OF nth-ORDER EQUATIONS AND SYSTEMS**

For the fundamental theory and the idea of the well-posed problem as applied to nth-order equations and systems, the system (4.12) is the superior vehicle. We need no separate analysis of (4.11), for, obviously, any assertion we are able to make about solutions of (4.12) specializes via (4.13) to (4.11). The proofs of existence, uniqueness, and continuity in parameters of solutions of (4.12) can be repeated almost verbatim from the corresponding proofs in Chapter 2, provided we introduce vector notation and analysis. Our notation for a vector is

$$\mathbf{Y} = (y_1, y_2, \ldots y_n);$$

that for the derivative of a vector,

$$\mathbf{Y}' = (y_1', y_2', \ldots y_n');$$

and that for a vector-valued function,

$$\mathbf{F}(x, \mathbf{Y}) = [f_1(x, \mathbf{Y}), f_2(x, \mathbf{Y}), \ldots f_n(x, \mathbf{Y})].$$

With all this we can write the system (4.12) as

$$\mathbf{Y}' = \mathbf{F}(x, \mathbf{Y}).$$

Defining the length of $\mathbf{Y}$ as

$$|\mathbf{Y}| = (y_1^2 + y_2^2 + \ldots + y_n^2)^{\frac{1}{2}},$$

we now have all of the notions of analysis; e.g.,

$$\lim_{x \to a} \mathbf{Y}(x) = \mathbf{A}$$

means that given $\epsilon > 0$, there is a $\delta > 0$ such that

$$|\mathbf{Y}(x) - \mathbf{A}| < \epsilon$$

if $|x - a| < \delta$. It is not hard to see that this is equivalent to

$$\lim_{x \to a} y_i(x) = a_i, \qquad i = 1, 2, \ldots n.$$

Our principal result is the exact analogue of Theorem 2.21.

Theorem 4.21. *Let* $\mathbf{F}(x, \mathbf{Y})$ *be continuous in* R, $|x - x_0| \leq a$, $|\mathbf{Y} - \mathbf{Y}_0| \leq b$, *and satisfy a Lipschitz condition in* R,

$$|\mathbf{F}(x, \mathbf{Y}_1) - \mathbf{F}(x, \mathbf{Y}_2)| \leq K|\mathbf{Y}_1 - \mathbf{Y}_2|$$

for all $|x - x_0| \leq a$, $|\mathbf{Y}_1 - \mathbf{Y}_0| \leq b$, *and* $|\mathbf{Y}_2 - \mathbf{Y}_0| \leq b$. *Then the initial value problem*

$$\mathbf{Y}' = \mathbf{F}(x, \mathbf{Y})$$
$$\mathbf{Y}(x_0) = \mathbf{Y}_0 \tag{4.21}$$

has a unique solution.

Note that $\mathbf{F}(x, \mathbf{Y})$ is continuous if each component is continuous in the $n + 1$ variables $(x, y_1, \ldots y_n)$, and that $\mathbf{F}(x, \mathbf{Y})$ satisfies a Lipschitz condition if each of the components in $y_1, \ldots y_n$ does. The standard hypothesis which implies this is that each component of $\mathbf{F}(x, \mathbf{Y})$ has continuous partial derivatives with respect to each y_i in R.

The proof proceeds quite simply. Let $M = \max |\mathbf{F}(x, \mathbf{Y})|$ in R. If $\mathbf{Y}_1(x)$ is continuous on $|x - x_0| \leq \alpha = \min \{a, b/M\}$ and if

$$|\mathbf{Y}_1(x) - \mathbf{Y}_0| \leq M|x - x_0|,$$

then the sequence of repeated approximations

$$\mathbf{Y}_n(x) = \mathbf{Y}_0 + \int_{x_0}^{x} \mathbf{F}(t, \mathbf{Y}_{n-1}(t)) \, dt, \qquad n = 2, 3, \ldots$$

converges uniformly to the unique solution on $|x - x_0| \leq \alpha$. We omit further details, but remark that $\int_{x_0}^{x} \mathbf{F}(t, \mathbf{Y}(t)) \, dt$ means the vector

$$\left(\int_{x_0}^{x} f_1(t, \mathbf{Y}(t)) \, dt, \int_{x_0}^{x} f_2(t, \mathbf{Y}(t)) \, dt, \ldots, \int_{x_0}^{x} f_n(t, \mathbf{Y}(t)) \, dt \right)$$

and that the essential inequality

$$\left| \int_{a}^{b} \mathbf{F}(t) \, dt \right| \leq \left| \int_{a}^{b} |\mathbf{F}(t)| \, dt \right|$$

holds for this vector integration.

For example, with no attention to details such as M, K, R, and α, consider the following problem:

$$y' = v \qquad y(0) = 0$$
$$v' = -y \qquad v(0) = 1.$$

The sequence of approximants is generated by the pair of equations

$$y_n(x) = \int_{0}^{x} v_{n-1}(t) \, dt$$

$$v_n(x) = 1 - \int_{0}^{x} y_{n-1}(t) \, dt.$$

Choosing $y_1(x) \equiv 0$, $v_1(x) \equiv 1$, we find in succession

$$y_2(x) = x \qquad\qquad v_2(x) = 1,$$

$$y_3(x) = x \qquad\qquad v_3(x) = 1 - \frac{x^2}{2},$$

$$y_4(x) = x - \frac{x^3}{3} \qquad v_4(x) = 1 - \frac{x^2}{2},$$

and so forth. Indeed, few more steps are needed, to make it clear that $\mathbf{Y}_n(x)$ is converging to $(\sin x, \cos x)$, and quite independently of the above we may verify directly that this is the solution of the given initial value problem.

The analogue of the continuity properties of the first-order equation, i.e., Theorems 3.31 through 3.34, is the following theorem.

Theorem 4.22. *If* $\mathbf{F}(x, \mathbf{Y}, \lambda)$ *is continuous in* λ *and otherwise satisfies the conditions of Theorem 4.21 in R, then the solution of*

$$\mathbf{Y}' = \mathbf{F}(x, \mathbf{Y}, \lambda)$$

$$\mathbf{Y}(x_0) = \mathbf{Y}_0$$

is continuous in x_0, $\mathbf{Y}_0$, *and* λ.

The proof is omitted, but just to indicate ideas, the proofs of uniqueness of solutions of (4.15) and continuity in $\mathbf{Y}_0$ can be reduced to a study of the differential inequality

$$|\,|U|'| \leq K|U|.$$

Let us state these results as a generally useful result for equation (4.11). The proof, of course, proceeds via (4.13).

Theorem 4.23. *If* $f(x, y_1, \ldots y_n)$ *and* $\partial f/\partial y_i$, $i = 1, 2, \ldots n$, *are continuous for* $|x - x_0| \leq a$, $|y_1 - y_0| \leq b_1$, $|y_2 - v_0| \leq b_2, \ldots, |y_n - z_0| \leq b_n$, *then the problem*

$$y^{(n)} = f(x, y, y', y'', \ldots, y^{(n-1)})$$

$$y(x_0) = y_0$$

$$y'(x_0) = v_0 \qquad\qquad\qquad\qquad (4.22)$$

$$\cdot$$
$$\cdot$$
$$\cdot$$

$$y^{(n-1)}(x_0) = z_0$$

is well posed.

The immediate result of the existence theorems given here is that the solution of (4.11)—or of (4.12)—is obtained on the interval $|x - x_0| \le \alpha \le a$. The idea of continuing the solution beyond this interval holds for nth-order equations as it did for the first-order equation. Indeed, we can continue the solution at least until we reach a point about which the hypotheses of the theorems do not hold. For example, it is shown that the solution of the linear equation (4.17) can be continued at least up to the nearest singularity or discontinuity of any of the coefficients. Indeed, certain higher order problems arising in physics and involving such discontinuous functions as impulses, square waves, etc., will force us to relax the definition of a solution so as to allow continuation through a discontinuity (cf. Section 3.4).

Conditions under which solutions of (4.11) and (4.12) are analytic remain much the same. That each component of $\mathbf{F}(x, \mathbf{Y})$ be analytic in $x, y_1, y_2, \ldots y_n$ at (x_0, y_0) is sufficient for the analyticity of the solution (i.e., each component) at x_0. Applying this to, say, the second-order equation

$$y'' - y = 0$$
$$y(0) = 0, \quad y'(0) = 1,$$

$$(4.23)$$

we see that the solution must be analytic. In that case it is given by its Taylor's series,

$$\sum_{n=0}^{\infty} \frac{y^{(n)}(0)}{n!} x^n.$$

We are given $y(0) = 1$ and $y'(0) = 1$, and we obtain from the differential equation

$$y''(0) = y(0) = 0$$
$$y'''(0) = y'(0) = 1$$
$$y^{iv}(0) = y''(0) = 0$$
$$\vdots$$

In fact, it is clear that $y^{(2n)}(0) = 0$ and $y^{(2n+1)}(0) = 1$ for all n; hence

$$y(x) \equiv \sum_{n=0}^{\infty} \frac{x^{2n+1}}{(2n + 1)!} \equiv \sinh x$$

is the solution. The same result could also be obtained by substituting $\sum_{n=0}^{\infty} a_n x^n$ into the equation and determining the a_n. In other words,

110

exactly the same formal techniques are employed for higher order equations and systems as those for the first-order equation.

PROBLEMS

1. Solve

$$y' = v \qquad y(0) = 1$$
$$v' = y \qquad v(0) = 1$$

by repeated approximations. Put the result in closed form, and verify directly that it is a solution.

2. Solve

$$y' = v \qquad y(0) = 1$$
$$v' = -2y \qquad v(0) = 0$$

by repeated approximations. Put the result in closed form.

3. Solve

$$y' = y + 4v \qquad y(0) = 2$$
$$v' = y + v \qquad v(0) = 1$$

by repeated approximations. Put the result in closed form.

4. Solve

$$y'' - y' - 2y = 0$$
$$y(0) = 1, \quad y'(0) = -1$$

by power series. Put the result in closed form and show directly that it is the solution.

5. Solve

$$y' = 2y - v \qquad y(0) = 0$$
$$v' = y \qquad v(0) = 1$$

by power series; i.e., determine the Taylor's series

$$\left(\sum_{n=0}^{\infty} \frac{y^{(n)}(0)}{n!} x^n, \qquad \sum_{n=0}^{\infty} \frac{v^{(n)}(0)}{n!} x^n \right).$$

6. Show that the equation

$$y'' - 2y' - 3y = 0$$

is equivalent to the system

$$y' = y + 4v$$
$$v' = y + v.$$

111

7. Solve

$$y'' + y = 0$$

$$y(x_0) = y_0, \quad y'(x_0) = v_0$$

by power series. Put the result in closed form.

8. Solve

$$y' = v \qquad y(0) = 1$$
$$v' = w \qquad v(0) = 1$$
$$w' = y \qquad w(0) = 1$$

by power series.

9. Find a single second-order equation which is equivalent to the system

$$y' = y + v$$
$$v' = y - v.$$

10. Solve by power series

$$y'' = 2yy'$$

$$y(0) = 0, \quad y'(0) = 1.$$

11. If $(y(x), v(x))$ is a solution of

$$y' = a_{11}y + a_{12}v$$
$$v' = a_{21}y + a_{22}v,$$

show that $y(x)$ is a solution of

$$y'' - (a_{11} + a_{22})y' + (a_{11}a_{22} - a_{12}a_{21})\, y = 0.$$

12. In view of Problem 11, solutions of

$$y' = y$$
$$v' = v$$

$$(4.24)$$

are, in a sense, contained in those of

$$y'' - 2y' + y = 0. \tag{4.25}$$

Find all solutions of (4.24) and then exhibit at least one solution of (4.25) which is in no sense a solution of (4.24).

▶ 4.3 SECOND-ORDER AUTONOMOUS CASE

The special system of equations

$$y' = g(y, v)$$
$$v' = h(y, v),$$

$$(4.31)$$

being independent of x, is called *autonomous*, and we also apply the term to a second-order equation of the type

$$y'' = f(y, y').\tag{4.32}$$

The formulation of a wide range of physical problems results in such a system or equation; for example, the many physical experiments which depend on the passage of time but are quite indifferent to when the experiment begins. To put this idea in analytic terms: if $(y(x), v(x))$ is the solution of (4.31) which satisfies $y(0) = y_0, v(0) = v_0$, then $(y(x - x_0), v(x - x_0))$ is the solution of (4.31) which satisfies $y(x_0) = y_0, v(x_0) = v_0$. This is easily seen. Certainly, $(y(x - x_0), v(x - x_0))$ satisfies the initial conditions at x_0; moreover,

$$\frac{dy(x - x_0)}{dx} = \frac{dy(t)}{dt}\frac{dt}{dx} = g(y(t), v(t)) \cdot 1 = g(y(x - x_0), v(x - x_0))$$

and

$$\frac{dv(x - x_0)}{dx} = \frac{dv(t)}{dt}\frac{dt}{dx} = h(y(t), v(t)) \cdot 1 = h(y(x - x_0), v(x - x_0)),$$

where for clarity we set $t = x - x_0$.

This property, that every translate of a solution is again a solution, is an analytic characterization of the autonomous case and is obviously useful. There is, as well, a geometric property which is unique to the autonomous system. To see this, we turn to the yv plane, often called the *phase plane*. Any solution $(y(x), v(x))$ of (4.31) can be realized as a curve in the yv plane, given parametrically by

$$\begin{aligned} y &= y(x) \\ v &= v(x). \end{aligned}\tag{4.33}$$

These curves, directed by increasing x, are called the *trajectories* of (4.31). The loci of the trajectories relate y and v, and these loci can often be explicitly described in cases where solutions themselves cannot be found. From these relations we can infer qualitative and sometimes quantitative knowledge of the solutions when no other techniques exist. The point of the autonomous case is that these loci are a fixed family of curves for a given system. In fact, they are the solution curves of the first-order equation

$$\frac{dv}{dy} = \frac{h(y, v)}{g(y, v)},\tag{4.34}$$

113

so that any available first-order techniques can be employed in their description. The development of (4.34) is as follows. As is well known, a vector tangent to a curve given by (4.33) has horizontal and vertical

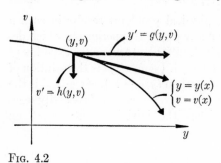

FIG. 4.2

components $y'(x)$ and $v'(x)$, respectively. We see at once, then, the geometric content of the equations in (4.31); they define a field of tangent vectors of the trajectories. The distinction between the autonomous system and the nonautonomous system, which also has this interpretation, is that the tangent field defined by (4.31) is stationary in x while that defined by the nonautonomous system is not.

At each point in the yv plane, (4.31) defines one tangent vector, and, if uniqueness of solutions holds for (4.31), through each point there is one and only one trajectory. Observe that the slope of such a tangent vector is

$$\frac{v'(x)}{y'(x)}$$

(see Fig. 4.2). In view of the chain rule for differentiation, if any portion of a trajectory is given by $v = v(y)$, then

$$\frac{dv(y)}{dy} = \frac{v'(x)}{y'(x)} = \frac{h(y, v)}{g(y, v)}.$$

In other words, trajectories are solution curves of equation (4.34). They are, as well, solution curves of

$$\frac{dy}{dv} = \frac{g(y, v)}{h(y, v)}. \tag{4.35}$$

The ideas for solving, or attempting to solve, (4.31) will now be stated simply. We derive from (4.34) by available techniques a functional representation for a trajectory or portion of a trajectory

$$v = v(y).$$

The first equation in (4.31) then becomes the ordinary, first-order equation

$$y' = g(y, v(y)). \tag{4.36}$$

114

A solution of (4.31) is then $(y(x), v(y(x)))$, where $y(x)$ is a solution of (4.36) and $v(y)$ is a solution of (4.34). *Note:* There will also be reasons for solving (4.35) first for $y(v)$, and then finding $v(x)$ from

$$v' = h(y(v), v).$$

For example, let us solve the initial value problem

$$\begin{aligned} y' &= v & y(0) &= 1 \\ v' &= y & v(0) &= 1 \end{aligned} \tag{4.37}$$

by this method. The appropriate trajectory is given by

$$\frac{dv}{dy} = -\frac{y}{v} \tag{4.38}$$

$$v(0) = 1,$$

and this problem is easily solved:

$$v(y) = \sqrt{1 - y^2}.$$

(*Note:* The complete trajectory is the circle $v^2 + y^2 = 1$.) The first component of the solution is then given by the problem

$$y' = v = \sqrt{1 - y^2} \tag{4.39}$$

$$y(0) = 0.$$

This also is a separable first-order equation, and we obtain $y(x) \equiv \sin x$. The component $v(x)$ is recovered from $v(x) = \sqrt{1 - \sin^2 x} = \cos x$, and thus $(\sin x, \cos x)$ is indeed the solution of (4.37). It is obviously a solution defined for all x, but, technically, this is not contained in the above argument, where we must be careful to stay within the domains of the equations involved, e.g., $v > 0$ in (4.38), $|y| < 1$ in (4.39). The reader should note the lack of uniqueness of solutions of the differential equation in (4.39); indeed, note the spurious solution $y(x) \equiv 1$, which is in no sense a solution of

$$y' = v$$

$$v' = -y.$$

The problem

$$\begin{aligned} y' &= v & y(0) &= 1 \\ v' &= y & v(0) &= 0 \end{aligned} \tag{4.310}$$

115

shows us the role of equation (4.35) since the problem

$$\frac{dv}{dy} = \frac{y}{v}$$

$$v(1) = 0$$

is not at all appropriate for obvious reasons. Instead, we pose

$$\frac{dy}{dv} = \frac{v}{y}$$

$$y(0) = 1,$$

which has the solution $y(v) = \sqrt{1 + v^2}$. We determine $v(x)$ from

$$v' = \sqrt{1 + v^2}$$

$$v(0) = 0;$$

thus $v(x) = \sinh x$, and in turn, $y(x) = \cosh x$.

It is easy to see, by finding the general solution of

$$\frac{dv}{dy} = -\frac{y}{v},$$

that the trajectories of the system in (4.37) are the family of concentric circles

$$v^2 + y^2 = c^2$$

directed in the clockwise direction (Fig. 4.3). An immediate inference is

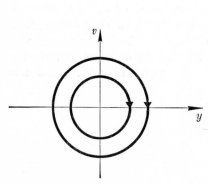

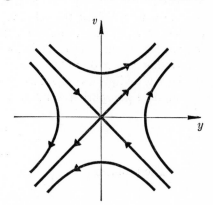

FIG. 4.3   FIG. 4.4

116

that all the solutions are periodic. The trajectories of the system in (4.31) are the family of hyperbolas

$$v^2 - y^2 = c$$

directed as shown in Figure 4.4.

We have, in principle, a systematic technique for finding the solution of (4.31) which satisfies $y(x_0) = y_0$, $v(x_0) = v_0$. We proceed, via (4.34) if $h(y_0, v_0) \neq 0$ and via (4.35) if $g(y_0, v_0) \neq 0$, to reduce the problem to two first-order problems. We notice, of course, a missing case,

$$h(y_0, v_0) = g(y_0, v_0) = 0.$$

Such a point is called a *singular point* of (4.31), but no complicated technique is necessary. We see the solution and trajectory involved, namely, the *constant* solution $(y(x), v(x)) \equiv (y_0, v_0)$ and the point trajectory (y_0, v_0).

While we have made no explicit comment on equation (4.32), it is evident that all ideas and techniques apply to the system

$$y' = v$$
$$v' = f(y, v)$$

which is equivalent to (4.32). For example, to solve

$$y'' - 2y'^2 y = 0$$
$$y(0) = 0, \quad y'(0) = 1,$$

we write, for reference, the equivalent problem

$$y' = v \qquad y(0) = 0$$
$$v' = 2v^2 y \qquad v(0) = 1.$$

The trajectory involved is given by

$$\frac{dv}{dy} = 2vy$$
$$v(0) = 1;$$

whence,

$$v(y) = e^{y^2}.$$

The solution $y(x)$ is given by

$$y' = e^{y^2}$$
$$y(0) = 0.$$

We can only give the solution of this in implicit form,

$$\int_0^{y(x)} e^{-y^2}\, dy = x,$$

117

noting, among the properties of this solution, the singularity

$$\lim_{x \to \sqrt{\pi/2}} y(x) = +\infty.$$

PROBLEMS

1. Find the solution of

$$y' = v \qquad\qquad y(0) = 1$$
$$v' = -y + 2v \qquad v(0) = -1.$$

2. Find the solution of

$$y'' = y'^2 - yy'$$
$$y(0) = 0, \quad y'(0) = 1.$$

3. Find the solution of

$$y'' = 2yy'$$
$$y(0) = 0, \quad y'(0) = 1.$$

4. Find the solution of

$$y'' = y'^2 - y^2$$
$$y(0) = -\tfrac{1}{2}, \quad y'(0) = \tfrac{1}{2}.$$

5. Find the solution of

$$y'' - e^y = 0$$
$$y(0) = 0, \quad y'(0) = 0.$$

6. If $y(x)$ is a solution of $y'' + e^y = 0$, show that

$$y(e^{-c}x) - 2c$$

is also a solution.

7. Find the explicit equation of the trajectories of

$$y' = v$$
$$v' = y;$$

i.e., find the general solution of

$$\frac{dv}{dy} = \frac{y}{v},$$

and sketch the trajectories.

8. Find the equation of the trajectories of

$$y' = v$$
$$v' = -y^3$$

and sketch them.

118

9. Find the equation of the trajectories of

$$y' = v$$
$$v' = -\sin y.$$

Sketch them. Note different cases and note singular points.

10. Find the equation of trajectories of

$$y' = y - v$$
$$v' = y + v.$$

Sketch them.

11. Given

$$y' = v$$
$$v' = f(y, v)$$

and given the trajectory T of this system shown in Figure 4.5 (a), explain, step by step, why $y(x)$ must have the behavior shown in Figure 4.5 (b). What further information would be needed in order to estimate the distances $x_1 - x_0$, $x_2 - x_1$, and $x_3 - x_2$?

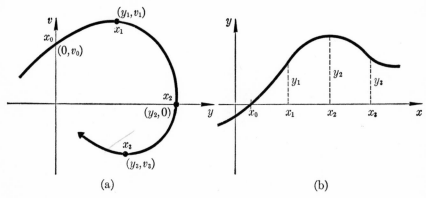

(a)   (b)

FIG. 4.5

12. Note the following point of view toward (4.32). Let $y' = p$; then

$$y'' = \frac{dp}{dx} = \frac{dp}{dy}\frac{dy}{dx} = \frac{dp}{dy} p,$$

and thus (4.32) becomes the first-order equation

$$\frac{dp}{dy} p = f(y, p)$$

119

which is in fact (4.34). The point of mentioning this is that this technique applies to the autonomous third-order equation

$$y''' = f(y, y', y'')$$

where geometric ideas would not be clear. Indeed, show that if $y' = p$, then this last equation becomes the second-order equation

$$p^2 \frac{d^2p}{dy^2} = -p\left(\frac{dp}{dy}\right)^2 + f\left(y, p, p\frac{dp}{dy}\right).$$

5
LINEAR EQUATIONS

▶ 5.1 SECOND-ORDER, LINEAR, HOMOGENEOUS EQUATIONS

We consider first the equation

$$y'' + ay' + by = 0, \tag{5.11}$$

which is *linear* and *homogeneous* (i.e., if $y(x)$ is a solution, then $cy(x)$ is also a solution) and has *constant* coefficients. To write the equivalent autonomous system

$$\begin{aligned} y' &= v \\ v' &= -av - by \end{aligned} \tag{5.12}$$

and solve it by the methods of the preceding chapter is but one of several methods of solving (5.11). There are, however, more effective methods, among them the application of the Laplace transform.

Recall that
$$L[f'(x)] = -f(0) + sL[f(x)];$$
hence,
$$L[f''(x)] = -f'(0) + sL[f'(x)] = -f'(0) - sf(0) + s^2L[f(x)].$$
Let $y(x)$ be the solution of (5.11) which satisfies
$$y(0) = y_0$$
$$y'(0) = v_0$$
and suppose that it has a transform. Then
$$L[y''(x) + ay'(x) + by(x)] \equiv 0.$$
By the properties of the transform, we find
$$-y'(0) - sy(0) + s^2L[y(x)] - ay(0) - asL[y(x)] + bL[y(x)] = 0,$$
or
$$L[y(x)] = \frac{v_0 + ay_0 + sy_0}{s^2 + as + b}. \tag{5.13}$$
In order to infer the form of $y(x)$ from this, we note three cases:

(i) $a^2 - 4b > 0$ so that $s^2 + as + b$ has real, distinct linear factors,
$$s^2 + as + b = (s - r_1)(s - r_2);$$

(ii) $a^2 - 4b = 0$, in which case
$$s^2 + as + b = \left(s - \frac{a}{2}\right)^2;$$

(iii) $a^2 - 4b < 0$ so that
$$s^2 + as + b = \left(s + \frac{a}{2}\right)^2 + \omega^2, \quad \omega = \sqrt{b - \frac{a^2}{4}}.$$

If (i) holds, we write, by the methods of partial fractions,
$$L[y(x)] = \frac{c_1}{s - r_1} + \frac{c_2}{s - r_2},$$
whence, from any table of transforms,
$$y(x) = c_1e^{r_1x} + c_2e^{r_2x}. \tag{5.14}$$
For example, the transform of the solution of
$$y'' - y' + 2y = 0$$
$$y(0) = 1, \quad y'(0) = 1$$

is

$$L[y(x)] = \frac{s}{s^2 - s + 2} = \frac{\frac{2}{3}}{s - 2} + \frac{\frac{1}{3}}{s + 1}$$

and,

$$y(x) = \tfrac{2}{3}e^{2x} + \tfrac{1}{3}e^{-x}.$$

If (ii) holds, then again by partial fractions,

$$L[y(x)] = \frac{c_1}{\left(x + \dfrac{a}{2}\right)} + \frac{c_2}{\left(x + \dfrac{a}{2}\right)^2}.$$

From this and tables,

$$y(x) = c_1 e^{-(a/2)x} + c_2 x e^{-(a/2)x}. \tag{5.15}$$

For example, in

$$y'' + 2y' + y = 0$$
$$y(0) = 1, \quad y'(0) = 1,$$
$$L[y(x)] = \frac{3 + s}{(s + 1)^2} = \frac{1}{s + 1} + \frac{2}{(s + 1)^2};$$

thus,

$$y(x) = e^{-x} + 2xe^{-x}.$$

Finally, when (iii) holds and $s^2 + as + b$ is irreducible, we must write

$$L[y(x)] = \frac{c_1\omega}{\left(s + \dfrac{a}{2}\right)^2 + \omega^2} + \frac{c_2\left(s + \dfrac{a}{2}\right)}{\left(s + \dfrac{a}{2}\right)^2 + \omega^2},$$

whence,

$$y(x) = c_1 e^{-(a/2)x} \sin \omega x + c_2 e^{-(a/2)x} \cos \omega x. \tag{5.16}$$

For example, if $y(x)$ is the solution of

$$y'' + 2y' + 2y = 0$$
$$y(0) = 1, \quad y'(0) = 0,$$

then

$$L[y(x)] = \frac{2 + s}{s^2 + 2s + 2} = \frac{1}{(s + 1)^2 + 1} + \frac{1 + s}{(s + 1)^2 + 1},$$

and

$$y(x) = e^{-x} \sin x + e^{-x} \cos x.$$

While it was clear from the beginning, by Theorem 2.21, that (5.11) has a unique solution which satisfies the initial conditions, it has not been

123

shown that this solution has a Laplace transform. This is now also clear, for we may verify directly that the functions exhibited in (5.14), (5.1)5, and (5.16) are solutions of (5.11), and they certainly have transforms.

We may use the translation property of the autonomous equation in order to get away from the initial value $x_0 = 0$. We note that if $y(x)$ is the solution of

$$y'' + ay' + by = 0$$
$$y(0) = y_0, \quad y'(0) = v_0,$$

then $y(x - x_0)$ is the solution of

$$y'' + ay' + by = 0$$
$$y(x_0) = y_0, \quad y'(x_0) = v_0.$$

PROBLEMS

1. Find the solution of
$$y'' + 3y' + 2y = 0$$
$$y(1) = 0, \quad y'(1) = 1.$$

2. Find the solution of
$$y'' - y' + y = 0$$
$$y(0) = 1, \quad y'(0) = 0.$$

3. Find the solution of
$$y'' + 4y' + 4y = 0$$
$$y(2) = 1, \quad y'(2) = 2.$$

4. Find a change of variable $u = y + c$ which brings
$$y'' + 3y' + 3y = 1$$
to an equivalent homogeneous equation. Find, therefore, the solution which satisfies $y(0) = 0$, $y'(0) = 0$.

5. Show that the change of variable $u = y + x - \frac{1}{2}$ transforms
$$y'' + 2y' + y = x$$
to a homogeneous equation. In view of this, find a similar change of variable which brings
$$y'' + 3y' - 2y = 2x$$
into homogeneous form.

6. If $y(x)$ is a solution of
$$y'' + ay' + by = 0,$$

124

show that $y(-x)$ is a solution of

$$y'' - ay' + by = 0,$$

e.g., let $u(x) = y(-x) = y(t)$, $u'(x) = -y'(t)$, etc.

7. Show that the change of variable $u = e^{-(a/2)x} y$ transforms

$$y'' + ay' + by = 0$$

into

$$u'' + \left(b - \frac{a^2}{4}\right) u = 0.$$

8. Find the Laplace transform of the solution of

$$y'' - 2y' - 3y = \sin x$$
$$y(0) = 0, \quad y'(0) = 1.$$

9. Find the Laplace transform of the solution of

$$y'' + y' - 2y = e^x$$
$$y(0) = 0, \quad y'(0) = 1.$$

10. Find the Laplace transform of the solution of

$$y'' + 2y' + y = e^{-x}$$
$$y(0) = 0, \quad y'(0) = 0.$$

11. Show that $\lim_{x \to +\infty} y(x) = 0$ holds for every solution of

$$y'' + ay' + by = 0$$

if, and only if, $a > 0$ and $b > 0$.

12. Show that the substitution $u = -y'/y$ transforms

$$y'' + ay' + by = 0$$

into the first-order equation

$$u' = u^2 + au + b,$$

which is called a *Riccati* equation. (This is another approach to the solution of (5.11).)

13. Show that if $a^2 - 4b \geq 0$, the only solution to the *boundary value* problem

$$y'' + ay' + by = 0$$
$$y(0) = y(1) = 0$$

is $y(x) \equiv 0$.

14. Find values of the parameter b such that the problem

$$y'' + y' + by = 0$$
$$y(0) = y(L) = 0$$

does have a solution which is not identically zero.

▶ **5.2 SECOND-ORDER, LINEAR, HOMOGENEOUS EQUATIONS** (Continued)

Formulas (5.14), (5.15), and (5.16) give the structure of solutions of (5.11) quite apart from initial value problems. They give solutions for all values of c_1 and c_2, and they give each possible solution if c_1 and c_2 are suitably chosen. In contrast, the linear equation

$$y'' + p(x)y' + q(x)y = 0, \tag{5.21}$$

whose coefficients are given, continuous functions is not often explicitly solvable in terms of elementary functions, but the structure of solutions is easily investigated.

Theorem 5.21. *If $y_1(x)$ and $y_2(x)$ are solutions of (5.21), then $c_1y_1(x) + c_2y_2(x)$ is also a solution for every c_1 and c_2.*

This is clear, for

$$[c_1y_1''(x) + c_2y_2''(x)] + p(x)[c_1q_1'(x) + c_2y_2'(x)] + q(x)[y_1(x) + y_2(x)]$$
$$\equiv c_1[y_1''(x) + p(x)y_1'(x) + q(x)y_1(x)]$$
$$+ c_2[y_2''(x) + p(x)y_2'(x) + q(x)y_2(x)] \equiv 0 + 0.$$

In dealing with linear combinations we shall need the notion of linear independence. The functions $f_1(x), f_2(x), \ldots, f_n(x)$ are said to be *linearly independent* on the interval $x_0 \leq x \leq x_1$ if

$$c_1f_1(x) + c_2f_2(x) + \ldots + c_nf_n(x) \equiv 0$$

on $x_0 \leq x \leq x_1$ implies that $c_1 = c_2 = \ldots = c_n = 0$. Otherwise, they are said to be *linearly dependent*. In the case of $n = 2$, we see that $f_1(x)$ and $f_2(x)$ are linearly independent if and only if one is not a constant multiple of the other. Thus e^x and e^{-x} are linearly independent for all x as are the functions 1 and x.

Theorem 5.22. *Equation (5.21) has a pair of linearly independent solutions. Every solution of (5.21) is a unique linear combination of any two linearly independent solutions.*

Let x_0 be any point in the interval $\alpha < x < \beta$ on which $p(x)$ and $q(x)$ are continuous. The solution $y_1(x)$ of the problem

$$y'' + p(x)y' + q(x)y = 0$$

$$y(x_0) = 0, \quad y'(x_0) = 1$$

and the solution $y_2(x)$ of

$$y'' + p(x)y' + q(x)y = 0$$

$$y(x_0) = 1, \quad y'(x_0) = 0$$

are linearly independent. For suppose that

$$c_1 y_1(x) + c_2 y_2(x) \equiv 0$$

then also

$$c_1 y_1'(x) + c_2 y_2'(x) \equiv 0.$$

Let $x = x_0$; the first identity becomes $c_2 = 0$ and the second $c_1 = 0$. This proves the first part of the theorem.

Let now $y_1(x)$ and $y_2(x)$ be any pair of linearly independent solutions and $y(x)$ an arbitrary solution. If there are constants c_1 and c_2 such that

$$\begin{aligned} y(x_0) &= c_1 y_1(x_0) + c_2 y_2(x_0) \\ y'(x_0) &= c_1 y_1'(x_0) + c_2 y_2'(x_0), \end{aligned} \tag{5.22}$$

where x_0 is an arbitrary point, then

$$y(x) \equiv c_1 y_1(x) + c_2 y_2(x).$$

This follows from the uniqueness theorem, for the solutions $y(x)$ and $c_1 y_1(x) + c_2 y_2(x)$ satisfy the same initial conditions. Now, either there is a unique pair of numbers (c_1, c_2) which satisfy (5.22) or, by the well-known algebraic result, there are numbers d_1 and d_2, not both zero, for which

$$\begin{aligned} d_1 y_1(x_0) + d_2 y_2(x_0) &= 0 \\ d_1 y_1'(x_0) + d_2 y_2'(x_0) &= 0. \end{aligned}$$

If the latter holds, the solution $u(x) = d_1 y_1(x) + d_2 y_2(x)$ satisfies $u(x_0) = 0$, $u'(x_0) = 0$. By uniqueness, $u(x)$ can only be the identically vanishing solution; whence

$$d_1 y_1(x) + d_2 y_2(x) \equiv 0,$$

which contradicts the assumption of linear independence. This completes the proof.

Since (5.22) has a unique solution, we also have the explicit algebraic result

$$\begin{vmatrix} y_1(x_0) & y_2(x_0) \\ y_1'(x_0) & y_2'(x_0) \end{vmatrix} \neq 0.$$

As x_0 is arbitrary, it must be that this determinant, called the Wronskian

127

of $y_1(x)$ and $y_2(x)$, is never zero if $y_1(x)$ and $y_2(x)$ are linearly independent. The converse is also true; if $y_1(x)$ and $y_2(x)$ are linearly dependent, then their Wronskian is identically zero. Indeed, we can evaluate the Wronskian in the following sense:

$$\begin{vmatrix} y_1(x) & y_2(x) \\ y_1'(x) & y_2'(x) \end{vmatrix} \equiv \overline{w}(x) \equiv \overline{w}(x_0) e^{-\int_{x_0}^{x} p(t)\, dt}. \tag{5.23}$$

This is immediate when we observe that

$$\overline{w}'(x) \equiv \begin{vmatrix} y_1'(x) & y_2'(x) \\ y_1'(x) & y_2'(x) \end{vmatrix} + \begin{vmatrix} y_1(x) & y_2(x) \\ y_1''(x) & y_2'' \end{vmatrix}$$

$$\equiv 0 + \begin{vmatrix} y_1(x) & y_2(x) \\ -p(x)y_1'(x) \quad -q(x)y_1(x) & -p(x)y_2'(x) \quad -q(x)y_2(x) \end{vmatrix}$$

$$\equiv -p(x)\overline{w}(x);$$

that is, $\overline{w}(x)$ is a solution of a first-order, linear, homogeneous, differential equation, and (5.23) follows.

If $y_1(x)$ and $y_2(x)$ were linearly dependent solutions of (5.21), then there would be constants c_1 and c_2, not both zero, such that

$$c_1 y_1(x) + c_2 y_2(x) \equiv 0;$$

consequently,

$$c_1 y_1'(x) + c_2 y_2'(x) \equiv 0.$$

In particular, these would hold at x_0, which implies that $\overline{w}(x_0) = 0$, but then (5.23) implies that $\overline{w}(x) \equiv 0$.

The above theory yields an effective technique of solution of (5.21), apart from such special methods as the Laplace transform. We need only find two independent solutions of such an equation, by any means, in order to have them all. Indeed, we can show by the identity (5.23) that one nontrivial solution $y_1(x) \not\equiv 0$, will generate an independent pair. For observe that if $y(x)$ satisfies

$$y_1(x)y'(x) - y_1'(x)y(x) \equiv \overline{w}(x) \equiv e^{-\int_{x_0}^{x} p(t)\, dt} \equiv r(x) \tag{5.24}$$

where $y_1(x)$ is a solution of (5.21) and x_0 is such that $y_1(x_0) \neq 0$, then $y(x)$ is a solution of (5.21). To prove this we exhibit such a function $y(x)$ by the methods of Section 1.3; i.e., solve the first-order linear equation (5.24),

$$y(x) \equiv y_1(x) \int_{x_0}^{x} \frac{r(t)}{y_1^2(t)}\, dt. \tag{5.25}$$

128

First,

$$y'(x) \equiv y_1'(x) \int_{x_0}^{x} \frac{r(t)}{y_1{}^2(t)} \, dt + \frac{r(x)}{y_1(x)},$$

then

$$y''(x) \equiv y_1''(x) \int_{x_0}^{x} \frac{r(t)}{y_1{}^2(t)} \, dt + \frac{y_1'(x)r(x)}{y_1{}^2(x)} - \frac{y_1'(x)r(x)}{y_1{}^2(x)} + \frac{r'(x)}{y_1(x)};$$

whence,

$$y''(x) + p(x)y'(x) + q(x)y(x)$$

$$\equiv [y_1''(x) + p(x)y_1'(x) + q(x)y_1(x)] \int_{x_0}^{x} \frac{r(t)}{y_1{}^2(t)} + \frac{p(x)r(x)}{y_1(x)} - \frac{p(x)r(x)}{y_1(x)}$$

$$\equiv 0.$$

Since $\overline{w}(x_0) = 1$, $y_1(x)$ and $y(x)$ are independent.

For example, one well-known method of solving an equation with constant coefficients, say

$$y'' + 2y + y = 0, \tag{5.26}$$

is to look for exponential solutions. Thus, e^{mx} is a solution if

$$m^2 e^{mx} + 2m e^{mx} + e^{mx} \equiv 0;$$

i.e., if $m^2 + 2m + 1 = 0$ or $m = -1$. With the one exponential solution, e^{-x}, we find an independent solution from (5.25):

$$y(x) \equiv e^{-x} \int_{0}^{x} \frac{e^{-2t}}{e^{-2t}} \, dt \equiv xe^{-x}.$$

[Recall (5.15).]

In another example, we observe that $y_1(x) \equiv x$ is a solution of

$$y'' - 2xy' + 2y = 0. \tag{5.27}$$

An independent solution is evidently

$$y(x) \equiv x \int_{1}^{x} \frac{e^{t^2}}{t^2} \, dt.$$

There only appears to be a singularity at $x = 0$. If we integrate by parts once, we obtain

$$y(x) \equiv x \left(-\frac{e^{x^2}}{x} + e - \int_{1}^{x} e^{t^2} \, dt \right),$$

which not only is well-behaved as $x \to 0$, but defines a solution of (5.27) for all x.

PROBLEMS

1. Show that $e^{r_1 x}$ and $e^{r_2 x}$ are independent solutions of
$$y'' + ay' + by = 0$$
when r_1 and r_2 are distinct real roots of $s^2 + as + b = 0$.

2. Show that $e^{r_1 x}$ and $x e^{r_1 x}$ are independent solutions of
$$y'' + ay' + by = 0$$
when r_1 is a double root of $s^2 + as + b = 0$.

3. Show that $e^{\alpha x} \sin \omega x$ and $e^{\alpha x} \cos \omega x$ are independent solutions of
$$y'' + ay' + by = 0$$
when $\alpha + i\omega$ and $\alpha - i\omega$ are roots of $s^2 + as + b = 0$.

4. Let $y(x)$ be a solution of
$$y'' + ay' + by = 0;$$
then, as we know, $y(x + c)$ is also a solution. Give two examples, one for which $y(x)$ and $y(x + c)$ are linearly independent and one for which they are not.

5. If $y(x)$ is a solution of
$$y'' + ay' + by = 0,$$
show that $y'(x)$ is also a solution. When are $y'(x)$ and $y(x)$ linearly dependent?

6. Let $y_1(x)$ and $y_2(x)$ be nontrivial solutions of (5.21) such that $y_1(x_0) = 0$. Show that $y_1(x)$ and $y_2(x)$ are linearly dependent if and only if $y_2(x_0) = 0$. If $y_1'(x_1) = 0$, show that $y_1(x)$ and $y_2(x)$ are linearly dependent if and only if $y_2'(x_1) = 0$.

7. Show that if $y(x)$ is a solution of
$$y'' + ay' + b = 0,$$
then $y(x)$ and $y(x + c)$ are linearly dependent for every c, if and only if neither $y(x)$ nor $y'(x)$ ever vanishes.

8. If $y_1(x)$ and $y_2(x)$ are independent solutions of (5.21) with Wronskian $\overline{w}(x)$, show that
$$\frac{y_1(x_0)y_2(x) - y_2(x_0)y_1(x)}{\overline{w}(x_0)} = y_0(x, x_0)$$
is the solution of
$$y'' + p(x)y' + q(x)y = 0$$
$$y(x_0) = 0, \quad y'(x_0) = 1.$$

130

9. Show that $u(t) = y_0(x, t)$ is a solution of the *adjoint* equation to (5.21),

$$\frac{d^2u}{dt^2} - \frac{d}{dt}[p(t)u] + q(t)u = 0.$$

10. Show that $2x^2 - 1$ is a solution of

$$y'' - 2xy' + 4y = 0,$$

and hence find a second independent solution.

11. Show that x is a solution of

$$y'' + y' - \frac{y}{x} = 0,$$

and find a second solution. Show that, in spite of the singularity of the coefficients of the equation at $x = 0$, all solutions are well-behaved at $x = 0$.

12. Show that x is a solution of

$$y'' - \frac{y'}{x} + \frac{y}{x^2} = 0,$$

and find a second solution. Note that the second solution has a singularity at $x = 0$.

▶ 5.3 NONHOMOGENEOUS EQUATIONS

Recall the first-order problem

$$\begin{aligned} y' + ay &= f(x) \\ y(0) &= y_0, \end{aligned} \tag{5.31}$$

where a is a constant. If we take Laplace transforms, we obtain

$$L[y(x)] = \frac{y_0}{s + a} + \frac{L[f(x)]}{s + a}.$$

Observe that $\dfrac{1}{s + a}$ is the transform of the solution,

$$y_0(x) \equiv e^{-ax},$$

of

$$\begin{aligned} y' + ay &= 0 \\ y(0) &= 1; \end{aligned}$$

hence, we can write the transform of the solution of (5.31) as

$$L[y(x)] = y_0 L[y_0(x)] + L[y_0(x)]L[f(x)].$$

On the other hand, we know independently that the solution of (5.31) is given by

$$y(x) = y_0 e^{-ax} + \int_0^x e^{-a(x-t)} f(t) \, dt \equiv y_0 y_0(x) + \int_0^x y_0(x - t) f(t) \, dt.$$

If we transform this, we get

$$L[y(x)] = y_0 L[y_0(x)] + L \left(\int_0^x y_0(x - t) f(t) \, dt \right).$$

From these two representations of $L[y(x)]$ we obtain the identity

$$L[y_0(x)] L[f(x)] \equiv L \left(\int_0^x y_0(x - t) f(t) \, dt \right).$$

This identity makes plausible the following general result, called the *Convolution Theorem*, which we state without proof.

Theorem 5.31. *In the common domain of $L[g(x)]$ and $L[f(x)]$,*

$$L[g(x)] L[f(x)] \equiv L[(g * f)(x)] \equiv L \left(\int_0^x g(x - t) f(t) \, dt \right).$$

The functional operation

$$(g * f)(x) \equiv \int_0^x g(x - t) f(t) \, dt$$

on two functions $g(x)$ and $f(x)$ defined on $[0, +\infty)$ occurs sufficiently often in mathematics to be given a name, one name being the *convolution* of $f(x)$ and $g(x)$. It is an easy exercise, for example, to show that

$$(g * f)(x) \equiv (f * g)(x).$$

Let us apply these ideas to the problem

$$y'' + ay' + by = f(x)$$
$$y(0) = y_0, \quad y'(0) = v_0. \tag{5.32}$$

Taking Laplace transforms, we have after some simplification

$$L[y(x)] = \frac{v_0}{s^2 + as + b} + \frac{y_0(a + s)}{s^2 + as + b} + \frac{L[f(x)]}{s^2 + as + b}.$$

Now we observe that $\dfrac{1}{s^2 + as + b}$ is the transform of the solution $y_0(x)$ of

$$y'' + ay' + by = 0$$
$$y(0) = 0, \quad y'(0) = 1,$$

and that $\dfrac{a+s}{s^2+as+b}$ is the transform of the solution $y_1(x)$ of

$$y'' + ay' + by = 0$$
$$y(0) = 1, \quad y'(0) = 0.$$

In view of these,

$$L[y(x)] = v_0 L[y_0(x)] + y_0 L[y_1(x)] + L[y_0(x)]L[f(x)],$$

and, by the Convolution Theorem,

$$L[y(x)] = v_0 L[y_0(x)] + y_0 L[y_1(x)] + L\left[\int_0^x y_0(x-t)f(t)\,dt\right].$$

Finally, by the linearity and uniqueness of the transform, we obtain

$$y(x) = v_0 y_0(x) + y_0 y_1(x) + \int_0^x y_0(x-t)f(t)\,dt. \tag{5.33}$$

This result stands independent of the Laplace transform, for we may verify directly that (5.33) is the solution of (5.32), as follows.   First,

$$y(0) = v_0 y_0(0) + y_0 y_1(0) + \int_0^0 y_0(x-t)f(t)\,dt = y_0$$

and

$$y'(x) = v_0 y_0'(x) + y_0 y_1'(x) + y_0(x-x)f(x) + \int_0^x \frac{\partial}{\partial x} y_0(x-t)f(t)\,dt \text{ *}$$

$$= v_0 y_0'(x) + y_0 y_1'(x) + 0 \cdot f(x) + \int_0^x y_0'(x-t)f(t)\,dt.$$

From this, $y'(0) = v_0$, and

$$y''(x) = v_0 y_0''(x) + y_0 y_1''(x) + y_0'(x-x)f(x) + \int_0^x y_0''(x-t)f(t)\,dt$$

$$= v_0 y_0''(x) + y_0 y_1''(x) + 1 \cdot f(x) + \int_0^x y_0''(x-t)f(t)\,dt.$$

Thus,

$$y''(x) + ay'(x) + by(x)$$
$$= v_0[y_0''(x) + ay_0'(x) + by_0(x)] + y_0[y_1''(x) + ay_1'(x) + by_1(x)]$$
$$\qquad + f(x) + \int_0^x [y_0''(x-t) + ay_0'(x-t) + by_0(x-t)]f(t)\,dt$$
$$= f(x).$$

* Recall Leibnitz' rule from analysis,

$$\frac{d}{dx}\left(\int_a^x g(x,t)\,dt\right) = g(x,x) + \int_a^x \frac{\partial g}{\partial x}(x,t)\,dt.$$

133

Notice the essential way in which the initial values $y_0(0) = 0$ and $y_0'(0) = 1$ enter. Notice also that

$$y(x) = v_0 y_0(x - x_0) + y_0 y_1(x - x_0) + \int_{x_0}^{x} y_0(x - t) f(t)\, dt \quad (5.34)$$

is the solution of

$$y'' + ay' + by = f(x)$$

$$y(x_0) = y_0, \quad y'(x_0) = v_0.$$

The verification is identical with the above, and this frees us of dependence on initial values given at $x = 0$.

Consider the example

$$y'' + y = \sin x$$
$$y(0) = 1, \quad y'(0) = 1. \qquad (5.35)$$

The normalized solution $y_0(x)$ of the homogeneous equation

$$y'' + y = 0$$

is of the form

$$y_0(x) = c_1 \sin x + c_2 \cos x$$

(see Theorem 5.22), but $y_0(0) = c_2 = 0$ and $y_0'(0) = c_1 = 1$; hence $y_0(x) = \sin x$. Similarly, $y_1(x) = \cos x$; thus, the solution is given by

$$y(x) = \sin x + \cos x + \int_0^x \sin(x - t) \sin t\, dt$$

$$= \sin x + \cos x + \int_0^x (\sin x \cos t - \cos x \sin t) \sin t\, dt$$

$$= \tfrac{3}{2} \sin x + \cos x - \tfrac{1}{2}x \cos x.$$

To depart even further from the original idea of the Laplace transform, we note that $y_0(x - t)$ is the solution of

$$y'' + ay' + by = 0$$
$$y(t) = 0, \quad y'(t) = 1,$$

and that $y_1(x - t)$ is the solution for the initial values $y(t) = 1$, $y'(t) = 0$. By analogy, let $y_0(x, t)$ be the solution of

$$y'' + p(x)y' + q(x)y = 0$$
$$y(t) = 0, \quad y'(t) = 1,$$

and let $y_1(x, t)$ be the solution of

$$y'' + p(x)y' + q(x)y = 0$$
$$y(t) = 1, \quad y'(t) = 0.$$

134

It is then plausible that

$$y(x) = v_0 y_0(x, x_0) + y_0 y_1(x, x_0) + \int_{x_0}^{x} y_0(x, t) f(t) \, dt \qquad (5.36)$$

is the solution of

$$y'' + p(x)y' + q(x)y = f(x)$$

$$y(x_0) = y_0, \quad y'(x_0) = v_0.$$

The verification of this follows exactly the same lines as that for (5.33). We must only be careful to note the initial values $y_0(x, x) = 0$ and $y_0'(x, x) = 1$.

In summary then, the solutions of any linear, nonhomogeneous equation can be obtained from appropriate solutions of the reduced, homogeneous equation. These appropriate solutions, moreover, are not as special as they appear. The normalized solutions $y_0(x, t)$ and $y_1(x, t)$ of equation (5.31) are easily written in terms of any pair of independent solutions, $u_1(x)$ and $u_2(x)$ of (5.31). Thus, by Theorem 5.22,

$$y_0(x, t) = c_1 u_1(x) + c_2 u_2(x);$$

whence

$$y_0(t, t) = 0 = c_1 u_1(t) + c_2 u_2(t)$$

$$y_0'(t, t) = 1 = c_1 u_1'(t) + c_2 u_2'(t).$$

Solving these for c_1 and c_2, we find

$$c_1 = \frac{-u_2(t)}{\overline{w}(t)}, \qquad c_2 = \frac{u_1(t)}{\overline{w}(t)}.$$

As a consequence,

$$y_0(x, t) = \frac{-u_2(t)u_1(x) + u_1(t)u_2(x)}{\overline{w}(t)}.$$

Similarly,

$$y_1(x, t) = \frac{u_2'(t)u_1(x) - u_1'(t)u_2(x)}{\overline{w}(t)}.$$

The first of these gives us a form of the integral representation in (5.36) which is sometimes more usable and transparent:

$$u(x) = \int_{x_0}^{x} y_0(x, t) f(t) \, dt$$

$$= -u_1(x) \int_{x_0}^{x} \frac{u_2(t)}{\overline{w}(t)} f(t) \, dt + u_2(x) \int_{x_0}^{x} \frac{u_1(t)}{\overline{w}(t)} f(t) \, dt. \qquad (5.37)$$

Consider the example

$$y'' - \frac{y'}{x} + \frac{y}{x^2} = 1$$

$$y(1) = 0, \quad y'(1) = 0.$$

We can verify that x and $x \log x$ are independent solutions of the reduced equation (cf. Problem 12, Section 5.2). Since $y_0 = v_0 = 0$, the solution is

$$y(x) = -x \int_1^x \frac{t \log t}{t}\, dt + (x \log x) \int_1^x \frac{t}{t}\, dt,$$

where we have computed $\overline{w}(t) \equiv t$. The integrations are easily carried out, and

$$y(x) = x^2 - x - x \log x.$$

In many instances, particularly in the constant coefficient case, the most efficient technique does not involve (5.36) or (5.37) at all but is based on the following result.

Theorem 5.32. *If $y(x)$ is any solution of the nonhomogeneous equation*

$$y'' + p(x)y' + q(x)y = f(x), \tag{5.38}$$

and if $u_1(x)$ and $u_2(x)$ are independent solutions of the reduced equation, then every solution of (5.38) is contained in the formula

$$c_1 u_1(x) + c_2 u_2(x) + y(x).$$

This is certainly suggested by (5.36) and also by the corresponding result for first-order equations. That the above functions are solutions is immediate when we substitute in (5.38). The formula contains all solutions because, for every x_0, y_0, and v_0, the pair of equations

$$c_1 u_1(x_0) + c_2 u_2(x_0) + y(x_0) = y_0$$

$$c_1 u_1'(x_0) + c_2 u_2'(x_0) + y'(x_0) = v_0$$

has a solution (c_1, c_2).

For example, we see that $y(x) \equiv 1$ is a solution of

$$y' - 2y' + y = 1. \tag{5.39}$$

We know that e^x and xe^x are independent solutions of the reduced equation; thus, the general solution of (5.39) is

$$y(x) = c_1e^x + c_2xe^x + 1.$$

The solution of the initial value problem, $y(1) = 0$ and $y'(1) = 1$, is obtained from

$$0 = c_1e + c_2e + 1$$
$$1 = c_1e + 2c_2e,$$

or $c_1 = -3$, $c_2 = 2$.

PROBLEMS

1. Find, one way or another, the solution of

$$y'' + 3y' - 4y = x + 1$$
$$y(1) = 0, \quad y'(1) = 1.$$

2. Find the solution of

$$y'' - y = \cosh x$$
$$y(0) = 0, \quad y'(0) = 0.$$

3. Find the general solution of

$$y'' + y = \tan x.$$

4. One method of finding a solution of

$$y'' + p(x)y' + q(x)y = f(x) \qquad (5.310)$$

is to determine $v_1(x)$ and $v_2(x)$ such that

$$v_1(x)y_1(x) + v_2(x)y_2(x) = y(x)$$

is a solution, where $y_1(x)$ and $y_2(x)$ are independent solutions of

$$y'' + p(x)y' + q(x)y = 0. \qquad (5.311)$$

By analogy with the general solution of (5.311), $c_1y_1(x) + c_2y_2(x)$, this is called the method of *variation of parameters*. Substitute $y(x)$ in (5.310) and show that it is a solution if

$$v_1'(x) \equiv \frac{-y_2(x)}{w(x)} f(x) \quad \text{and} \quad v_2'(x) \equiv \frac{y_1(x)}{w(x)} f(x)$$

hold. Note the relation to formula (5.37).

5. Show that $(1/\sqrt{x}) \sin x$ is a solution of *Bessel's equation of order* $\frac{1}{2}$,

$$y'' + \frac{y'}{x} + \left(1 - \frac{1}{4x^2}\right) y = 0.$$

Find an independent solution, and then find the general solution, of

$$y'' + \frac{y'}{x} + \left(1 - \frac{1}{4x^2}\right)y = \frac{1}{\sqrt{x}}.$$

6. Find the general solution of

$$y'' + ay' + by = \cos \omega t.$$

Find the periodic solution.

7. If $a > 0$ and $b > 0$ and $E(t)$ is bounded, show that

$$y_p(x) = \int_{-\infty}^{x} y_0(x, t) E(t)\, dt$$

is a solution of

$$y'' + ay' + by = E(x). \tag{5.312}$$

If $E(x)$ is periodic of period t, show that $y_p(x)$ is also.

8. Show that $y_p(x)$ is the unique periodic solution of (5.312).

▶ **5.31 UNDETERMINED COEFFICIENTS**

Perhaps the most efficient method of finding a particular solution of the inhomogeneous equation

$$y'' + y = 1$$

is to see one: $y(x) \equiv 1$. This equation is a simple example drawn from a broad class of inhomogeneous equations with constant coefficients whose solutions can, in a sense, be systematically seen. For these, the most efficient method of finding particular solutions is to assume that a solution has a certain form and then find the solution in detail by substituting the form in the equation. The development of this technique is left to the reader in the following sequence of problems.

1. If $y(x)$ is a polynomial of degree 3, show that

$$y''(x) + ay'(x) + by(x)$$

is a polynomial of degree 3, 2, or 1. When does each possibility hold?

2. Find a polynomial solution of

$$y'' + 3y' + 3y = x^2 + 1.$$

Ans. $\dfrac{x^2}{3} - \dfrac{2x}{3} + \dfrac{7}{9}.$

3. Find a polynomial solution of
$$y'' + 3y' = 6x^2 + x.$$
   Ans. $\dfrac{2x^3}{3} - \dfrac{x^2}{2} + \dfrac{x}{3}.$

4. Sketch a procedure for finding a solution of
$$y'' + ay' + by = P_n(x),$$
   where $P_n(x)$ is a polynomial of degree n.

5. If $y(x) \equiv (a_0 + a_1x + a_2x^2)e^x$, find
$$y''(x) + 3y'(x) + y(x).$$
   Ans. $[(5a_0 + 5a_1 + 2a_2) + (10a_2 + 5a_1)x + 5a_2x^2]e^x.$

6. For the same function $y(x)$ find
$$y''(x) - 3y'(x) + 2y(x).$$
   Ans. $[(2a_2 - a_1) - 2a_2x]e^x.$
   Why is the result independent of a_0?

7. For $y(x)$ as given in Problem 5, find
$$y''(x) - 2y'(x) + y(x).$$
   Ans. $2a_2e^x.$
   Why is the result independent of a_1 and a_0?

8. Show that the equation
$$y'' + ay' + by = f(x)e^{kx}$$
   transforms into
$$u'' + (2k + a)u' + (k^2 + ak + b)u = f(x)$$
   under the change of variable $u = e^{kx}y$.

9. Discuss a procedure for finding a solution of
$$y'' + ay' + by = P_n(x)e^{kx},$$
   where $P_n(x)$ is a polynomial of degree n. Note all cases.

10. Find
$$y''(x) + ay'(x) + by(x)$$
    if $y(x) = e^{kx}(c_1 \cos \omega x + c_1 \sin \omega x)$.
    Ans. $[(k^2 + ak + b - \omega^2)c_1 + (2k + a)\omega c_2]e^{kx} \cos \omega x$
    $+ [(k^2 + ak + b - \omega^2)c_2 - (2k + a)\omega c_1]e^{kx} \sin \omega x.$

11. Find a solution of
$$y'' + 2y' + y = e^{-x} \cos x.$$
    Ans. $-e^{-x} \cos x.$

12. Sketch a proof of the fact that if
$$y(x) = P_n(x) \cos \omega x + Q_n(x) \sin \omega x,$$
    then $y''(x) + ay'(x) + by(x) = R_m(x) \cos \omega x + S_m(x) \sin \omega x,$
    where $P_n(x)$ and $Q_n(x)$ are polynomials of degree n and $R_m(x)$ and $S_m(x)$ are polynomials of degree n or $n-1$.

13. Find a solution of
$$y'' + y' + y = x \sin x.$$
    Ans. $\sin x + (2 - x) \cos x$

14. Find a solution of
$$y'' + 2y' + 2y = e^{-x} \cos x.$$
    (One method is as follows: The substitution $y = e^{-x}u$ reduces this to
$$u'' + u = \cos x.)$$
    Ans. $e^{-x} \dfrac{x}{2} \sin x.$

15. Find a solution of
$$y'' + 4y = \sin 2x.$$
    Ans. $-(x/4) \cos 2x.$

16. Discuss, on the basis of all the preceding problems, a systematic method of solving
$$y'' + ay' + by = e^{kx}P_n(x) \sin \omega x,$$
    where $P_n(x)$ is a polynomial of degree n.

17. Find a solution of
$$y'' - y = xe^x + \sin x.$$
    Ans. $\left(\dfrac{x^2}{4} - \dfrac{x}{4}\right) e^x - \tfrac{1}{2} \sin x.$

18. What is the general rule in finding a solution of
$$y'' + ay' + by = f_1(x) + f_2(x)?$$

▶ 5.4 LINEAR SYSTEMS

We consider here the somewhat special problem of three first-order, linear equations with constant coefficients, in order to illustrate ideas for higher-order systems and equations.

$$y' = a_{11}y + a_{12}v + a_{13}u + f(x)$$
$$v' = a_{21}y + a_{22}v + a_{23}u + g(x) \tag{5.41}$$
$$u' = a_{31}y + a_{32}v + a_{33}u + h(x).$$

We shall discuss briefly the specialization of the results of the single third-order equation. The extension of techniques to higher order systems and equations is left for a few exercises.

For example, let $\mathbf{Y}(x) = [y(x), v(x), u(x)]$ be the solution of

$$y' = v \qquad y(x_0) = y_0$$
$$v' = u \qquad v(x_0) = v_0 \tag{5.42}$$
$$u' = y \qquad u(x_0) = u_0.$$

If each component of the solution has a Laplace transform, then

$$L[y'(x)] = -y_0 + sL[y(x)] = L[v(x)]$$
$$L[v'(x)] = -v_0 + sL[v(x)] = L[u(x)]$$
$$L[u'(x)] = -u_0 + sL[u(x)] = L[y(x)]$$

all hold. $L[y(x)]$, $L[v(x)]$, and $L[u(x)]$, therefore, satisfy the system of three algebraic equations

$$-sL[y(x)] + \ L[v(x)] \qquad\qquad = -y_0$$
$$-sL[v(x)] + \ L[u(x)] = -v_0$$
$$L[y(x)] \qquad\qquad -sL[u(x)] = -u_0.$$

Solving them, we have

$$L[y(x)] = \frac{y_0 s^2 + v_0 s + u_0}{s^3 - 1}$$

$$L[v(x)] = \frac{y_0 + v_0 s^2 + u_0 s}{s^3 - 1} \tag{5.43}$$

$$L[u(x)] = \frac{y_0 s + v_0 + u_0 s^2}{s^3 - 1}.$$

By the methods of partial fractions, we obtain

$$L[y(x)] = \frac{\alpha_1}{s-1} + \frac{\beta_1 s + \gamma_1}{s^2 + s + 1}$$

where $\alpha_1 = \dfrac{y_0 + v_0 + u_0}{3}, \quad \beta_1 = \dfrac{2y_0 - v_0 - u_0}{3}, \quad \gamma_1 = \dfrac{y_0 + v_0 - 2u_0}{3},$

and there is a similar decomposition of $L[v(x)]$ and $L[u(x)]$.

From tables, then,

$$y(x) = \alpha_1 e^x + \beta_1 e^{-x/2} \cos \sqrt{\tfrac{3}{4}}x + \sqrt{\tfrac{4}{3}}\left(\gamma_1 - \frac{\beta_1}{2}\right) e^{-x/2} \sin \sqrt{\tfrac{3}{4}}x.$$

We may also find $v(x)$ and $u(x)$ from (5.43), but note that the identities $v(x) \equiv y'(x)$ and $u(x) \equiv v'(x) \equiv y''(x)$ offer a somewhat more practical method.

For (5.41) the technique is straightforward. Let $\mathbf{Y}(x)$ be the solution which satisfies $[y(0), v(0), u(0)] = (y_0, v_0, u_0)$. Taking transforms, we reduce (5.41) to the system of algebraic equations

$$(a_{11} - s)L[y(x)] + a_{12}L[v(x)] + a_{13}L[u(x)] = -y_0 - L[f(x)]$$

$$a_{21}L[y(x)] + (a_{22} - s)L[v(x)] + a_{23}L[u(x)] = -v_0 - L[g(x)] \qquad (5.44)$$

$$a_{31}L[y(x)] + a_{32}L[v(x)] + (a_{33} - s)L[u(x)] = -u_0 - L[h(x)].$$

From this,

$$L[y(x)] = (y_0 + L[f(x)])L[y_1(x)]$$
$$\qquad\qquad + (v_0 + L[g(x)])L[y_2(x)] + (u_0 + L[h(x)])L[y_3(x)],$$

$$L[v(x)] = (y_0 + L[f(x)])L[v_1(x)]$$
$$\qquad\qquad + (v_0 + L[g(x)])L[v_2(x)] + (u_0 + L[h(x)])L[v_3(x)],$$

$$L[u(x)] = (y_0 + L[f(x)])L[u_1(x)]$$
$$\qquad\qquad + (v_0 + L[g(x)])L[u_2(x)] + (u_0 + L[h(x)])L[u_3(x)].$$

Here, after a great deal of computation, $\mathbf{Y}_1(x) = [y_1(x), v_1(x), u_1(x)]$ is the solution of the reduced, homogeneous $[f(x) \equiv g(x) \equiv h(x) \equiv 0]$ system, which satisfies $\mathbf{Y}_1(0) = (1, 0, 0)$; $y_2(x) = [y_2(x), v_2(x), u_2(x)]$ is the solution which satisfies $\mathbf{Y}_2(0) = (0, 1, 0)$; and finally, $\mathbf{Y}_3(0) = [y_3(0), v_3(0), u_3(0)] = (0, 0, 1)$. For example, the normalized solution $\mathbf{Y}_1(x)$ of (5.42) is determined by

$$L[y_1(x)] = \frac{s^2}{s^3 - 1}, \quad L[v_1(x)] = \frac{1}{s^3 - 1}, \quad L[u_1(x)] = \frac{s}{s^3 - 1},$$

or

$$\mathbf{Y}_1(x) = \Big(\tfrac{1}{3}e^x + \tfrac{2}{3}e^{-x/2} \cos \sqrt{\tfrac{3}{4}}x,$$

$$\tfrac{1}{3}e^x - \tfrac{1}{3}e^{-x/2} \cos \sqrt{\tfrac{3}{4}}x - \frac{1}{\sqrt{3}} e^{-x/2} \sin \sqrt{\tfrac{3}{4}}x, \quad \tfrac{1}{3}e^x + \tfrac{2}{3}e^{-x/2} \cos \sqrt{\tfrac{3}{4}}x \Big).$$

With this recognition and applying the convolution theorem to such terms as $L[y_1(x)]L[f(x)]$, we find on inversion that

$$\mathbf{Y}(x) = y_0\mathbf{Y}_1(x) + v_0\mathbf{Y}_2(x) + u_0\mathbf{Y}_3(x) + \mathbf{Y}_0(x), \tag{5.45}$$

where the components of $Y_0(x)$ are

$$y_0(x) = \int_0^x [y_1(x - t)f(t) + y_2(x - t)g(t) + y_3(x - t)h(t)]\, dt,$$

$$v_0(x) = \int_0^x [v_1(x - t)f(t) + v_2(x - t)g(t) + v_3(x - t)h(t)]\, dt,$$

and

$$\tag{5.46}$$

$$u_0(x) = \int_0^x [u_1(x - t)f(t) + u_2(x - t)g(t) + u_3(x - t)h(t)]\, dt.$$

Finally, to free ourselves from the special initial point $x = 0$, we should observe that the $\mathbf{Y}_i(x - x_0)$, $i = 1, 2, 3$, are solutions of the reduced system with normalized initial values at $x = x_0$. If the end point $t = 0$ is replaced by $t = x_0$ in $\mathbf{Y}_0(x)$ and if we call the result $\mathbf{Y}_0(x, x_0)$, then the solution of (5.41) which satisfies $\mathbf{Y}(x_0) = (y_0, v_0, u_0)$ is given by

$$\mathbf{Y}(x) = y_0\mathbf{Y}_1(x - x_0) + v_0\mathbf{Y}_2(x - x_0) + u_0\mathbf{Y}_3(x - x_0) + \mathbf{Y}_0(x, x_0). \tag{5.47}$$

In a sense, all necessary knowledge of (5.41) is contained in (5.45), (5.46), and (5.47); however, there are both practical and theoretical considerations which justify further analysis. For example, the form of solutions of the reduced system is of interest. Let $\mathbf{Y}(x)$ be any solution of (5.41) when $f(x) \equiv g(x) \equiv h(x) \equiv 0$. From (5.44) we have

$$L[y(x)] = \frac{\alpha_1 s^2 + \beta_1 s + \gamma_1}{s^3 + as^2 + bs + c}$$

$$L[v(x)] = \frac{\alpha_2 s^2 + \beta_2 s + \gamma_2}{s^3 + as^2 + bs + c}$$

$$L[u(x)] = \frac{\alpha_3 s^2 + \beta_3 s + \gamma_3}{s^3 + as^2 + bs + c},$$

where

$$s^3 + as^2 + bs + c = - \begin{vmatrix} (a_{11} - s) & a_{12} & a_{13} \\ a_{21} & (a_{22} - s) & a_{23} \\ a_{31} & a_{32} & (a_{33} - s) \end{vmatrix} \cdot \qquad (5.48)$$

The form is determined by specific cases. If the *characteristic polynomial* (5.48) has three real, distinct factors

$$s^3 + as^2 + bs + c = (s - r_1)(s - r_2)(s - r_3),$$

then

$$L[y(x)] = \frac{a_1}{s - r_1} + \frac{b_1}{s - r_2} + \frac{c_1}{s - r_3},$$

and there are similar decompositions of $L[v(x)]$ and $L[u(x)]$. From this,

$$y(x) = a_1 e^{r_1 x} + b_1 e^{r_2 x} + c_1 e^{r_3 x},$$

etc. Another possibility is illustrated by the system (5.42), that of one real factor and an irreducible quadratic. If

$$s^3 + as^2 + bs + c = (s - r)^3,$$

then

$$L[y(x)] = \frac{a_1}{s - r} + \frac{b_1}{(s - r)^2} + \frac{c_1}{(s - r)^3},$$

and

$$y(x) = a_1 e^{rx} + b_1 x e^{rx} + \frac{c_1}{2} x^2 e^{rx},$$

etc. If, finally,

$$s^3 + as^2 + bs + c = (s - r_1)^2(s - r_2), \qquad r_1 \neq r_2,$$

then

$$y(x) = a_1 e^{r_1 x} + b_1 x e^{r_1 x} + c_1 e^{r_2 x},$$

and so forth.

Formula (5.45) suggests the following: *if* $\mathbf{Y}_1(x)$, $\mathbf{Y}_2(x)$, *and* $\mathbf{Y}_3(x)$ *are any three solutions of the reduced system, then any linear combination*

$$c_1 \mathbf{Y}_1(x) + c_2 \mathbf{Y}_2(x) + c_3 \mathbf{Y}_3(x)$$

is also a solution. The proof is omitted. Somewhat deeper is the analogue of Theorem 5.22: *Let* $\mathbf{Y}_1(x)$, $\mathbf{Y}_2(x)$, $\mathbf{Y}_3(x)$ *be any three linearly independent solutions, that is,*

$$c_1 \mathbf{Y}_1(x) + c_2 \mathbf{Y}_2(x) + c_3 \mathbf{Y}_3(x) \equiv (0, 0, 0)$$

only if $c_1 = c_2 = c_3 = 0$. *Then every solution is a unique linear combination of* $\mathbf{Y}_1(x)$, $\mathbf{Y}_2(x)$, *and* $\mathbf{Y}_3(x)$. (The three normalized solutions appearing in

(5.45) are linearly independent, for example.) The idea of the proof is that the determinant of the system

$$y_1(x_0)c_1 + y_2(x_0)c_2 + y_3(x_0)c_3 = y_0$$
$$v_1(x_0)c_1 + v_2(x_0)c_2 + v_3(x_0)c_3 = v_0$$
$$u_1(x_0)c_1 + u_2(x_0)c_2 + u_3(x_0)c_3 = u_0$$

shall be different from zero, where x_0 is any point, and $[y_1(x), v_1(x), u_1(x)]$, $[y_2(x), v_2(x), u_2(x)]$, and $[y_3(x), v_3(x), u_3(x)]$ are independent. Indeed, it is left as an exercise to show that

$$\overline{w}(x) = \begin{vmatrix} y_1(x) & y_2(x) & y_3(x) \\ v_1(x) & v_2(x) & v_3(x) \\ u_1(x) & u_2(x) & u_3(x) \end{vmatrix} \equiv \overline{w}(x_0)\exp\left[-(a_{11}+a_{22}+a_{33})(x-x_0)\right].$$

$$(5.49)$$

We can see explicitly how all of this applies to the single third-order equation

$$y''' + ay'' + by' + cy = f(x), \tag{5.410}$$

via the equivalent system,

$$y' = v$$
$$v' = u \tag{5.411}$$
$$u' = -cy - bv - au + f(x).$$

The characteristic polynomial is

$$-\begin{vmatrix} -s & 1 & 0 \\ 0 & -s & 1 \\ -c & -b & -a-s \end{vmatrix} = s^3 + as^2 + bs + c.$$

(*Note:* If we look for exponential solutions of (5.410) when $f(x) \equiv 0$, then e^{mx} is a solution if

$$m^3 + am^2 + bm + c = 0.)$$

The form of the general solution of the homogeneous equation is then determined by cases as previously discussed.

For example, the general solution of

$$y''' + 6y'' + 11y' + 6y = 0 \tag{5.412}$$

is

$$y(x) = c_1 e^{-x} + c_2 e^{-2x} + c_3 e^{-3x}.$$

Since $y_0(x) \equiv \frac{1}{6}$ is evidently a solution of

$$y''' + 6y'' + 11y' + 6y = 1, \tag{5.413}$$

the general solution of this equation is

$$y(x) = c_1 e^{-x} + c_2 e^{-2x} + c_3 e^{-3x} + \frac{1}{6}.$$

When we write out formula (5.47) we note that

$$y_0(x, x_0) = \int_{x_0}^{x} y_3(x - t) f(t) \, dt$$

is a solution of (5.410) where $y_3(x)$ is the solution of

$$y''' + ay'' + by' + cy = 0$$

$$y(0) = 0, \quad y'(0) = 0, \quad y''(0) = 1.$$

To find this normalized solution $y_3(x)$ for (5.412), we must solve

$$0 = c_1 e^{-0} + c_2 e^{-0} + c_3 e^{-0}$$

$$0 = -c_1 - 2c_2 - 3c_3$$

$$1 = c_1 + 4c_2 + 9c_3;$$

thus,

$$y_3(x) = \tfrac{1}{2} e^{-x} - e^{-2x} + \tfrac{1}{2} e^{-3x}.$$

PROBLEMS

1. Find the solution of

$$y''' + y = 1$$

$$y(0) = y'(0) = y''(0) = 0.$$

2. Find the general solution of

$$y' = v - w$$

$$v' = w$$

$$w' = y - 2v + 3w.$$

3. Find the general solution of the system

$$y'' = 2y + v$$

$$v' = -y$$

Note three possible approaches to the problem: as is, as a single third-order equation, or as a system of three first-order equations.

146

4. Solve

$$y'''' - y = 0$$
$$y(0) = y'(0) = y''(0) = 0$$
$$y'''(0) = 1.$$

5. Prove formula (5.49).

6. Find, by the method of undetermined coefficients, a solution of

$$y''' - y = \sin x.$$

7. Show that if $y_0(x)$ is the solution of Problem 4, then

$$y(x) = \int_0^x y_0(x - t)f(t)\, dt$$

is a solution of

$$y'''' - y = f(x).$$

What initial values does $y(x)$ satisfy at $x = 0$?

8. Apply the Laplace transform to the description of the form of solutions of the system

$$y' + v' = v + w$$
$$v' + w' = w + y$$
$$y' = v.$$

9. Apply the Laplace transform so as to reduce the system

$$y'' = y + v$$
$$v' = w$$

$$w = -v + \cos t$$

to a system of three algebraic equations in three unknowns.

10. Discuss the form of solutions of

$$y'''' + ay''' + by'' + cy' + dy = 0.$$

▶ **5.5 POWER SERIES**

The solution in power series of

$$y'' + p(x)y' + q(x)y = 0$$
$$y(x_0) = y_0, \quad y'(x_0) = v_0$$

$$(5.51)$$

147

is straightforward if x_0 is a point at which $p(x)$ and $q(x)$ are analytic. The function

$$y(x) \equiv \sum_{n=0}^{\infty} a_n(x - x_0)^n$$

is a solution if it converges, and if

$$\sum_{n=2}^{\infty} n(n-1)a_n(x - x_0)^{n-2} + \left(\sum_{n=0}^{\infty} p_n(x - x_0)^n \right) \left(\sum_{n=1}^{\infty} na_n(x - x_0)^{n-1} \right)$$
$$+ \left(\sum_{n=0}^{\infty} q_n(x - x_0)^n \right) \left(\sum_{n=0}^{\infty} a_n(x - x_0)^n \right) \equiv 0.$$

In detail, we must have

$$2a_2 + p_0 a_1 + q_0 a_1 = 0$$
$$3 \cdot 2a_3 + 2p_0 a_2 + a_1 p_1 + q_0 a_1 + q_1 a_0 = 0 \qquad (5.52)$$
$$4 \cdot 3a_4 + 3p_0 a_3 + 2p_1 a_2 + q_0 a_2 + q_1 a_1 + q_2 a_0 = 0$$
$$\vdots$$

etc. The coefficients a_0 and a_1 are determined by the initial values $a_0 = y_0$, $a_1 = v_0$; thereafter, the coefficients are determined recursively by (5.52) in a unique way. In many cases we can derive from (5.52) a simple, usable formula for a_n from which we can deduce the radius of convergence.

For example, consider

$$y'' + xy = 0$$
$$y(0) = y_0, \quad y'(0) = v_0. \qquad (5.53)$$

If $\sum_{n=0}^{\infty} a_n x^n \equiv y(x)$ is a solution, then $a_0 = y_0$, $a_1 = v_0$, and

$$2a_2 = 0, \qquad\qquad a_2 = 0$$

$$3 \cdot 2a_3 = -a_0 = -y_0, \qquad a_3 = -\frac{y_0}{2 \cdot 3}$$

$$4 \cdot 3a_4 = -a_1 = -v_0, \qquad a_4 = -\frac{v_0}{3 \cdot 4}$$

$$5 \cdot 4a_5 = -a_2 = 0, \qquad a_5 = 0$$

$$6 \cdot 5a_6 = -a_3 = \frac{y_0}{2 \cdot 3}, \qquad a_6 = \frac{y_0}{2 \cdot 3 \cdot 5 \cdot 6}$$

$$\vdots$$

148

Indeed, it is a simple inference that

$$a_{3n+2} = 0, \qquad\qquad n = 0, 1, \ldots,$$

$$a_{3n+1} = \frac{(-1)^n v_0}{3 \cdot 4 \cdot 6 \cdot 7 \cdots (3n)(3n+1)}, \quad n = 1, 2, \ldots,$$

$$a_{3n} = \frac{(-1)^n y_0}{2 \cdot 3 \cdot 5 \cdot 6 \cdots (3n-1)(3n)}, \quad n = 1, 2, \ldots.$$

We see further that $\sum_{n=0}^{\infty} a_n x^n$ separates naturally into two linearly independent series solutions,

$$y_0 y_1(x) \equiv y_0 \left(1 + \sum_{n=1}^{\infty} \frac{(-1)^n x^{3n}}{2 \cdot 3 \cdot 5 \cdot 6 \cdots (3n-1)(3n)} \right)$$

and

$$v_0 y_2(x) \equiv v_0 \left(x + \sum_{n=1}^{\infty} \frac{(-1)^n x^{3n+1}}{3 \cdot 4 \cdot 6 \cdot 7 \cdots (3n)(3n+1)} \right),$$

each of which converges for all x (by the ratio test).

A variant of the majorant method proves the following result, which explains why the series solution of (5.53), for example, must converge for all x.

Theorem 5.51. *If $p(x) \equiv \sum_{n=0}^{\infty} p_n(x - x_0)^n$ and $q(x) \equiv \sum_{n=0}^{\infty} q_n(x - x_0)^n$ converge for $|x - x_0| < r$, then the series solution $\sum_{n=0}^{\infty} a_n(x - x_0)^n$, determined by (5.52), converges, at least for $|x - x_0| < r$.*

Let $0 < k < r$; then

$$\sum_{n=0}^{\infty} |p_n| k^n = A, \qquad \sum_{n=0}^{\infty} |q_n| k^n = B.$$

Consequently,

$$|p_n| \leq \frac{A}{k^n}, \qquad |q_n| \leq \frac{B}{k^m}.$$

The problem

$$y'' = A \left[\sum_{n=0}^{\infty} \left(\frac{x - x_0}{k} \right)^n \right] y' + B \left[\sum_{n=0}^{\infty} \left(\frac{x - x_0}{k} \right)^n \right]^2 y$$

$$= \frac{A}{1 - \left(\dfrac{x - x_0}{k} \right)} y' + \frac{B}{\left[1 - \left(\dfrac{x - x_0}{k} \right) \right]^2} y \qquad (5.54)$$

$$y(x_0) = y_0, \quad y'(x_0) = v_0$$

majorizes (5.51). (The verification of this is left as an exercise.) Equation (5.54) is an example of Euler's equation. At least one solution is of the form

$$\left[1 - \left(\frac{x - x_0}{k}\right)\right]^m,$$

and we determine m by substitution,

$$\frac{m(m - 1)}{k^2}\left[1 - \left(\frac{x - x_0}{k}\right)\right]^{m-2}$$

$$= -\frac{m}{k}A\left[1 - \left(\frac{x - x_0}{k}\right)\right]^{m-2} + B\left[1 - \left(\frac{x - x_0}{k}\right)\right]^{m-2}.$$

This holds if either $m = m_1$ or $m = m_2$, where

$$m_1 = \frac{1 - Ak + \sqrt{(1 - Ak)^2 + 4k^2B}}{2},$$

$$m_2 = \frac{1 - Ak - \sqrt{(1 - Ak)^2 + 4k^2B}}{2}.$$

The solution of (5.54) is a linear combination of

$$\left[1 - \left(\frac{x - x_0}{k}\right)\right]^{m_1} \quad \text{and} \quad \left[1 - \left(\frac{x - x_0}{k}\right)\right]^{m_2};$$

each of these functions has a (binomial) series expansion about x_0 which converges for $|x - x_0| < k$; therefore, by the majorant principle,

$$\sum_{n=0}^{\infty} a_n(x - x_0)^n$$

converges for $|x - x_0| < k$. As k is arbitrary and less than r, the convergence holds for $|x - x_0| < r$. This completes the proof.

For example, this assures us that the series expansion of any solution of

$$y'' + \frac{y}{x} = 0 \tag{5.55}$$

about $x = 1$ must converge at least for $|x - 1| < 1$. Such a series, $\sum_{n=0}^{\infty} a_n(x - 1)^n$, is determined by

$$\sum_{n=2}^{\infty} n(n - 1)a_n(x - 1)^n + \left(\sum_{n=0}^{\infty} (-1)^n(x - 1)^n\right)\left(\sum_{n=0}^{\infty} a_n(x - 1)^n\right) \equiv 0$$

since

$$\frac{1}{x} \equiv \frac{1}{1 + (x - 1)} \equiv \sum_{n=0}^{\infty} (-1)^n(x - 1)^n, \qquad |x - 1| < 1.$$

150

On multiplying out the series involved, we obtain

$$2a_2 = -a_{0_1}$$
$$3 \cdot 2 a_3 = a_0 - a_1$$
$$4 \cdot 3 a_4 = -a_0 + a_1 - a_2 \qquad (5.56)$$

$$\cdot$$
$$\cdot$$
$$\cdot$$

$$n(n - 1)a_n = (-1)^{n+1}[a_0 - a_1 + a_2 + \ldots + (-1)^n a_{n-2}].$$

It is evident that

$$\sum_{n=0}^{\infty} a_n(x - 1)^n = a_0 \sum_{n=0}^{\infty} f_n(x - 1)^n + a_1 \sum_{n=1}^{\infty} g_n(x - 1)^n,$$

but simple, explicit formulas for the f_n and g_n cannot be obtained. More careful analysis of (5.56) would show that

$$|g_n| \leq \frac{1}{n}, \quad |f_n| \leq \frac{1}{n}, \quad n \geq 1,$$

which would show, independently of Theorem 5.51, that the radius of convergence is at least one.

PROBLEMS

1. Show that, in fact, (5.54) does majorize (5.51).

2. Find the series solution of

$$y'' - x^2 y = 0$$
$$y(0) = 0, \quad y'(0) = 1.$$

3. The solution of Problem 2 is an odd function. Pose a suitable initial value problem so as to obtain an even solution of

$$y'' - x^2 y = 0.$$

Find the series expansion of this solution.

4. Show that the function x^n is a solution of Euler's equation

$$y'' + \frac{a}{x} y' + \frac{b}{x^2} y = 0$$

if

$$n(n - 1) + an + b = 0. \qquad (5.57)$$

151

LINEAR EQUATIONS

If the two roots of this equation are real and distinct, we have two independent
solutions. Find two independent solutions if the roots are real and equal.

5. If the two roots of (5.57) are complex $\alpha \pm i\beta$, then, in some sense $x^{\alpha+i\beta}$ are
solutions. Interpret $x^{i\beta}$ as $e^{i\beta \log x}$, and thus find real solutions by means of
Euler's formulas.

6. Prove that for f_n and g_n defined by formulas (5.56),

$$|f_n| \leq \frac{1}{n}, \qquad |g_n| \leq \frac{1}{n}.$$

7. Show that in the series expansion $\sum_{n=0}^{\infty} a_n x^n$ of the solution of

$$y'' + \sin xy = 0,$$

the a_n satisfy

$$|a_n| \leq \frac{1}{n(n-1)} \left\{ \frac{|a_0|}{(n-2)!} + \frac{|a_2|}{(n-4)!} + \ldots + |a_{n-3}| \right\},$$

$$n \text{ odd}, \geq 3$$

$$|a_n| \leq \frac{1}{n(n-1)} \left\{ \frac{|a_1|}{(n-3)!} + \frac{|a_3|}{(n-5)!} + \ldots + |a_{n-3}| \right\},$$

$$n \text{ even}, \geq 4.$$

Show from these that if $a_0 = 1$ and $a_1 = 1$, then

$$|a_n| \leq \frac{2^n}{n!}.$$

▶ 5.6 BESSEL'S FUNCTIONS

That we can find the series expansion of solutions of (5.56) about x_0, where
$x_0 \neq 0$, is not surprising and, in fact, not as interesting as the description
of solutions at the *singular* point, $x = 0$. Although it does not often
happen for such a singular differential equation, equation (5.56) does have
an analytic solution,

$$y(x) \equiv \sum_{n=0}^{\infty} a_n x^n.$$

The technique is no different; $y(x)$ is a solution if it converges and if

$$\sum_{n=2}^{\infty} n(n-1)a_n x^n + \sum_{n=0}^{\infty} a_n x^{n-1} \equiv 0,$$

152

that is, if

$$a_0 = 0$$
$$2a_2 + a_1 = 0$$
$$3 \cdot 2a_3 + a_2 = 0$$
$$\cdot$$
$$\cdot$$
$$\cdot$$

It is easy to derive a formula for the nth term

$$a_n = a_1(-1)^n \frac{n}{(n!)^2}, \qquad n = 1, 2, \ldots,$$

and the ratio test shows that

$$a_1 y_1(x) = a_1 \sum_{n=1}^{\infty} (-1)^n \frac{nx^n}{(n!)^2}$$

converges for all x. But, to within a multiplicative constant, $y_1(x)$ is evidently the only solution which is analytic at the origin. To obtain a formula for an independent solution, we must proceed indirectly. Recall Section 5.3; an independent solution is given by

$$y_1(x) \int_{x_0}^{x} \frac{dt}{y_1{}^2(t)} = y_1(x) \int_{x_0}^{x} \frac{dt}{[t - (t^2/2) + \ldots]^2} = y_1(x) \int_{x_0}^{x} \frac{dt}{t^2 - t^3 + \ldots}$$

$$= y_1(x) \int_{x_0}^{x} \frac{1}{t^2} (1 + t + b_2 t^2 + \ldots)\, dt$$

$$= -\frac{y_1(x)}{x} + y_1(x) \log x + b_2 x + \frac{b_3}{2} x^2 + \ldots + c_1 y_1(x),$$

where c_1 is a constant which depends on x_0, and the b_ν can be computed. We see that the essential structure of an independent solution is

$$y_2(x) \equiv y_1(x) \log x + u_1(x),$$

where $u_1(x) \equiv -\dfrac{y_1(x)}{x} + b_2 x + \dfrac{b_3}{2} x^2 + \ldots$ is analytic.

It turns out that a correct problem to pose for an equation whose coefficients are singular at x_0 is not the existence and computation of an analytic solution but rather the computation of a solution of the form

$$(x - x_0)^r \sum_{n=0}^{\infty} a_n(x - x_0)^n.$$

The class of equations for which this problem always makes sense contains many equations which have been of the greatest importance in pure and applied mathematics. In a sense, this class is bounded by Euler's equation,

$$y'' + \frac{a}{x} y' + \frac{b}{x^2} y = 0. \tag{5.61}$$

That is, an equation cannot have worse singularities than (5.61). This equation has a solution x^r which we find by substitution:

$$r(r-1)x^{r-2} + arx^{r-2} + bx^{r-2} \equiv 0.$$

Thus, x^r is a solution if $r(r-1) + ar + b = 0$. The general result is: any equation of the form

$$y'' + \frac{p(x)}{x - x_0} y' + \frac{q(x)}{(x - x_0)^2} y = 0, \tag{5.62}$$

where $p(x)$ and $q(x)$ are analytic at x_0, has at least one solution of the form $(x - x_0)^r \sum_{n=0}^{\infty} a_n(x - x_0)^n$. We can compute r and the a_n by substituting in the equation. We call x_0 a *regular* singular point; of course, however, it could happen that x_0 is not a singular point at all (e.g., $p(x) = (x - x_0)$ and $q(x) = (x - x_0)^2$ is a possibility).

We shall not give a general discussion of (5.62); instead, we concentrate on an important special case, *Bessel's equation of order n*,

$$y'' + \frac{y'}{x} + \left(1 - \frac{n^2}{x^2}\right) y = 0, \tag{5.63}$$

which will illustrate the ideas and the technique. We exhibit a solution of the form $x^r \sum_{m=1}^{\infty} a_m x^m$; indeed,

$$\sum_{m=0}^{\infty} (m+r)(m+r-1)a_m x^{m+r-2} + \sum_{m=0}^{\infty} (m+r) a_m x^{m+r-2}$$
$$+ \sum_{m=0}^{\infty} a_m x^{m+r} - n^2 \sum_{m=0}^{\infty} a_m x^{m+r-2} \equiv 0$$

must hold. We observe that the lowest power of x present is x^{r-2} and the coefficient of this power must be zero:

$$a_0[r(r-1) + r - n^2] = 0.$$

An equation of this type will always occur in the corresponding analysis of (5.62). It determines r; although it is clear that $a_0 = 0$ will suffice, it should also be clear that $a_0 = 0$ may be an unnecessary restriction on the computation of succeeding a_m. In this case, we have $r^2 - n^2 = 0$, or

$$r = \pm n.$$

It is standard practice always to choose the larger root. Suppose it is n; then the coefficients of all the higher powers of x must also vanish, and this means

$$(1 + n)na_1 + (1 + n)a_1 - n^2a_1 = (1 + 2n)a_1 = 0,$$

or

$$a_1 = 0.$$

Then,

$$(2 + n)(1 + n)a_2 + (2 + n)a_2 + a_0 - n^2a_2 = 0,$$

or

$$a_2 = \frac{-a_0}{2(2n + 2)}.$$

A computation shows that a_3 vanishes with a_1; in fact, all of the odd-numbered coefficients a_m are zero. Next,

$$(4 + n)(3 + n)a_4 + (4 + n)a_4 + a_2 - n^2a_4 = 0,$$

or

$$a_4 = \frac{-a_2}{4(4 + 2n)} = \frac{a_0}{4(4 + 2n)2(2n + 2)} = \frac{a_0}{2^4 \cdot 2(n + 1)(n + 2)},$$

then, omitting the details, we have

$$a_6 = 2^6 \frac{-a_0}{1 \cdot 2 \cdot 3(n + 1)(n + 2)(n + 3)}.$$

From

$$(2k + n)(2k + n - 1)a_{2k} + (2k + n)a_{2k} + a_{2k-2} - n^2a_{2k} = 0,$$

it follows that

$$[(2k + n)^2 - n^2]a_{2k} = -a_{2k-2},$$

or,

$$a_{2k} = \frac{-a_{2k-2}}{(2k + 2n) \cdot 2k} = \frac{-a_{2k-2}}{2^2 k(k + n)};$$

hence, it is easily proved by induction that

$$a_{2k} = \frac{(-1)^k a_0}{2^{2k} k!(n + 1)(n + 2) \cdots (n + k)}.$$

155

By the ratio test, the series $\sum_{k=0}^{\infty} a_{2k} x^{2k}$ converges for all x; the solution

$$J_n(x) = (x/2)^n \sum_{k=0}^{\infty} (-1)^k \frac{(x/2)^{2k}}{\Gamma(n+k+1)k!} \quad *$$ (5.64)

is called the Bessel function of the first kind of order n, where we have introduced a customary normalization

$$a_0 = \frac{1}{2^n \Gamma(n+1)}.$$

The series expansion of $J_n(x)$ clearly converges for all x (by the ratio test). We want now an independent solution for each n. We have assumed that $n \geq 0$. If n is not an integer, then

$$J_{-n}(x) = (x/2)^{-n} \sum_{k=0}^{\infty} \frac{(-1)^k (x/2)^{2k}}{\Gamma(-n+k+1)k!}$$ (5.65)

is well defined for all x except $x = 0$. The power series portion converges for all x; we may differentiate and substitute in equation (5.63) to show directly that it is a solution. From their behavior near $x = 0$, $J_n(x)$ and $J_{-n}(x)$ are clearly independent. For example,

$$J_{\frac{1}{2}}(x) = (x/2)^{\frac{1}{2}} \sum_{k=0}^{\infty} \frac{(-1)^k (x/2)^{2k}}{\Gamma(\frac{3}{2})(\frac{1}{2}+1)(\frac{1}{2}+2)\cdots(\frac{1}{2}+k)k!}$$

$$= (x/2)^{\frac{1}{2}} \frac{1}{\Gamma(\frac{3}{2})} \sum_{k=0}^{\infty} \frac{(-1)^k (x/2)^{2k}}{2\cdot 3\cdots(2k+1)} = \sqrt{\frac{2}{\pi x}} \sin x,$$

and

$$J_{-\frac{1}{2}}(x) = (x/2)^{-\frac{1}{2}} \sum_{k=0}^{\infty} \frac{(-1)^k (x/2)^{2k}}{\Gamma(-\frac{1}{2})(-\frac{1}{2}+1)(-\frac{1}{2}+2)(-\frac{1}{2}+3)\cdots(-\frac{1}{2}+k)k!}$$

$$= \sqrt{\frac{2}{\pi x}} \cos x,$$

are seen to be independent solutions of (5.63) for $n = \frac{1}{2}$.

---

* Recall the gamma function,

$$\Gamma(k) = \int_0^{\infty} e^{-x} x^{k-1} \, dx, \qquad k > 0,$$

and its elementary property $\Gamma(k+1) = k\Gamma(k)$, which holds for all k except the nonnegative integers. From this, we find by induction

$$\Gamma(n+k+1) = \Gamma(n+1)(n+1)(n+2) \cdots (n+k),$$

or

$$(n+1)(n+2) \cdots (n+k) = \frac{\Gamma(n+k+1)}{\Gamma(n+1)}.$$

When n is an integer, we must proceed to find a second solution in the form

$$Z_n(x) = J_n(x) \int_{x_0}^{x} \frac{dt}{tJ_n{}^2(t)}$$

$$= J_n(x) \int_{x_0}^{x} \frac{dt}{t^{2n+1}(a_0{}^2 + 2a_0a_2t^2 + \ldots)}$$

$$= J_n(x) \int_{x_0}^{x} \frac{1}{t^{2n+1}} (b_0 + b_2t^2 + b_4t^4 + \ldots)\, dt$$

$$= J_n(x) \left[\left(\frac{c_0}{x^{2n}} + \frac{c_2}{x^{2n-2}} + \ldots + c_{2n} \log x + c_{2n+2}x^2 + \ldots \right) - d_0 \right],$$

where d_0 is a constant depending on x_0. As $J_n(x)$ has the factor x^n, we see the essential form of the independent solution as

$$x^{-n}y_n(x) + J_n(x) \log x,$$

where $y_n(x)$ is an analytic function.

PROBLEMS

1. Show that the change of variable $y = (1/\sqrt{x})z$ transforms Bessel's equation into the linear (Whittaker) equation

$$z'' + \left(1 + \frac{\frac{1}{4} - n^2}{x^2}\right)z = 0. \tag{5.66}$$

2. Show from (5.66) that $(1/\sqrt{x})\cos x$ and $(1/\sqrt{x})\sin x$ are solutions of Bessel's equation of order $\frac{1}{2}$.

3. Show that if $y(x)$ is any solution of Bessel's equation of order zero, then $u(x) = y'(x)$ is a solution of Bessel's equation of order 1.

4. Prove, in fact, that

$$J_{n+1}(x) \equiv -x^n \left(\frac{J_n(x)}{x^n}\right)'.$$

5. Compute in detail a solution of Bessel's equation of order zero which is independent of $J_0(x)$; i.e., work out

$$J_0(x) \int_{x_0}^{x} \frac{dt}{tJ_0{}^2(t)} \equiv J_0(x) \log x + b_2x^2 + b_4x^4 + b_6x^6 + \ldots.$$

157

6. Show that if $y(x)$ is a solution of Bessel's equation of order one,

$$y'' + \frac{1}{x}y' + \left(1 - \frac{1}{x^2}\right)y = 0,$$

then $u(x) = \sqrt{x}\,y\,(2\sqrt{x})$ is a solution of

$$u'' + \frac{1}{x}u = 0.$$

Explain how this might be inferred from the power series solution that we obtained for equation (5.56) and the series expansion of $J_1(x)$.

7. Show that if $y(x)$ is a solution of Bessel's equation of order $\frac{1}{3}$,

$$y'' + \frac{y'}{x} + \left(1 - \frac{1}{9x^2}\right)y = 0$$

then $\sqrt{x}\,y\,(\frac{2}{3}x^{3/2}) = u(x)$ is a solution of

$$u'' + xu = 0.$$

8. The equation

$$y'' + \frac{y}{x^4} = 0$$

does not have a regular singular point at $x = 0$; however, show that with the change of variable $x = 1/t$, this equation becomes

$$\frac{d^2y}{dt^2} + \frac{2}{t}\frac{dy}{dt} + y = 0$$

which comes under our heading. Solve this, and thus exhibit the form of solutions of the original equation.

▶ 5.7 SPECIAL TOPICS

With rapidly convergent series for $\sin x$, e^x, $J_0(x)$ and other functions which are solutions of second-order, linear, homogeneous equations it is feasible to compute values of these functions at a large number of points. Graphing these values, we may see in this way the essential characteristics of these functions. However, the content of such equations themselves is often sufficient to permit qualitative descriptions by elementary means without the effort of extensive computations. We illustrate some of these techniques and ideas which are sometimes geometric, sometimes analytic, and always somewhat special.

For illustrative purposes, let us set aside our previous knowledge of the function $\cos x$ and derive its essential behavior by discussing the solution of

$$y'' + y = 0$$
$$y(0) = 1, \quad y'(0) = 0. \tag{5.71}$$

Of the solution $y(x)$ we observe the obvious,

$$y''(x) = -y(x).$$

From this, $y(x)$ is a concave function wherever $y(x) > 0$ and a convex function wherever $y(x) < 0$. In view of the initial condition $y(0) = 1$, $y(x)$ is concave at $x = 0$ and will remain so as x increases—or decreases— until $y(x)$ changes sign. We sketch this in Figure 5.1, employing also the condition $y'(0) = 0$. Recall that a concave curve lies beneath any of its tangent lines. In particular, by looking at T_0 at x_0 where $y'(x_0)$ has become negative, we are certain that $y(x_1) = 0$ for some finite point x_1. As x increases from x_1, $y(x)$ is negative and convex.

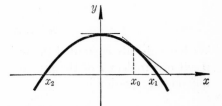

FIG. 5.1

The solution curve begins to bend back toward the x axis. We leave it there for the moment.

As x decreases from zero, $y(x)$ exhibits essentially the same behavior, vanishing at x_2. Indeed, there is enough evidence of symmetry to justify the conjecture that $y(x)$ is an even function, $y(-x) \equiv y(x)$. To check this, let $u(x) = y(-x)$. Then

$$u'(x) \equiv -y'(-x),$$

and

$$u''(x) \equiv y''(-x) \equiv -y(-x) \equiv -u(x);$$

thus, $u(x)$ is a solution of the same differential equation. Moreover, $u(0) = y(0) = 1$, and $u'(0) = -y'(0) = 0$; therefore, by uniqueness, $y(x) \equiv u(x)$. This yields the information that $x_2 = -x_1$ and also $y'(x_2) = -y'(x_1)$.

Now observe that the equation is autonomous. There should be a symmetry of geometric arguments about x_1 as well. In other words, as x increases from x_1, $-y(x)$ should be identical to $y(x)$, as x decreases from x_1. Analytically, we should prove that $y(x) \equiv -y(2x_1 - x)$. Let $u(x) = -y(2x_1 - x)$. First $y(-x)$ is a solution, as we have shown; $y(-x + 2x_1)$

159

is a solution by the translation property of autonomous equations; and $-y(-x + 2x_1)$ is a solution by Theorem 5.31. In particular, $u(x_1) = -y(x_1) = 0 = y(x_1)$ and $u'(x_1) = -[-y'(x_1)] = y'(x_1)$; therefore, $u(x) \equiv y(x)$ by uniqueness. This symmetry property says that the continuation of $y = y(x)$ past x_1 is the negative duplicate of the arch between $-x_1$ and x_1. It also appears that

$$y(3x_1) = -y(-x_1) = 0 = y(-x_1)$$

and

$$y'(3x_1) = -[-y'(-x_1)] = y'(-x_1),$$

from which we see that $y(x)$ is periodic of period $4x_1$.

Consider a less simple example,

$$y'' + xy = 0$$
$$y(0) = 0, \quad y'(0) = 1. \tag{5.72}$$

We have already computed the series solution of this problem and by the result of Problem 7 of the preceding section, the general solution of this differential equation is

$$\sqrt{x}[c_1 J_{1/3}(\tfrac{2}{3}x^{3/2}) + c_2 J_{-1/3}(\tfrac{2}{3}x^{3/2})].$$

We keep these facts in reserve and turn to the direct description of the solution of (5.72).

Again we begin with convexity arguments, which, in fact, are standard for any second-order equation of the form

$$y'' + q(x)y = 0. \tag{5.73}$$

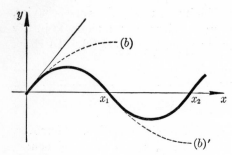

FIG. 5.2

As x increases from zero, $y(x)$ increases from zero, since initially $y'(0) = 1 > 0$. From this, $y''(x) = -xy(x)$ is negative, and the solution curve is concave. Either $y(x)$ continues to be concave until it vanishes at x_1, or $y(x)$ is monotonely increasing for all $s \geq 0$ [(b) in Fig. 5.2]. If the latter were the case, then $xy(x) \to \infty$ as $x \to \infty$. On the other hand, $y'(x)$ would remain bounded, in fact positive and decreasing, as $x \to \infty$, which is impossible in view of

$$y'(x) = y'(0) + \int_0^x y''(t)\, dt = 1 - \int_0^x ty(t)\, dt.$$

160

Not only is (b) impossible, but so also is (b′) beyond x_1. The same argument applies; indeed, we may use it repeatedly to show that $y(x)$ vanishes infinitely often as $x \to +\infty$.

For $x < 0$, the convexity property of bending toward the x axis, which is observed for $x > 0$, is reversed. Now $y''(x) = -xy(x)$ is of the same sign as $y(x)$. Solution curves bend away from the x axis. The solution in question has the behavior shown in Figure 5.3. In particular, as a convex curve lies beneath its tangent,

$$y(x) \leq x$$

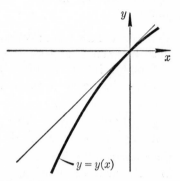

for $x \leq 0$. We drop further consideration of $y(x)$ for $x \leq 0$.

We wish now to refine our knowledge for $x \geq 0$ answering, if possible, the following questions: How fast does $y(x)$ oscillate—specifically, how does the distance between consecutive zeros vary as $x \to \infty$? How does the amplitude of oscillations vary as $x \to \infty$? Finally,

FIG. 5.3

although this question does not directly concern (5.72), is the behavior of $y(x)$ typical, in any sense, of the behavior of every solution of

$$y'' + xy = 0? \tag{5.74}$$

Speaking to the last question first, the convexity properties of any solution are the same, and thus the argument which eliminated (b) and (b′) as possibilities will hold for any solution. Thus, all solutions oscillate on $x \geq 0$. As to the comparative behavior of two solutions, we may infer this from (5.71). For note that in terms of the solution $\cos x$, every solution of

$$y'' + y = 0$$

can be written in the form $a \cos (x - b)$, and we see that the zeros of independent solutions intertwine, or separate one another. The result remains true for all second-order, linear, homogeneous equations, although we do not, in general, have this translation property to prove it.

Let $y_1(x)$ be a solution of (5.74) which is independent of $y(x)$. Between two consecutive zeros of $y(x)$ there is exactly one zero of $y_1(x)$.

From the Wronskian of $y(x)$ and $y_1(x)$,

$$\overline{w}(x) = \begin{vmatrix} y(x) & y_1(x) \\ y'(x) & y_1'(x) \end{vmatrix} \equiv c$$

where $c \neq 0$. Notice that $\overline{w}(x_1) = -y_1(x_1)y'(x_1) = c$ and

$$(\overline{w}x_2) = -y_1(x_2)y'(x_2) = c$$

since $y(x_1) = y(x_2) = 0$. Further, $y'(x_1)$ and $y'(x_2)$ are opposite in sign. It then follows from

$$-y_1(x_1)y'(x_1) = -y_1(x_2)y'(x_2) \neq 0$$

that $y_1(x_1)$ and $y_1(x_2)$ are opposite in sign. Therefore, $y(x)$ is zero at least once between x_1 and x_2. But there cannot be two—or more—zeros of $y(x)$ on this interval, for if so we could simply interchange the roles of $y(x)$ and $y_1(x)$ in the above to show that $y(x)$ has a (nonexistent) zero between x_1 and x_2.

When stated and proved for

$$y'' + p(x)y' + q(x)y = 0,$$

the above result is known as the *Sturm Separation Theorem*. This answers, in part, our third question.

To get at the first question, we ask how a half period of oscillation, π, of solutions of

$$y'' + y = 0$$

compares with that, π/a, of solutions of

$$y'' + a^2y = 0.$$

It is clear how we get π and π/a from the solutions of these equations, and it is likewise clear that the distance between zeros goes down as the coefficient of y goes up. This is true in general and the result is known as the *Sturm Comparison Theorem*:

Let $q_1(x) \leq q_2(x)$ for $x \geq x_0$. Let $y_1(x)$ be a nontrivial solution of

$$y'' + q_1(x)y = 0$$

which is zero at x_0, and let $y_2(x)$ be a nontrivial solution of

$$y'' + q_2(x)y = 0$$

which is zero at x_0. Then, beyond x_0, $y_2(x)$ vanishes before $y_1(x)$ does, if, indeed, either vanishes again.

The point of this is that the behavior shown in Figure 5.4 is not possible. But suppose it is; then we write

$$y_1''(x)y_2(x) + q_1(x)y_1(x)y_2(x) \equiv 0$$
$$y_2''(x)y_1(x) + q_2(x)y_2(x)y_1(x) \equiv 0,$$

162

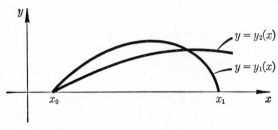

FIG. 5.4

where we have multiplied each equation by the solution of the other. We subtract one of these from the other and integrate the result from x_0 to x_1,

$$\int_{x_0}^{x_1} [y_1''(x)y_2(x) - y_2''(x)y_1(x)] \, dx = \int_{x_0}^{x} [q_2(x) - q_1(x)y_1(x)y_2(x)] \, dx.$$

The term on the left can be integrated by parts to yield

$$y_1'(x)y_2(x) - y_2'(x)y_1(x) \Big|_{x_0}^{x_1} - \int_{x_0}^{x_1} [y_1'(x)y_2'(x) - y_2'(x)y_1'(x)] \, dx.$$

In view of $y_1(x_0) = y_1(x_1) = y_2(x_0) = 0$, this reduces to

$$y_1'(x_1)y_2(x_1) = \int_{x_0}^{x_1} [q_2(x) - q_1(x)]y_1(x)y_2(x) \, dx.$$

We may assume, as is implicit in Figure 5.4, that $y_1(x)$ and $y_2(x)$ are nonnegative on $[x_0, x_1]$; thus $y'(x_1) < 0$, and $y_2(x_1) > 0$. We also have $q_2(x) \geq q_1(x)$. From these, the right-hand side is non-negative and the left is negative, which is a contradiction.

To apply this, let x_1 and x_2 be consecutive zeros of the solution of (5.72) such that $x_1 > 0$. For $x \geq x_1$, we have $x \geq x_1$; hence if we find a solution of

$$y'' + x_1 y = 0$$

which vanishes at x_1, its next zero must be beyond x_2. An appropriate solution is $\sin[\sqrt{x_1}(x - x_1)]$, which we obtain by standard solution methods. The next zero is seen to be $x_1 + \pi/x_1$; thus

$$x_2 \leq x_1 + \pi/\sqrt{x_1}.$$

We can reverse the argument. For $x_1 \leq x \leq x_1 + (\pi/\sqrt{x_1})$ (which is all that matters), $x \leq x_1 + (\pi/\sqrt{x_1})$. We use the Sturm theorem again to compare

$$y'' + xy = 0$$

163

with

$$y'' + \left(x_1 + \frac{\pi}{\sqrt{x_1}} \right) y = 0,$$

in the reverse way. This yields

$$x_1 + \frac{\pi}{\sqrt{x_1 + \dfrac{\pi}{\sqrt{x_1}}}} \leq x_2.$$

We see that to assume

$$x_2 - x_1 = \frac{\pi}{\sqrt{x_1}}$$

involves an error which goes to zero more rapidly than $x_2 - x_1$. We also add to the structure shown in Figure 5.2 that the solution oscillates more and more rapidly as $x \to \infty$ and, in fact, the "period" goes to zero.

The question of whether $y(x)$ is bounded as $x \to \infty$, or is unbounded, or, perhaps, goes to zero can be partially answered in the context of (5.72) and more fully answered by using the relation to Bessel's equation of order $\frac{1}{3}$. We choose the latter means. We also note, parenthetically, that this idea of the equivalence of one equation to another, perhaps better-known equation has been thoroughly investigated. An encyclopedic collection of such results as well as solutions is found in the book of Kamke.* With one general exception, it is very difficult to see in advance which way to go in trying to transform a given equation to a more useful equivalent form, and here we simply accept the known result for (5.72). The exception occurs for the linear equation

$$y'' + p(x)y' + q(x)y = 0;$$

namely, the simple change of variable

$$y = e^{-\frac{1}{2}\int_{x_0}^{x} p(t)\, dt} z = u(x)z$$

always eliminates the y' term and thus makes geometric arguments somewhat simpler. To see this, we have

$$y' = u(x)z' - \tfrac{1}{2}p(x)u(x)z$$

and

$$y'' = u(x)z'' - p(x)u(x)z' - \tfrac{1}{2}p'(x)u(x)z + \tfrac{1}{4}p^2(x)u(x)z.$$

---

* E. Kamke, *Differentialgleichungen, Lösungsmethoden und Lösungen* (Ann Arbor' Michigan: J. W. Edwards, 1945).

From these,

$$y'' + p(x)y' + q(x)y = u(x)\{z'' + [q(x) - \tfrac{1}{2}p'(x) - \tfrac{1}{4}p^2(x)]z\},$$

and the equivalent equation is therefore

$$z'' + [q(x) - \tfrac{1}{2}p'(x) - \tfrac{1}{4}p^2(x)]z = 0. \tag{5.75}$$

For example, Bessel's equation of order $\tfrac{1}{3}$,

$$y'' + \frac{y'}{x} + \left(1 - \frac{1}{9x^2}\right)y = 0, \tag{5.76}$$

is equivalent, under $y = \dfrac{1}{\sqrt{x}}\, z$, $x \geq 0$, to the equation

$$z'' + \left(1 + \frac{5}{36x^2}\right)z = 0. \tag{5.77}$$

In discussing, say, $J_{1/3}(x)$, we may look to the series expansion

$$a_0 x^{1/3}(1 - \ldots)$$

for the description for small x and to (5.77) for large x. The latter is clear, since for large x the equation (5.77) is closely approximated by the solvable equation

$$z'' + z = 0. \tag{5.78}$$

It remains to be seen whether the approximation holds for solutions.

To compare solutions of (5.78) to those of (5.77), let $z_1(x)$ be any particular solution of (5.77) and let $x_1 > 0$. Let $z_2(x)$ be the solution of (5.78) which satisfies

$$z_2(x_1) = z_1(x_1), \qquad z_2'(x_1) = z_1'(x_1).$$

We know the form of this solution, $z_2(x) = a\sin(x - b)$. If we let $w(x) = z_2(x) - z_1(x)$, then

$$w''(x) + w(x) = \frac{5}{36x^2}\, z_1(x)$$

$$w(x_1) = 0, \quad w'(x_1) = 0.$$

As we know,

$$w(x) = \int_{x_1}^{x} \sin(x - t)\, \frac{5}{36t^2}\, z_1(t)\, dt.$$

If we knew only that $z_1(x)$ were bounded for $x > x_1$, i.e., $|z(x)| \leq M$, then we would have the estimate

$$|w(x)| \leq \int_{x_1}^{x} |\sin (x - t)| \frac{5}{36t^2} |z_1(t)| \, dt$$

$$\leq \frac{5M}{36} \int_{x_1}^{x} \frac{dt}{t^2} = \frac{5M}{36} \left(\frac{1}{x_1} - \frac{1}{x} \right).$$

In other words, if we go far enough out before fitting a sine curve to $z_1(x)$, the difference between $z_1(x)$ and $a \sin (x - b)$ is small for all larger x.

The boundedness of solutions of (5.77) is shown as follows. Let $z_1(x)$ be a solution of (5.77). Multiply equation (5.77) by $z'(x)$,

$$z'(x)z''(x) + \left(1 + \frac{5}{36x^2} \right) z(x)z'(x) = 0.$$

We integrate this from $x_0 > 0$ to x, and integrate the second term by parts. We obtain

$$\frac{z'^2(x)}{2} + \left(1 + \frac{5}{36x^2} \right) \frac{z^2(x)}{2} + \int_{x_0}^{x} \frac{5}{36x^3} z^2(x) \, dx$$

$$= \frac{z'^2(x_0)}{2} + \left(1 + \frac{5}{36x_0^2} \right) \frac{z^2(x_0)}{2} = \frac{M^2}{2}.$$

Each term on the left is non-negative; therefore, among other things

$$\left(1 + \frac{5}{36x^2} \right) \frac{z^2(x)}{2} \leq \frac{M^2}{2},$$

and, consequently,

$$|z(x)| \leq M.$$

Very careful analysis would show that $z(x)$ does not go to zero, however, so that the approximation on $x \geq x_1$ by $a \sin (x - b)$ is significant.

Evidently, solutions of (5.76) are approximated by

$$\frac{1}{\sqrt{x}} (c_1 \cos x + c_2 \sin x)$$

for large x. We infer that solutions of (5.74) are approximated by

$$\sqrt{x} \cdot \frac{1}{\sqrt{x^{3/2}}} \left(c_1 \cos \frac{2x^{3/2}}{3} + c_2 \sin \frac{2x^{3/2}}{3} \right) = x^{-1/4} \left(c_1 \cos \frac{2x^{3/2}}{3} + c_2 \sin \frac{2x^{3/2}}{3} \right),$$

for large x.

166

PROBLEMS

1. Show by means of the comparison theorem that if a solution of (5.77) has a zero at x_1, then the next zero x_2 satisfies

$$x_1 + \frac{\pi}{\sqrt{1 + (5/36x_1^2)}} \leq x_2 \leq x_1 + \pi.$$

2. Show that for large x, all solutions of Bessel's equation of all orders behave alike.

3. Analyze the behavior of the solution of

$$y'' + \frac{1}{x} y = 0$$

$$\quad (5.79)$$

$$y(1) = 0, \quad y'(1) = 1,$$

for $x > 0$. Show in particular that it oscillates, though slowly.

4. The technique of multiplying the equation

$$y'' + p(x)y = 0 \qquad (5.710)$$

through by y' and integrating the result is known as the *energy integral*. The result is similar to that obtained for (5.77); namely, the identity

$$\frac{y'^2(x)}{2}\bigg|_{x_0}^{x} + \frac{p(x)y^2(x)}{2}\bigg|_{x_0}^{x} - \int_{x_0}^{x} \frac{p'(t)y^2(t)}{2}\, dt \equiv 0,$$

for solutions of (5.710). A variation is obtained by integrating

$$\frac{y''y'}{p(x)} + yy' = 0.$$

Show that if $p(x)$ is positive and increasing for $x \geq x_0$, all solutions of (5.710) are bounded on $[x_0, +\infty)$. Show that if $p(x)$ is positive and decreasing for $x \geq x_0$, all solutions are bounded by

$$|y(x)| \leq \frac{M}{\sqrt{p(x)}}.$$

5. Discuss in some detail solutions of the equation

$$y'' + (x^2 - 1)y = 0.$$

6. For $x \geq 0$ discuss and sketch the solution of

$$y'' - xy = 0$$

$$y(0) = 1, \quad y'(0) = a$$

for various values of a.　Give plausible reasons for the existence of a value of a, a_0, such that the solution $y(x)$ involved satisfies

$$\lim_{x \to \infty} y(x) = 0.$$

Note: A useful guide, perhaps, is the known behavior of the solution of

$$y'' - y = 0$$

$$y(0) = 1, \quad y'(0) = a.$$

7. Sketch the solution of

$$y'' + \lambda xy = 0$$

$$y(0) = 0, \quad y'(0) = 1,$$

where λ is a positive constant.　How does the solution change as λ increases?

8. Show that $e^{-x^2/2}$ is the solution of

$$y'' + (1 - x^2)y = 0$$

$$y(0) = 1, \quad y'(0) = 0.$$

Argue geometrically that no other solution of the same differential equation can be bounded.

6
NONLINEAR EQUATIONS

▶ 6.1 GEOMETRIC ARGUMENTS

We turn now to nonlinear, autonomous systems of such a nature that we can reasonably obtain information about solutions only by means of geometric ideas and techniques in the phase plane. The arguments have two general steps. First we describe trajectories by suitable first-order techniques—explicit solution, slope field arguments, approximate solutions, or other. Then, we must infer from trajectories the behavior of the functions $y(x)$ and $v(x)$ which form a solution.

Consider the example

$$y'' - y + y^2 = 0. \tag{6.11}$$

An equivalent system is

$$y' = v$$
$$v' = y - y^2. \tag{6.12}$$

In this case, we can solve

$$\frac{dv}{dy} = \frac{y - y^2}{v}$$

for the trajectories,

$$v^2 - y^2 + \tfrac{2}{3}y^3 = c, \qquad (6.13)$$

which are easily sketched. The difficulty here lies in recovering solutions of (6.11) by integrating along trajectories; thus,

$$\int_{y_0}^{y(x)} \frac{dy}{v(y)} = \int_{y_0}^{y(x)} \frac{dy}{\sqrt{y^2 - \tfrac{2}{3}y^3 + c}} = x - x_0$$

in accordance with the technique described in Section 4.3. Instead of attacking such integrals by analytic methods, which would lead us to the study of certain elliptic functions, we turn to inferences from the trajectories. A few are sketched in Figure 6.1.

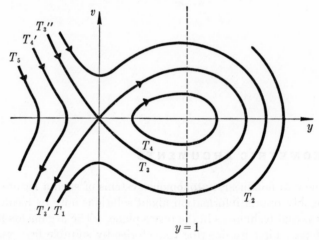

Fig. 6.1

T_1 and T_2 correspond to positive values of c in (6.13). T_3, T_3', and T_3'' are given by $c = 0$, but note that they are distinct trajectories separated by the singular point $(0, 0)$. T_4 and T_4' are both given by some c, $-\tfrac{1}{3} < c < 0$, and T_5 is given by some $c \leq \tfrac{1}{3}$. There are two singular points, $(0, 0)$ and $(1, 0)$. Among general characteristics, we see that all trajectories have a horizontal tangent when $y = 1$ or $y = 0$ $(v' = 0)$, and all have vertical tangents along the y axis $(y' = 0)$. At the origin the

170

limiting values of the slopes of T_3, $T_3{}'$, and $T_3{}''$ are ± 1. This follows from the equation of these trajectories,

$$v = \pm y \sqrt{1 - \frac{2y}{3}}.$$

We now translate these trajectories into graphs of the corresponding solutions of (6.11). Let $y(x)$ correspond to T_1, where, say, $y(x_0) = y_0$ and $y'(x_0) = 0$. At x_0, $y(x)$ has a max-imum. As x increases from x_0, $y(x)$ decreases and $y'(x)$ decreases; thus $y(x)$ is concave until x_1, where $y(x_1) = 1$. As x increases from x_1, $y(x)$ continues to decrease, but $y'(x)$ increases; hence, $y(x)$ is con-vex and decreasing until x_2, where $y(x_2) = 0$. Thereafter, $y(x)$ is de-creasing and concave. Finally, ob-serve the obvious symmetry of T_3 (indeed, of all trajectories) about

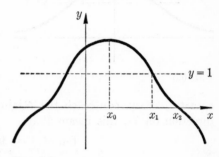

FIG. 6.2

the y axis. This implies that $y = y(x)$ is symmetric about $x = x_0$. All of this is embodied in the sketch of $y(x)$ in Figure 6.2.

Missing from this is any knowledge of the values $x_1 - x_0$ and $x_2 - x_1$ (by the translation property, the value x_0 is irrelevant). We can write these down in integral form,

$$x_1 - x_0 = \int_{y_0}^{1} - \frac{dy}{\sqrt{y^2 - \frac{2}{3}y^3 - y_0{}^2 + \frac{2}{3}y_0{}^3}}$$

and a similar expression for $x_2 - x_1$. Here we are using the fact that T_1 is given in terms of the initial value $y_0 > \frac{3}{2}$ by

$$v^2 - y^2 + \tfrac{2}{3}y^3 = -y_0{}^2 + \tfrac{2}{3}y_0{}^3.$$

Since $v \leq 0$ on the position considered, we must choose

$$v(y) = -\sqrt{y^2 - \tfrac{2}{3}y^3 - y_0{}^2 + \tfrac{2}{3}y_0{}^3}$$

in forming

$$x_1 - x_0 = \int_{y_0}^{1} \frac{dy}{v}.$$

Observe that the integral for $x_1 - x_0$ is, in fact, improper at the endpoint y_0, but for y near y_0,

$$y^2 - \tfrac{2}{3}y^3 - y_0{}^2 + \tfrac{2}{3}y_0{}^3 \sim (y_0 - y)(2y_0{}^2 - 2y_0),$$

171

so that the integral exists. Its evaluation is a matter for approximate methods or a suitable table. By very tedious and somewhat delicate analysis it can be shown that $x_1 - x_0$ decreases as y_0 increases.

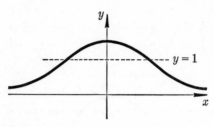

The locus of T_3 passes through the origin; however, as noted, the singular point $(0, 0)$ is not a part of the trajectory T_3. This is a consequence of uniqueness of solutions of (6.12). For any finite x_0 there is only one solution, namely, $[y(x), v(x)] \equiv (0, 0)$, which satisfies $[y(x_0), v(x_0)] = (0, 0)$.

Fig. 6.3

Therefore, no nontrivial solution, as a trajectory, can reach the origin at a finite time. In view of the direction on T_3, this means that

$$\lim_{x \to \infty} y(x) = \lim_{x \to -\infty} y(x) = 0$$

and

$$\lim_{x \to \pm\infty} v(x) = 0$$

for the solution which generates T_3. It is easy to sketch $y(x)$ where $y(0) = y_0$ (see Fig. 6.3).

Indeed, this is the one case in which (6.11) can be solved in terms of elementary functions. T_3 is given by

$$v^2 = y^2 - \tfrac{2}{3}y^3,$$

whence, $y(x)$ satisfies

$$y' = -\sqrt{y^2 - \tfrac{2}{3}y^3}$$

$$y(0) = \tfrac{3}{2}.$$

We must reject the constant solution, $y(x) = \tfrac{3}{2}$, since it is not a solution of (6.11). We then find on carrying out the integration,

$$y(x) = \frac{3}{2}\left(1 - \tanh^2\frac{x}{2}\right).$$

This is a solution of (6.11), as may be verified.

The trajectories inside T_3, e.g., T_4, are simple closed curves surrounding the singular point $(1, 0)$. Each corresponds to a *periodic* solution. For suppose that T_4 is given by $[y(x), v(x)]$, where $[y(x_0), v(x_0)] = (y_0, 0)$. T_4 is traversed in a finite time τ; thus,

$$[y(x_0 + \tau), v(x_0 + \tau)] = (y_0, 0).$$

172

By the translation property, $[y(x + \tau), v(x + \tau)]$ is a solution of (6.12). Since it satisfies the same initial conditions as $[y(x), v(x)]$, it must be identical with $[y(x), v(x)]$, hence the periodicity. A sketch is given in Figure 6.4, with $x_0 = 0$. By symmetry, we obtain the period

$$\tau = 2 \int_{y_1}^{y_0} \frac{dy}{\sqrt{y^2 - \frac{2}{3}y^3 - y_0{}^2 + \frac{2}{3}y_0{}^3}}$$

where $0 < y_1 < y_0 < \frac{3}{2}$, and

$$y_1{}^2 - \frac{2}{3}y_1{}^3 - y_0{}^2 + \frac{2}{3}y_0{}^3 = 0.$$

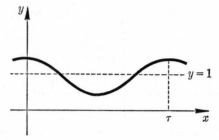

FIG. 6.4

We see that T_3 is the limiting position of T_4 as $y_0 \to \frac{3}{2}-$, from which it appears that $\tau \to \infty$ as $y_0 \to \frac{3}{2}-$. This is a heuristic continuity argument based on the infinite transit time for T_3. The result can be proved by direct analysis of the integral for τ.

PROBLEMS

1. Find the trajectories of

$$y' = v$$
$$v' = -\sin y.$$

Sketch them and note different cases. Indicate various possibilities for the behavior of $y(x)$.

2. In view of the manner of approach of T_3, T_3', and T_3'' to $(0, 0)$, argue plausibly that the corresponding solutions $y(x)$ are behaving exponentially as $x \to \pm\infty$.

3. It is clear that trajectories of (6.12) in the second and third quadrants of the yv plane run off to infinity. Show that they are traversed in a *finite* time. From this, sketch $y(x)$ corresponding to T_5.

4. Sketch the trajectories of

$$y' = v$$
$$v' = -\sin y + 1.$$

Show that there is no nontrivial periodic solution.

5. Sketch the trajectories of

$$y' = \sin v$$
$$v' = -\sin y.$$

173

Locate the singular points and locate the nonclosed trajectories. Sketch the graph of $y = y(x)$, where $y(x)$ is not a periodic solution.

6. Show that all solutions of

$$y'' + y^3 = 0$$

are periodic. Show that the period, as a function of amplitude y_0

$$[\text{i.e., } y(0) = y_0, \, y'(0) = 0],$$

goes to zero as $y_0 \to +\infty$.

▶ 6.2 LINEARIZATION

The other limiting case for periodic solutions of (6.11) is that of $y_0 \to 1_+$, and this brings us to the idea of approximating solutions of an autonomous system near singular points by linearizing the system. The idea requires careful justification by the theorems on continuity of solutions in parameters. In effect, for the system

$$y' = g(y, v)$$
$$v' = h(y, v) \qquad (6.21)$$

we must stay near enough to a singular point for the linear approximations to $g(y, v)$ and $h(y, v)$ to be valid and, at the same time, we must stay a finite distance away from the singular point itself. We omit the details.

Near the singular point $(1, 0)$ of (6.12), for example, we argue that $y - y^2 = y(1 - y)$ is, effectively, $(1 - y)$. The first equation in (6.12) is, of course, already linear; thus the linearized system is

$$y' = v$$
$$v' = 1 - y. \qquad (6.22)$$

The trajectories are the concentric circles

$$v^2 + (y - 1)^2 = c^2,$$

and solutions are also easily found to be

$$[1 + a \cos (x - x_0), \, -a \sin (x - x_0)].$$

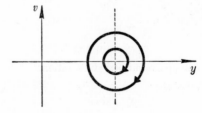

FIG. 6.5

174

We infer, on continuity, that for $y_0 \sim 1$, the trajectory of (6.12) is nearly circular,

$$v^2 + (y - 1)^2 = (y_0 - 1)^2,$$

and moreover that

$$[1 + (y_0 - 1) \cos (x - x_0), -(y_0 - 1) \sin (x - x_0)]$$

approximates the solution of (6.12). Another inference is that, as $y_0 \to 1$, τ approaches 2π. (This may be proved directly from the integral for τ.)

Near $(0,0)$, $y - y^2$ is effectively y; hence the linearized system is

$$y' = v$$
$$v' = y.$$
(6.23)

Here the trajectories are the hyperbolas

$$v^2 - y^2 = c$$

(Fig. 6.6). Note the similarity to the trajectories of (6.12) near $(0, 0)$ as shown in Figure 6.1. Solutions of (6.23) which correspond to various trajectories are found by linear methods. For example, T_4 corresponds to $(-e^{-x}, e^{-x})$ and T_5 to $(y_0 \cosh x, y_0 \sinh x)$. From this we infer that the solution $y(x)$ of (6.11) which corresponds to T_3' in Figure 6.1 has the asymptotic behavior

$$y(x) \sim -e^{-x}$$

as $x \to \infty$.

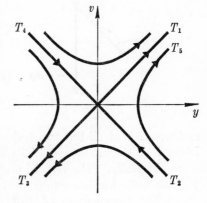

Fig. 6.6

This idea of linearizing in the neighborhood of a singularity is familiar in physics, where the results are often called the equilibrium case. For example, consider the spherical pendulum shown in Figure 6.7, where m is a point mass attached to a rigid, weightless rod of length l. With no friction, the only force on m in its path of travel is the component of gravitational force $-mg \sin y$. Since the acceleration along this path is

$$\frac{d^2 s}{dt^2} = l \frac{d^2 y}{dt^2},$$

175

we obtain the equation of motion

$$ml\,\frac{d^2y}{dt^2} = -mg\,\sin y, \tag{6.24}$$

which is nonlinear. However, near the *stable* equilibrium position (singular point) $(y, dy/dt) = (0, 0)$, we argue that

$$\sin y \equiv y - \frac{y^3}{3!} + \ldots \equiv y.$$

As a consequence, we have the well-known linear equation

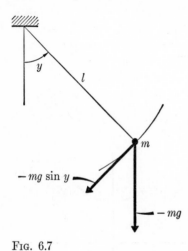

$$\ddot{y} + \frac{g}{l}\,y = 0$$

of simple harmonic motion.

Near the unstable equilibrium position $(y, dy/dt) = (\pi, 0)$, $\sin y$ is

$$\sin y = -\sin(y - \pi) \approx -(y - \pi).$$

The linearized system is

$$\dot{y} = v$$

$$\dot{v} = \frac{g}{l}\,(y - \pi).$$

Trajectories are the hyperbolas

FIG. 6.7

$$\frac{v^2}{2} - \frac{g}{2l}\,(y - \pi)^2 = c,$$

and we see that all but two trajectories leave the vicinity of $(\pi, 0)$ with increasing t (Figure 6.6 essentially illustrates this). This, of course, makes sense physically. The vertical position of the pendulum is an equilibrium position but a highly unstable one.

The linearization of (6.21) procedes similarly. Let $g(y_0, v_0) = h(y_0, v_0) = 0$ and assume that (6.21) has no other singular points in some neighborhood of (y_0, v_0); in other words, let (x_0, y_0) be an *isolated singular* point of (6.21). Let the partial derivatives g_y, g_v, h_y, and h_v be continuous at (y_0, v_0) (in fact, we assume this continuity everywhere so as to insure existence and uniqueness of solutions). The linearization of (6.21) is then

176

$$y' = \frac{\partial g}{\partial y}(y_0, v_0)(y - y_0) + \frac{\partial g}{\partial v}(y_0, v_0)(v - v_0) = a_{11}(y - y_0) + a_{12}(v - v_0)$$

$$(6.25)$$

$$v' = \frac{\partial h}{\partial y}(y_0, v_0)(y - y_0) + \frac{\partial g}{\partial v}(y_0, v_0)(v - v_0) = a_{21}(y - y_0) + a_{22}(v - v_0);$$

that is, we replace $g(y, v)$ and $h(y, v)$ by the linear terms of their Taylor's series. A further notational simplicity is achieved by the translation $u = y - v_0$, $w = v - v_0$ which moves the singular point to the origin and transforms (6.25) into

$$u' = a_{11}u + a_{12}w$$

$$(6.26)$$

$$w' = a_{21}u + a_{22}w.$$

Examples and the theory show that (6.26) is a useful approximation to (6.21) only if $(0, 0)$ is also an isolated singularity of (6.26), or, what is the same, if $(0, 0)$ is the only solution of

$$a_{11}u + a_{12}w = 0$$

$$a_{21}u + a_{22}w = 0.$$

To insure this, we assume that the determinant $\Delta = a_{11}a_{22} - a_{12}a_{21}$ is different from zero.

We now categorize the singular point according to the behavior of solutions, as trajectories, of (6.26). We may, for example, solve (6.26) by applying the Laplace transform, obtaining, after some algebra,

$$L[u(x)] = \frac{c_1 s + c_2}{s^2 - (a_{11} + a_{22})s + \Delta}$$

$$L[w(x)] = \frac{d_1 s + d_2}{s^2 - (a_{11} + a_{22})s + \Delta},$$

where c_1, c_2, d_1, and d_2 depend on initial values and the elements of Δ. From previous experience we see that the behavior of solutions depends on the roots, λ_1 and λ_2 of

$$s^2 - (a_{11} + a_{22})s + \Delta = 0.$$

Indeed, we may list the possibilities and describe the corresponding behavior as follows:

(i) λ_1 and λ_2 are complex, $\alpha \pm i\beta$; components of solutions have the form $e^{\alpha x}(k_1 \cos \beta x + k_2 \sin \beta x)$. Trajectories wrap around $(0, 0)$ infinitely often, spiraling in as $x \to \infty$ if $\alpha < 0$, spiraling out as $x \to +\infty$ if

$\alpha > 0$, and moving in closed curves if $\alpha = 0$. The origin is called a *stable focus*, an *unstable focus*, and a *vortex*, respectively.

  (*ii*) λ_1 and λ_2 are real, and $\lambda_1 < 0 < \lambda_2$. Components have the form $k_1 e^{\lambda_1 x} + k_2 e^{\lambda_2 x}$. Some trajectories [e.g., $(e^{-x}, -e^{-x})$ for (6.23)] approach the origin as $x \to +\infty$, but most recede. The singular point is called a *saddle point*.

  (*iii*) λ_1 and λ_2 are real and $0 < \lambda_1 \leq \lambda_2$. A component has the form $k_1 e^{\lambda_1 x} + k_2 e^{\lambda_2 x}$, or $k_1 e^{\lambda_1 x} + k_2 x e^{\lambda_1 x}$. All trajectories leave the vicinity of $(0, 0)$ as $x \to \infty$. This is called an *unstable node*.

  (*iv*) λ_1 and λ_2 are real, and $\lambda_1 \leq \lambda_2 < 0$. This is just the reverse of (*iii*); all trajectories tend to $(0, 0)$ as $x \to +\infty$. We call $(0, 0)$ a *stable node*.

  Further geometric interpretation of trajectories is left for the problems.

PROBLEMS

1. Show that the change of variable $x = \sqrt{g/l}\, t$, to dimensionless time, transforms (6.24) into

$$y'' + \sin y = 0.$$

2. Find the equilibrium points of

$$y'' + \sin y = \tfrac{1}{2}.$$

Linearize this equation at these points, and solve for and sketch the trajectories of the linearized system. Describe possible periodic solutions.

3. Suppose that (6.26) is, in fact,

$$\begin{aligned} y' &= v \\ v' &= a_{21}y + a_{22}v. \end{aligned} \tag{6.27}$$

Give conditions on a_{21} and a_{22} which characterize each of the types of singular points (*i*)–(*iv*).

4. The equation of trajectories of (6.26) is

$$\frac{dw}{du} = \frac{a_{21}u + a_{22}w}{a_{11}u + a_{12}w}. \tag{6.28}$$

Show that

$$\frac{d^2w}{du^2} = -\frac{\Delta\left(w - u\dfrac{dw}{du}\right)}{(a_{11}u + a_{12}w)^2}. \tag{6.29}$$

Show then that if $\Delta = 0$, trajectories are parallel lines. Find their slope. Where are the singular points of (6.26) if $\Delta = 0$?

5. Show that the w intercept of the tangent line to the curve $w = w(u)$ at (u, w) is $w - u(dw/du)$. With this fact and (6.29), show that if $\Delta < 0$, each trajectory of (6.26) is separated from the origin by any of its tangent lines.

6. Show that $(0, 0)$ is a saddle point if and only if $\Delta < 0$. Show that (6.28) has two distinct linear solutions, $w = \lambda_1 u$ and $w = \lambda_2 u$, if $\Delta < 0$. With these facts, the fact that trajectories are nonintersecting, the slope field of (6.28), and the convexity property of Problem 5, justify the term *saddle point* by a sketch. In other words, explain Figure 6.8.

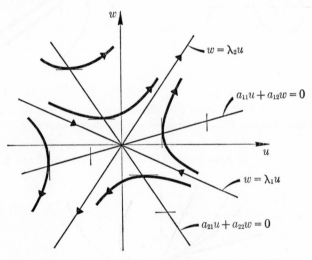

FIG. 6.8

7. If $\lambda_1 \leq \lambda_2 < 0$, show that

$$\lim_{x \to +\infty} \frac{v(x)}{y(x)} = \lambda_2$$

and

$$\lim_{x \to -\infty} \frac{v(x)}{y(x)} = \lambda_1$$

for every nontrivial solution $[y(x), v(x)]$ of (6.28).

8. Show that if $\Delta > 0$ each trajectory of (6.26) lies on the same side of any of its tangent lines as the origin.

179

9. If $\Delta > 0$ and (6.28) has no linear solutions of the form $w = mu$, show that $(0, 0)$ is a focus or a vortex. Explain the convexity properties shown for a focus in Figure 6.9.

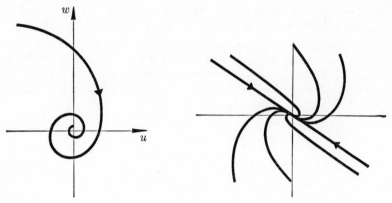

FIG. 6.9   FIG. 6.10

10. If $\Delta > 0$ and (6.28) has exactly one linear solution, $w = mu$, show that $(0, 0)$ is a node. Explain Figure 6.10 in view of Problems 7 and 8.

11. If $\Delta > 0$ and (6.28) has two distinct linear solutions, $w = mu$, show that $(0, 0)$ is a node. Explain Figure 6.11 in view of Problems 7 and 8.

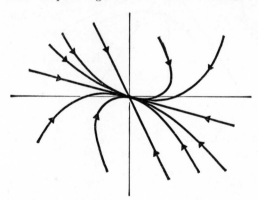

FIG. 6.11

12. Linearize

$$y' = v$$
$$v' = 3(1 - y^2)v - 2y$$

at $(0, 0)$. Sketch the trajectories.

180

13. Linearize

$$y' = \sin v$$
$$v' = -\sin y$$

in the neighborhood of each singular point.   Classify each.

14. Linearize

$$y' = v$$
$$v' = -v - \sin y$$

at $(0, 0)$.   Sketch the trajectories.

15. Linearize

$$y' = v$$

$$v' = -2v - \sin y$$

at $(0, 0)$.   Sketch the trajectories.

▶ 6.3 CONSERVATIVE AND NONCONSERVATIVE SYSTEMS

In discussing trajectories in the large (as opposed to "in the small," in equilibrium or singular-point analysis) we have looked only at systems whose trajectories are given by a simple, separable first-order equation, e.g., equation (6.11).   Typically, such a system has the form

$$y' = v$$
$$v' = -g(y), \tag{6.31}$$

or

$$y'' + g(y) = 0 \tag{6.32}$$

as a second-order equation.   We call such a system *conservative*.   The term comes from physics, for we may interpret (6.32) as the equation of a particle of unit mass moving with displacement y at time x, velocity $v = y'$, and under the force $-g(y)$.   Trajectories are given by

$$\frac{v^2}{2} + G(y) = c, \tag{6.33}$$

where $G'(y) = g(y)$.   We see in this formula that the sum of the kinetic energy, $v^2/2$, and of the potential energy, $G(y)$, is constant, i.e., that the total energy is conserved.   A trajectory is a curve of constant energy.

181

A *nonconservative* system related to (6.31) is

$$y' = v$$
$$v' = f(y, v) - g(y).$$

(6.34)

Trajectories of (6.34) are not simply given, since their equation is

$$\frac{dv}{dy} = \frac{f(y, v) - g(y)}{v},$$

which is solvable in few interesting cases other than the linear. We propose to retain, however, the notion of curves of constant energy given by (6.33) for the system (6.34). They are no longer trajectories for (6.34), but we are able to compare the trajectories of (6.34) with them by simple geometric and analytic arguments.

To illustrate, consider the nonconservative system

$$y' = v$$
$$v' = -av - \sin y,$$

(6.35)

arising from the circular pendulum when we assume a frictional force which is proportional to velocity and resistive $(a > 0)$. There are no methods for solving

$$\frac{dv}{dy} = \frac{-av - \sin y}{v},$$

but we can sketch trajectories of (6.35) relative to those of the conservative system

$$y' = v$$
$$v' = -\sin y,$$

(6.36)

which are given by

$$\frac{v^2}{2} - \cos y = c.$$

A few are sketched in Figure 6.12, and we note that as c increases, they recede from the origin. At the point P on the energy curve T_0, we sketch for comparison the tangent vectors $\mathbf{T}_0$ and $\mathbf{T}_1$ defined by (6.36) and (6.35), respectively. Observe the effect of the term $-av$ on the vertical component of $\mathbf{T}_1$ compared to the vertical component of $\mathbf{T}_0$. The horizontal components are the same. By considering all possible points on the energy curves, we see that the trajectories of (6.35) are directed toward curves of smaller energy. There is possibly an exception to this at points

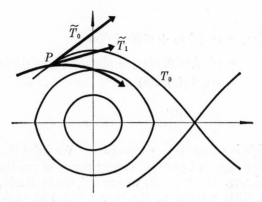

Fig. 6.12

on the y axis, where $\mathbf{T}_0$ and $\mathbf{T}_1$ are identical, but even here the trajectories of (6.35) "bend" to the interior.

This yields a sketch of typical trajectories, shown in Figure 6.13. The behavior near the singular points is a matter for linearizing (6.35). For example, $(0, 0)$ is a stable focus if $a < 2$ and a stable node if $a \geq 2$, and $(\pi, 0)$ is a saddle point for all a.

Fig. 6.13

Analytically, if we form the "energy" of a solution of (6.34),

$$E(x) = \frac{v^2(x)}{2} + G[y(x)],$$

183

then

$$\frac{dE}{dx}(x) = v(x)v'(x) + g[y(x)]y'(x) \qquad (6.37)$$
$$= v(x)f[y(x), v(x)] - g[y(x)] + g[y(x)]v(x)$$
$$= v(x)f[y(x), v(x)].$$

For example,

$$\frac{dE}{dx}(x) = -av^2(x)$$

for (6.35), which is everywhere nonpositive. We infer that trajectories of (6.35) are such as to cut constant energy curves of smaller and smaller energy as x increases. From (6.37) we can tell, qualitatively, the behavior trajectories of (6.34) relative to the curves (6.33) at each point of the yv plane.

Quantitatively, we can sometimes estimate the energy lost, or gained, over a portion of a trajectory by integrating (6.37):

$$E(x_1) - E(x_0) = \int_{x_0}^{x_1} v(x)f[y(x), v(x)]\, dx.$$

Other forms of this follow from

$$\frac{dE}{dy} = v\frac{dv}{dy} + g(y) = v\left[\frac{f(y, v) - g(y)}{v}\right] + g(y) = f(y, v),$$

or

$$E(y_1) - E(y_0) = \int_{y_0}^{y_1} f(y, v)\, dy;$$

and

$$\frac{dE}{dv} = v + g(y)\frac{dy}{dv} = v + g(y)\left[\frac{v}{f(y, v) - g(y)}\right] = \frac{vf(y, v)}{f(y, v) - g(y)}$$

or

$$E(v_1) - E(v_0) = \int_{v_0}^{v_1} \frac{vf(y, v)}{f(y, v) - g(y)}\, dv.$$

To illustrate, consider in Figure 6.14 the trajectory of (6.35) which starts at $(0, v_0)$, where T_0 is one of the closed trajectories of (6.36) given by

$$\frac{v^2}{2} - \cos y = c_0.$$

We want the energy, c_1, when the trajectory has reached the y axis. Since we do not know $x_1 - x_0$ or $y_0 - y_1$, the appropriate integral is

$$c_1 - c_0 = -a\int_{v_0}^{0} \frac{v^2}{-av - \sin y}\, dv.$$

184

To estimate this crudely, we note that $\sin y > 0$ in the range considered; thus

$$av + \sin y > av.$$

From this,

$$c_0 - c_1 = a \int_0^{v_0} \frac{v^2}{av + \sin y}\, dv \leq a \int_0^{v_0} \frac{v^2}{av}\, dv = \frac{v_0{}^2}{2}.$$

We conclude that the energy lost is less than $v_0{}^2/2$. It is easy to work out a lower estimate from

$$c_0 - c_1 \geq a \int_0^{v_0} \frac{v^2}{av + 1}\, dv,$$

for example.

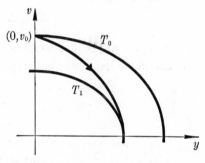

As a general rule, in the analysis of a nonconservative system by comparison with a conservative one, both systems should have the same singularities. For example, the equation of a damped circular pendulum which is driven by a constant torque of $\frac{1}{2}$,

FIG. 6.14

$$y + ay + \sin y = \tfrac{1}{2},$$

should be compared to the undamped driven pendulum and not to the undriven, undamped case.

PROBLEMS

1. Sketch the trajectories of

$$y' = v$$
$$v' = (1 - y^2 - v^2)v - y$$

compared to those of

$$y' = v$$
$$v' = y.$$

Discuss the behavior of the component $y(x)$. Characterize the singular point.

2. Sketch the trajectories of Van der Pol's equation

$$y'' + (1 - y^2)y' + y = 0,$$

185

in comparison with those of

$$y'' + y = 0.$$

Characterize the singular point.

3. Sketch the trajectories of

$$y' = v$$
$$v' = -v - \sin y + \tfrac{1}{2},$$

and identify the singular points by type. (The reader may want to use ordinary slope field methods for

$$\frac{dv}{dy} = \frac{-v - \sin y + \tfrac{1}{2}}{v}$$

instead of energy considerations.)

4. Sketch the trajectories of the system

$$y' = v$$
$$v' = \begin{cases} v - y, & |y| < 1 \\ -v - y, & |y| \geq 1. \end{cases} \tag{6.38}$$

(This is piecewise linear, but it must be classed as a nonlinear system.)

5. A trajectory T_1 of (6.38) which begins at $(-1, v_0)$ is shown in Figure 6.15. Show that T_1 lies beneath its tangent at $(-1, v_0)$; hence, show that the energy gained by the time T_1 reaches $(1, v_1)$ is less than

$$2\left(v_0 + \frac{v_0 + 1}{v_0}\right).$$

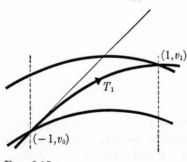

FIG. 6.15

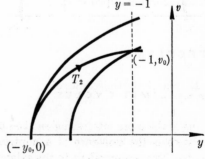

FIG. 6.16

6. A segment of a trajectory T_2 of (6.38) is shown as Figure 6.16. The energy lost over its course is

$$E = \int_{-y_0}^{-1} v \, dy.$$

186

Find a simple, integrable function $h(v)$ such that $0 \leq h(v) \leq v$ on the interval $[-y_0, -1]$, and from this show that

$$E \geq k v_0^2,$$

for some constant k.

7. Consider the trajectory of (6.38) shown in Figure 6.17 as a function of v_0. Show that for small v_0, $y_1 > y_0$.

8. Refer to Figure 6.17. With the results of Problems 5 and 6 show that for all sufficiently large v_0 that $y_1 < y_0$.

9. By the symmetries of the tangent field defined by (6.38) and the result of Problem 8, show that all solutions of (6.38) are bounded.

10. Referring to Figure 6.17, by the continuity of solutions in initial values, argue that there is at least one value v_0 such that $y_1 = y_0$. By symmetry show that this yields a periodic solution of (6.38), as shown in Figure 6.18.

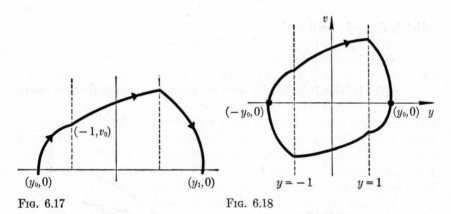

FIG. 6.17   FIG. 6.18

▶ 6.4 LIMIT CYCLES

One of the more interesting and important problems for a nonconservative system is the existence of a nontrivial periodic solution. As previously noted, this is equivalent to the existence of a closed trajectory in the phase plane. The effect of such a closed trajectory is the conservation of energy over the period τ of transit. For clearly, a closed trajectory begins and ends on the same energy curve; thus, the net gain of energy,

$$\int_{x_0}^{x_0 + \tau} v(x) f(y(x), v(x)) \, dx,$$

must be zero. We see also that for systems that are everywhere dissipative, in the sense that $vf(y,v) \leq 0$ at all points (e.g. the damped pendulum), there is little possibility of a closed trajectory. Indeed, except for the rare case where the locus $vf(y,v) = 0$ contains a closed trajectory, a necessary condition for the existence of periodic solutions is that $vf(y, v)$ change sign. Physically, we must be dealing with mechanisms which absorb energy in certain phases and dissipate energy in others.

A specific approach to this type of problem was developed in Problems 5 through 10 of the preceding section. Although energy considerations such as these are always useful, a somewhat more general, and theoretical, point of view grows from the following obvious remark: A trajectory of

$$y' = g(y,v)$$
$$v' = h(y,v),$$
(6.41)

which is defined for all x, either

  (i)   approaches a singular point as $x \to +\infty$,
  (ii) is unbounded as $x \to +\infty$,

or

  (iii) is bounded and also bounded away from every singular point
        as $x \to +\infty$.

(We may make these statements also for $x \to -\infty$, but for the moment we consider only the one case.) Property (iii) is a characteristic of a closed trajectory; however, it is not the principal property of being closed. Nonetheless, the conclusion of the Bendixson-Poincaré theorem is that if (iii) holds for some solution, then there exists a periodic solution.

We shall not prove this, but we can indicate the ideas involved for the special system

$$y' = v$$
$$v' = h(y, v).$$
(6.42)

Suppose that $(0, 0)$ is the only singular point and that (iii) holds for some solution. In view of the special form of (6.42) and the implicit assumption on $h(y, 0)$, the pattern of behavior of the trajectory involved is limited. Indeed, the spiral of Figure 6.19 is more or less indicated since trajectories move to the right in the upper half plane, and to the left in the lower half plane. Also, $h(y, 0)$ is zero only if $y = 0$, in order that $(0, 0)$ be the only singular point, and if $h(y, 0)$ is not of the same sign as y, no bounded solu-

188

tion is possible. (An inward winding spiral which stays a finite distance from $(0, 0)$ is, in fact, the only other possibility.)

We note the infinite sequence of intersections $\{P_i\}$ with the positive y axis. It is an increasing sequence, and it is bounded since T is bounded; therefore, the sequence converges to P. At the same time T has "swept out" a bounded region of the yv plane. Moreover, *the boundary of this region is a simple closed curve, specifically the trajectory through P.* To indicate a proof of this geometric assertion, let any trajectory T_y intersect the y axis between P_1 and P at y_0. From the behavior of T and the fact that trajectories cannot intersect, T_y will make a circuit of the origin and intersect the y axis again at $P(y_0)$ between P_1 and P. By the continuity

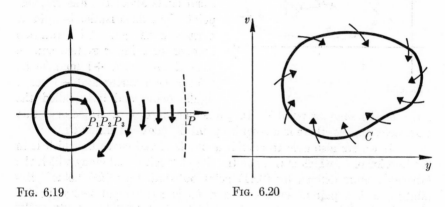

FIG. 6.19   FIG. 6.20

of solutions, and trajectories, in initial values, $P(y_0)$ is a continuous function of y_0, and this continuity holds also for $y_0 = P$. From Figure 6.19 we have

$$\lim_{y_0 \to P} P(y_0) = P,$$

that is, the trajectory through P returns to P. This is the outline of the proof for equations (6.42). In the general case, somewhat delicate continuity arguments are employed to reduce it, essentially, to a configuration similar to Figure 6.19.

We see that the nonclosed trajectory T winds onto the closed trajectory, or away from it, if (*iii*) holds as $t \to -\infty$. From this geometric description we derive the name *limit cycle* for such a closed trajectory.

A simple condition which insures that there is a bounded trajectory of (6.41) is shown in Figure 6.20; namely, a simple closed curve C at every point of which the tangent vector defined by (6.41) points to the interior of, or is tangent to, C. It is shown by various topological arguments that there must be at least one singular point in the interior of C. If there is just one—and we shall not consider more complicated cases—it must be a node, a focus, or a vortex. (The idea of this is that as we proceed in the counterclockwise direction around C the vectors defined by (6.41) make one counterclockwise rotation. As C is continuously deformed without intercepting a singular point, this rotation number of $+1$ remains the same. In fact, if we shrink C to a small circle about the one singular point where linearization is valid, it must still be $+1$. This rotation number for a linear system can be worked out. It is $+1$ for a node, a focus, or a vortex and -1 for a saddle point, and it is called the index of the singular point.) In particular, if C is a trajectory, this statement applies: there is a singular point of index $+1$ inside C.

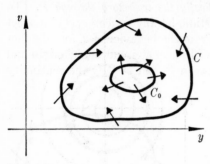

FIG. 6.21

If we are also able to exhibit a simple closed curve C_0 which is in the interior of C, which surrounds the singular point, and along which the tangent vectors defined by (6.41) point outward, then (iii) holds. Exhibiting such a pair of curves C and C_0 is a principal technique for showing the existence and rough location of at least one limit cycle. Energy considerations with respect to a simple one-parameter family of curves are a valuable tool in this. Consider the simplest possible example,

$$y' = v$$
$$v' = (1 - y^2 - v^2)v - y. \tag{6.43}$$

The energy curves are the concentric circles

$$\frac{v^2}{2} + \frac{y^2}{2} = C,$$

and we see that

$$\frac{dE}{dx} = v^2(1 - y^2 - v^2),$$

which is negative on the circle $y^2 + v^2 = a^2 > 1$ and positive on a circle $y^2 + v^2 = b^2 < 1$. These circles serve as C and C_0 respectively; therefore,

190

there is a limit cycle.   Indeed, we see one by inspection, the unit circle,

$$v^2 + y^2 = 1.$$

We see also that dE/dx is of one sign in the interior of this limit cycle and of the opposite sign in the exterior; hence, there can be no other closed trajectory.   We remark that, when used in a much more sophisticated manner, such energy considerations are, essentially, the only way of proving that there is exactly one limit cycle in a given domain.

Closely related to the uniqueness problem for limit cycles is the notion of *stability*. From Figure 6.19 a limit cycle is generated by a nonclosed trajectory spiraling onto the limit cycle from one side as $t \to \infty$, or, if (*iii*) holds, as $t \to -\infty$, spiraling away from it.   On that side of the limit cycle we would refer to it as *stable* or *unstable* according as it is approached for $t \to +\infty$ or $t \to -\infty$.   On the other side of the limit cycle, assuming there are no other limit cycles in the immediate neighborhood, we have the same two possibilities.   In total then, we have four classifications for isolated limit cycles, *stable* as illustrated by (6.43), *unstable* as illustrated by

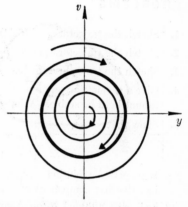

FIG. 6.22

$$
\begin{aligned}
y' &= v \\
v' &= -(1 - y^2 - v^2)v - y,
\end{aligned}
\tag{6.44}
$$

or *semistable* of two types, as illustrated by

$$
\begin{aligned}
y' &= v \\
v' &= |1 - y^2 - u^2|v - y
\end{aligned}
\tag{6.45}
$$

and

$$
\begin{aligned}
y' &= v \\
v' &= -|1 - y^2 - v^2|v - y.
\end{aligned}
\tag{6.46}
$$

It is, in general, extremely difficult to prove stability or instability of an isolated limit cycle.   However, a typical result relating stability and uniqueness is the following: Two isolated consecutive concentric limit cycles cannot both be stable. For example, for a given system we may be able to prove that all limit cycles are isolated and that all limit cycles are stable. We conclude that there is at most one limit cycle.

PROBLEMS

1. Sketch the trajectories of (6.44).

2. Sketch the trajectories of (6.45).

3. Sketch the trajectories of (6.46).

4. Give a geometric "proof" of the fact that two isolated, consecutive limit cycles cannot both be stable. What can they be?

5. Show that

$$y' = v$$
$$v' = (1 - y^2 - v^2)v - 2y$$

has a periodic solution. Show that the amplitude of a periodic solution $y(x)$—i.e., the first component of a periodic solution $[y(x), v(x)]$—is less than one and greater than $1/\sqrt{2}$. Assuming there is only one periodic solution, show that it is stable.

6. Sketch the trajectories of

$$y' = v - \frac{y^3}{3} + y$$
$$v' = -y. \qquad (6.47)$$

Show that (6.47) and

$$y' = w$$
$$w' = (1 - y^2)w - y \qquad (6.48)$$

are equivalent under the transformation

$$v = w + y^3 - y.$$

7. Sketch the trajectories of

$$y' = v$$
$$v' = \begin{cases} (1 - y^2 - v^2)v - y, & y^2 + v^2 \le 1 \\ -y, & y^2 + v^2 \ge 1. \end{cases}$$

8. Sketch the trajectories of

$$y' = v$$
$$v' = (1 - r) \sin\left(\frac{1}{1 - r}\right)v - y, \qquad r^2 = y^2 + v^2.$$

192

Identify limit cycles and classify them, if possible. (Both Problems 7 and 8 illustrate the result that *limits of limit cycles are limit cycles*.)

9. Assume that in

$$y' = g(y, v)$$
$$v' = h(y, v),$$

(6.49)

$$g(y + \tau, v) \equiv g(y, v) \quad \text{and} \quad h(y + \tau, v) \equiv h(y, v).$$

In view of this periodicity, the behavior of any trajectory in any part of the yv plane can, by a translation, be viewed in the strip $0 \le y \le \tau$. Indeed, if we identify edges of this strip so as to obtain a cylinder, all of the trajectories of (6.49) become a continuum of curves on the cylinder. For example, the trajectories T_1, T_2, and T_3 in the phase plane become one trajectory on the "phase cylinder" of Figure 6.23. The ideas of the Bendixson-Poincaré theorem

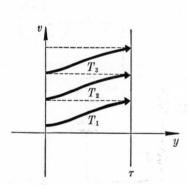
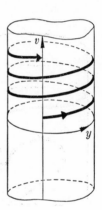

Fig. 6.23

remain the same as the idea of Figure 6.21, but now there are on the cylinder two different types of bounded regions, which are free of singular points, to consider, and with them two kinds of closed trajectories. They are shown in Figure 6.24. T_2 is of the usual type, which we now call a limit cycle of the *first kind*; T_1 is new, and it is called a limit cycle of the *second kind*. In general, it corresponds in the yv plane to a trajectory which is given by $v = f(y)$, where $f(y + \tau) \equiv f(y)$.

Notions of stability can be introduced. For example, if T_1 and T_2 are the only limit cycles of (6.49), one but not both can be stable.

Show that

$$y'' + y + \sin y = 2$$

193

has no limit cycles of the first kind and exactly one of the second kind. Note, it is not necessary to use the phase cylinder. What must be shown is that the first-order equation

$$\frac{dv}{dy} = \frac{-v - \sin y + 2}{v}$$

for trajectories has exactly one periodic solution $v(y)$ of period 2π. It may help to write this as

$$\frac{d(v^2/2)}{dy} = -v - \sin y + 2$$

and apply slope field arguments (cf. Section 3.5).

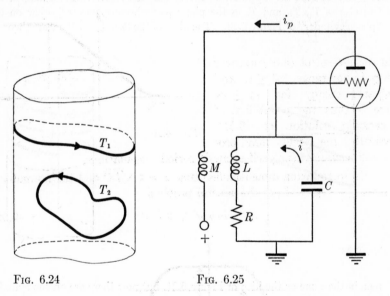

Fig. 6.24   Fig. 6.25

▶ 6.5 EXAMPLE

An example which calls for the application of the ideas of the preceding sections comes from the following plausible description of the vacuum tube circuit of Figure 6.25. We assume a symmetric tube characteristic, $f(e_g) = i_p$, shown in Figure 6.26, where e_s is the saturation potential and $-e_s$ the cutoff potential. We further assume that no grid current flows, so that the equations of the grid-tank circuit become

194

$$\frac{de_g}{dt} = \frac{i}{C}$$

$$L\frac{di}{dt} + Ri + e_g = M\frac{di_p}{dt} = Mf'(e_y)\frac{de_g}{dt}.$$

A second-order equation equivalent to this system is

$$\frac{d^2e_g}{dt^2} + \left[\frac{R}{L} - \frac{M}{LC}f'(e_g)\right]\frac{de_g}{dt} + \frac{1}{LC}e_g = 0. \qquad (6.51)$$

A graph of $f'(e_g)$ has the features shown in Figure 6.27. The value of $f'(0) = \mu$ is known as the transconductance of the tube, and if circuit constants are such that

$$\frac{R}{L} - \frac{M\mu}{LC} < 0,$$

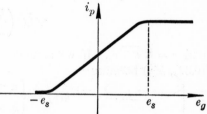

then the system of (6.51) absorbs energy in one range, $|e_g| \leq e_0$, and dissipates energy for $|e_g| \geq e_0$. There is thus the possibility of a periodic solution of (6.51). Physically, the circuit may pro-

FIG. 6.26

duce self-sustained (i.e., self-excited) periodic oscillations.

On introducing dimensionless time $x = t/\sqrt{LC}$ and the normalized variable $y = ce_g$, we have the general problem

$$y'' + h(y)y' + y = 0, \qquad (6.52)$$

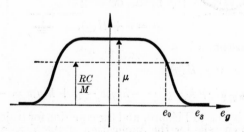

FIG. 6.27

where $h(y)$ is a continuous, or piecewise continuous, function with the following properties:

(a) $h(y) = h(-y)$

(b) $h(y) < 0$ for $|y| < a_0$,

$h(y) > 0$ for $|y| > a_0$

(c) $\displaystyle\int_0^y h(t)\,dt = H(y) \to +\infty$ as $y \to \infty$.

For example, if we assume a parabolic approximation to $f'(e_g)$,

$$f'(e_g) = \mu(1 - ke_g{}^2),$$

equation (6.52) becomes *Van der Pol's equation*

$$y'' + \lambda(1 - y^2)y' + y = 0, \tag{6.53}$$

where λ is the positive parameter

$$\sqrt{LC}\left(\frac{R}{L} - \frac{M}{LC}\right),$$

and $y = \sqrt{k/\lambda}\,e_g$. If we assume that $f(e_g)$ is piecewise linear, then in (6.52), $h(y)$ becomes

$$h(y) = \begin{cases} \alpha < 0, & y < a_0 \\ \beta > 0, & y > a_0 \end{cases}$$

(cf. Problems 4 through 10 of Section 6.3).

The mathematical result is that (6.52) has a unique, stable limit cycle, and to prove it we write (6.52) as the system

$$\begin{aligned} y' &= v \\ v' &= -h(y)v - y. \end{aligned} \tag{6.54}$$

We now change variables by means of

$$u = v + H(y),$$

whence (6.54) becomes

$$\begin{aligned} y' &= u - H(y) \\ u' &= v' + h(y)y' = -h(y)v - y + h(y)v = -y. \end{aligned} \tag{6.55}$$

This technique is due to Liénard, and the equation for trajectories of (6.55),

$$\frac{du}{dy} = \frac{y}{H(y) - u} \tag{6.56}$$

is sometimes called Liénard's equation. We remark that the transformation between (6.54) and (6.55) is one-to-one, and thus, closed stable trajectories go into closed stable trajectories.

196

The tangent field of (6.55) is shown in Figure 6.28, and the isocline, $u = H(y)$, of vertical tangents has been included. As $H(y)$ is an odd function, the slope field of (6.56) is symmetric about the origin; in other words, the reflection of a trajectory through the origin is again a trajectory. We need describe, therefore, only trajectories in the right half plane in order to have described them all. In particular, a trajectory is closed if

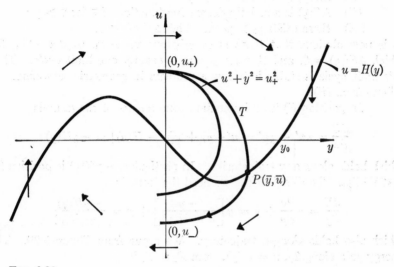

FIG. 6.28

and only if its intersections with the positive and negative u axes, u_+ and u_-, stand in the relation $u_+ = -u_-$.

We refer trajectories to the point $P(\bar{y}, \bar{u})$ of intersection with $u = H(y)$. For each P, the trajectory will indeed reach the u axis at finite points u_+ and u_-. It is clear that $0 \leq y \leq \bar{y}$ along this trajectory; thus, away from the curve $u = H(y)$ the slope of T is bounded, in view of (6.56). It could not, therefore, run off to infinity in either direction and avoid the u axis.

If we look at the energy curves for (6.55), the concentric circles

$$\frac{u^2}{2} + \frac{v^2}{2} = C,$$

and the energy of solutions

$$\frac{u^2(x)}{2} + \frac{v^2(x)}{2} = E,$$

197

we see that $u_+ = -u_-$ if and only if the total change of energy, ΔE, around T is zero. We conclude from continuity of solutions in initial values that $\Delta E(\bar{y})$, as a function of $\bar{y}$, is continuous. The idea of the proof, which is essentially due to Levinson and Smith,* can be given schematically. We show that

(i) $\Delta E(\bar{y}) > 0$ for $0 < \bar{y} \leq y_0$;
(ii) $\Delta E(\bar{y})$ is a strictly decreasing function of $\bar{y}$ for $\bar{y} > y_0$;
(iii) there exists $y_2 > y_0$ for which $\Delta E(y_2) < 0$.

It is now obvious that there is exactly one value y_1, $y_0 < y_1 < y_2$, for which $\Delta E(y_1) = 0$, and therefore there is exactly one limit cycle. That this limit cycle is stable is left as a problem in geometric reasoning. It follows from (ii).

Proposition (i) is an immediate consequence of the formula

$$\frac{dE}{dx} = uu' + yy' = u(-y) + y[u - H(y)] = -yH(y)$$

which holds along any trajectories. In particular, $-yH(y)$ is positive for $0 < y < y_0$. To establish (ii) we need the formula

$$\frac{dE}{dy} = u\frac{du}{dy} + y = u\left[\frac{-y}{u - H(y)}\right] + y = \frac{-yH(y)}{u - H(y)}$$

which also holds along a trajectory. We argue from Figure 6.29. The energy gain along T_1, $u = u_1(y)$, from P_1 to P_2 is

$$\int_0^{y_0} \frac{-yH(y)}{u_1(y) - H(y)}\, dy$$

and that along T_2 is

$$\int_0^{y_0} \frac{-yH(y)}{u_2(y) - H(y)}\, dy.$$

Since $u_2(y) < u_1(y)$, it is evident that more energy is gained along T_2 than along T_1. The same kind of argument shows that more energy is gained along T_2 between Q_3 and Q_4 than is gained along T_1 between P_3 and P_4. We complete the proof of (ii) by showing that more energy is lost on T_1 between P_2 and P_3 than is lost along T_2 between Q_2 and Q_3—indeed, the loss between P_2' and P_3' alone is greater. For this we need the formula

$$\frac{dE}{du} = u + y\frac{dy}{du} = u + y\left[\frac{u - H(y)}{-y}\right] = -H(y),$$

---

* N. Levinson and O. K. Smith, "A General Equation for Relaxation Oscillations," *Duke Mathematical Journal*, 1942, Vol. 9, pp. 382–403.

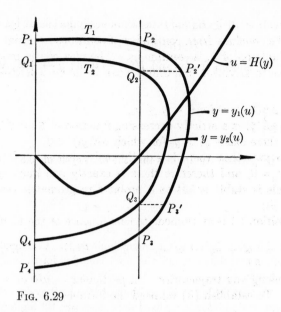

FIG. 6.29

and we have only to compare

$$\int_{u_3}^{u_2} H[y_1(u)] \, du \quad \text{and} \quad \int_{u_3}^{u_2} H[y_2(u)] \, du.$$

The comparison goes as indicated, since $y_1(u) > y_2(u)$ and $H(y)$ is an increasing function.

To prove (iii), we first note that in the above we have shown that the total energy gain over those portions of a trajectory between 0 and y_0 is a decreasing function $\bar{y}, \bar{y} > y_0$. This gain is therefore bounded. We now show that for large enough $\bar{y}$ the energy lost over a trajectory in the region $y > y_0$ is arbitrarily large. This would prove (iii). Consider the portion

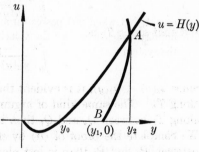

FIG. 6.30

of the trajectory shown in Figure 6.30 for $\bar{y} = y_2 > y_0$. The energy lost between A and B is given by

$$\int_0^{H(y_2)} H(y) \, du.$$

199

On this interval, $H(y) \geq H(y_1)$; thus, the energy lost is at least

$$H(y_1)H(y_2) \geq H^2(y_1).$$

Since y_1 may be chosen freely and $H(y) \to \infty$ as $y \to +\infty$, we have the result.

PROBLEMS

1. Show that proposition (ii) implies that the limit cycle of (6.55) is stable.

2. The system

$$y' = v$$

$$v' = \begin{cases} av - y, & y < 1 \\ -bv - y, & y > 1, \end{cases}$$

(6.57)

where a and b are positive, has a unique limit cycle. Carry out the Liénard transformation and thus compute the lower bound y_0 for the amplitude of the periodic solution.

3. Sketch the tangent field of (6.57) and indicate the limit cycle. Show by slope field comparison that if b remains fixed and a decreases, the limit cycle "shrinks" toward the origin. Argue that as $a \to 0$ the limiting position of the limit cycle is the unit circle.

4. Energy may be added to a dissipative system by means of impulses, as in the escapement mechanism of a clock. We may have a linear, damped oscillatory system, for example,

$$y'' + 2y' + 2y = 0,$$

except that when $y(t)$ passes through zero with positive velocity we apply an impulse which increases the velocity by one unit. In other words, we have the system

$$y' = v$$

$$v' = -2v - 2y$$

(6.58)

except along the positive v axis, where, if $y(t_-) = 0$, then

$$v(t_-) + 1 = v(t_+).$$

Sketch trajectories of (5.8). Show that it has a unique, stable limit cycle, and find it explicitly.

5. Consider the driven Van der Pol's equation

$$y'' + (y^2 - 1)y' + y = A,$$

where A is a constant. Show that under $u = y - A$ this is equivalent to

$$u'' + (u^2 + 2Au + A^2 - 1)u' + u = 0.$$

Discuss the existence of limit cycles for the cases $A^2 < 1$, $A^2 = 1$, and $A^2 > 1$.

7

APPLICATIONS OF HIGHER-ORDER EQUATIONS AND SYSTEMS

▶ 7.1 A DESCRIPTIVE APPLICATION

In a solution technique for certain problems involving the fourth-order partial differential equation

$$\frac{\partial^4 u}{\partial x^4} = -\frac{\partial u}{\partial t},$$ (7.11)

the function

$$u(x,t) = \int_{-\infty}^{\infty} e^{-\alpha^4 t} \cos \alpha x \, d\alpha, \qquad t > 0$$

is, in a sense, a fundamental solution (cf. Section 3.1). We let t be a fixed positive parameter and investigate the behavior of $u(x, t)$ as a function of x, called $u(x)$.

We note first that $u(x)$ is bounded for all x, since

$$|u(x)| \leq \int_{-\infty}^{\infty} e^{-\alpha^4 t} \, d\alpha = \frac{1}{\sqrt[4]{t}} \int_{-\infty}^{\infty} e^{-s^4} \, ds.$$

We form the derivatives of $u(x)$,

$$u'(x) = -\int_{-\infty}^{\infty} e^{-\alpha^4 t} \, \alpha \sin \alpha x \, dx$$

$$u''(x) = -\int_{-\infty}^{\infty} e^{-\alpha^4 t} \, \alpha^2 \cos \alpha x \, d\alpha$$

$$u'''(x) = \int_{-\infty}^{\infty} e^{-\alpha^4 t} \, \alpha^3 \sin \alpha x \, d\alpha,$$

and so forth. Each of these is likewise bounded for all x. In particular,

$$u'''(x) = -\frac{1}{4t} e^{-\alpha^4 t} \sin \alpha x \Big|_{-\infty}^{\infty} + \frac{x}{4t} \int_{-\infty}^{\infty} e^{-\alpha^4 t} \cos \alpha x \, d\alpha$$

$$= \frac{x}{4t} u(x);$$

that is, $u(x)$ is the solution of the third-order, linear, homogeneous equation

$$u''' - \frac{x}{4t} u = 0, \tag{7.12}$$

which satisfies the initial conditions

$$u(0) = \int_{-\infty}^{\infty} e^{-\alpha^4 t} \, d\alpha = u_0$$

$$u'(0) = 0$$

$$u''(0) = -\int_{-\infty}^{\infty} e^{-\alpha^4 t} \, \alpha^2 \, d\alpha = w_0.$$

With the knowledge that $u'''(x)$ is bounded, we have the immediate inference from (7.12) that

$$|u(x)| = \left| \frac{4t}{x} u'''(x) \right| \leq \frac{c}{x},$$

or that $u(x) \to 0$ as $x \to \infty$. Indeed, by differentiating (7.12) repeatedly, we could show that $u(x) \to 0$ faster than $1/x^n$ for every n.

The behavior of solutions of such a third-order equation is, in general, little known, but we can give a geometric, qualitative description of

202

$u(x)$ for $x \geq 0$ (this is sufficient since $u(x)$ is an even function). First, u''' is of the same sign as u, from (7.12). At $x = 0$, u is positive, u' is zero, u'' is negative, and u''' is positive. We infer that u'' increases from its negative initial value. While u'' is negative, u' decreases from zero. We sketch all of this out to a point x_1. We now list, and show in Figure 7.1, the four possibilities past x_1.

(1) u'' has become zero at x_1 and continues to increase at such a rate that u remains positive. If u has a positive relative minimum, then the solution curve is convex and increasing for all x. This is impossible, since u is bounded.

(2) u'' has become zero at x_1 and u remains convex, decreasing,

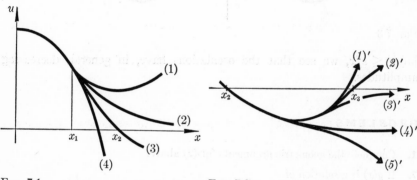

Fig. 7.1   Fig. 7.2

and positive for all $x > x_1$. This is possible since u is bounded, but in this case u''' is positive and u'' is positive and increasing past x_1. Therefore, u'' has a positive lower bound. We leave it as a geometric exercise to argue that this is impossible.

(3) What actually occurs is an inflection point at x_1. We show this by eliminating (4).

(4) The curve remains concave ($u'' < 0$) into the lower half plane. But when u is negative, u''' is negative, and then u'' will decrease from negative values. Such a curve will remain concave and hence unbounded.

If u' and u are zero at x_2, the solution curve will bend back into the upper half plane to remain convex and unbounded; therefore, the solution curve crosses the x axis at x_2. Thereafter, we have five possibilities. The basic situation is that u''' is negative, hence u'' is decreasing in the lower half plane. $(5)'$ is eliminated at once, $(4)'$ implies that $u''' = (x/4t)u$

203

is unbounded which is impossible, (3)' is eliminated by the arguments involved previously in (2), and (1)' is entirely similar to (4). From all this, (2)' must prevail.

The arguments can be repeated indefinitely to show that $u(x)$ oscillates infinitely often as shown in Figure 7.3. With the knowledge that

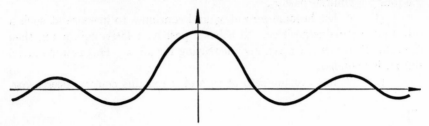

FIG. 7.3

$|u(x)| \leq c/x$, we see that the oscillations have, in general, decreasing amplitudes.

PROBLEMS

1. Complete the geometric arguments for (2) above.

2. If $y(x)$ is a solution of
$$y''' - xy = 0,$$
show that $y(x/\sqrt[4]{4t})$ is a solution of (7.12). Hence describe $u(x,t)$ for various values of $t > 0$.

3. Show that if
$$y(x) = -\int_{-\infty}^{\infty} \frac{e^{-|x-t|}}{2} f(t)\, dt$$
exists, it is a solution of
$$y'' - y = f(x).$$
Show that it is the only solution of this equation which can satisfy the condition: $|y(x)|$ is bounded for all x.

▶ 7.2 BUCKLING OF THIN COLUMNS

We consider a slender, ideal column of length l which is built in vertically at the base, is free at the top, and is subject to an axial force of magnitude

204

F applied at the top (Fig. 7.4). This force produces a bending moment $-F(y_0 - y)$ at point P in the column. Also, if it is significant compared to F, we may want to consider the bending moment produced at P by the weight of the column above P. If s is the arc length parameter of the column, such that $s = 0$ at the base, and $\delta(s)$ is the linear mass density, then this contribution to the bending moment is

$$-\int_s^l g\delta(t)[y(t) - y(s)]\, dt.$$

It is now shown that, as a consequence of Hooke's law, the column is in equilibrium when the bending moment at each point is proportional to the negative curvature:

$$k\frac{d\phi}{ds} = -\left\{-F(y_0 - y) - \int_s^l g\delta(t)[y(t) - y(s)]\, dt\right\}. \qquad (7.21)$$

The constant k is the flexural rigidity of the column in the plane of bending, and it is given by EI, where E is the modulus of elasticity of the material and I is the moment of inertia of the cross section with respect to the line which passes, perpendicular to the plane of bending, through the centroid of the cross section.

From (7.21) we derive, if E and I are constant,

$$EI\frac{d^2\phi}{ds^2} = -F\frac{dy}{ds} - \frac{dy}{ds}g\int_s^l \delta(t)\, dt, \qquad (7.22)$$

and, with the end conditions

$$y(l) = y_0 \quad \text{and} \quad \frac{d\phi}{ds}(l) = 0,$$

(7.22) is equivalent to (7.21) by integration. By the identity

$$\frac{dy}{ds} = \sin\phi$$

we finally have the nonlinear equation

$$EI\frac{d^2\phi}{ds^2} = -\left(F + g\int_s^l \delta(t)\, dt\right)\sin\phi \qquad (7.23)$$

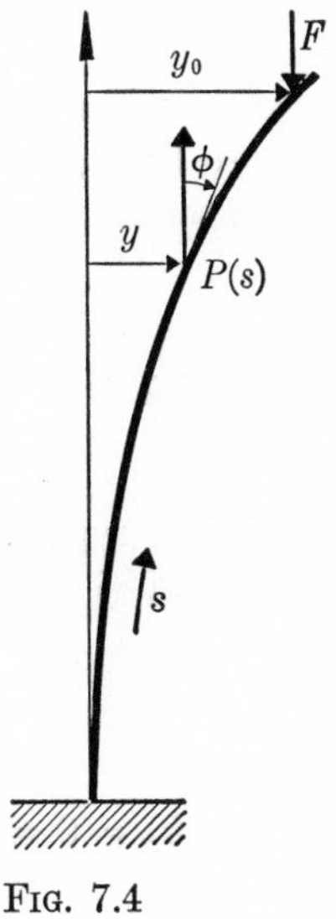

as the equation of equilibrium states. We must solve (7.23) subject to the boundary conditions

$$\frac{d\phi}{ds}(l) = 0, \qquad \phi(0) = 0,$$

FIG. 7.4

205

where the first condition expresses the fact that there is no bending moment at $s = l$ and the second, that the end ($s = 0$) is built in.

This boundary value problem always has a solution, namely $\phi(s) \equiv 0$, which is to say, the vertical position is always an equilibrium state. The deeper question is whether, for some critical values of F and/or $\delta(s)$, there is a nontrivial solution. If so, then the vertical equilibrium is in some sense unstable. The column would tend to buckle to the new equilibrium state and, indeed, collapse if the new state involved exceeding the elastic limits.

At its simplest, $\delta(s)$ would be a constant, so that (7.23) would become

$$\frac{d^2\phi}{ds^2} = -\left[\frac{F}{EI} + \frac{\delta}{EI}(l - s)\right]\sin \phi. \tag{7.24}$$

A further simplification is the practical assumption that ($\delta l/F$) is very small, whence

$$\frac{d^2\phi}{ds^2} + \frac{F}{EI}\sin \phi = 0, \tag{7.25}$$

is the equation of state. Finally, let us assume that deflections are very small so that ϕ is small. As a consequence, we may replace $\sin \phi$ by ϕ to obtain the linear, boundary value problem

$$\frac{d^2\phi}{ds^2} + \frac{F}{EI}\phi = 0,$$

$$\phi(0) = 0, \quad \frac{d\phi}{ds}(l) = 0, \tag{7.26}$$

which is a typical so-called Sturm-Liouville problem. The technique of solution of (7.26) is straightforward. The solution of (7.26) must have the form

$$\phi(s) = c_1 \cos \sqrt{\frac{F}{EI}}\, s + c_2 \sin \sqrt{\frac{F}{EI}}\, s.$$

Since $\phi(0) = 0 = c_1 \cos 0 + c_2 \sin 0 = c_1$, the only possible solution of (7.26) is

$$\phi(s) = c_2 \sin \sqrt{\frac{F}{EI}}\, s.$$

In addition,

$$\frac{d\phi}{ds}(l) = c_2 \sqrt{\frac{F}{EI}} \cos \sqrt{\frac{F}{EI}}\, l = 0$$

must hold.   Unless

$$\sqrt{\frac{F}{EI}}\, l = \frac{\pi}{2} + n\pi$$

for some integer n, this is possible only if $c_2 = 0$, that is, if the only solution is the trivial one.   We see then that buckling is first possible if the vertical force has the critical value

$$F = \frac{\pi^2}{4l^2} EI$$

called the Euler load, and corresponding to it,

$$\phi(s) = c_2 \sin \frac{\pi}{2l} s,$$

where c_2 is small.

According to the linear model, nonvertical equilibrium states are possible also, if and only if F has the values

$$F = (2n + 1)^2 \frac{\pi^2}{4l^2} EI, \qquad n = 1, 2, \ldots.$$

In some Sturm-Liouville problems, these higher *characteristic values* and the corresponding solutions are of great importance, but here it is clear physically that either the column will collapse for $F \geq (\pi^2/4l^2)EI$ or that there is a nonvertical equilibrium state for each $F \geq (\pi^2/4l^2)EI$.   Another physical inconsistency of the linear model is that, except for being known to be small, c_2 is indeterminate.   It does not seem likely that if the column does not collapse under the Euler load, it can assume any one of the continuum of positions indicated.

We turn to the nonlinear problem in order to clarify this.   We let

$$\lambda = \frac{F}{EI}$$

and consider the problem

$$\phi'' + \lambda \sin \phi = 0$$
$$\phi(0) = 0, \quad \phi'(l) = 0. \tag{7.27}$$

To solve this, recall the methods of Section 4.2.   A solution which satisfies $\phi(0) = 0$ satisfies

$$\phi'^2(s) - 2\lambda \cos \phi(s) = -2\lambda + \phi'^2(0) = -2\lambda \cos \phi_0,$$

and, if $\phi'(0) > 0$, is given by

$$\int_0^{\phi(s)} \frac{d\phi}{\sqrt{2\lambda \cos \phi - 2\lambda \cos \phi_0}} = s.$$

Viewing this in the $\phi\phi'$ plane (see Fig. 7.5), we are integrating along one of the closed trajectories of equation (7.25) beginning at the point $[0, \phi'(0)]$. If possible, we are to choose $\phi'(0)$—or, what is the same, ϕ_0—so that

$$\frac{1}{\sqrt{\lambda}} \int_0^{\phi_0} \frac{d\phi}{\sqrt{2 \cos \phi - 2 \cos \phi_0}} = l, \qquad (7.28)$$

in other words, so that $\phi'(l) = 0$.

To examine this integral as a function of ϕ_0 we transform it to the elliptic integral

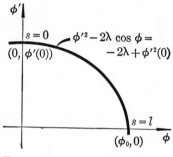

FIG. 7.5

$$\int_0^1 \frac{dt}{\sqrt{1 - t^2} \sqrt{1 - (a/2)t^2}}$$

by means of the change of variable

$$\cos \phi = 1 - (1 - \cos \phi_0)t^2 = 1 - at^2.$$

As ϕ_0 increases from 0 to π, a increases from 0 to 2. The above integral is clearly an increasing, continuous function of a, since the integrand becomes larger as a increases. As $a \to 0_+$, the limiting value is

$$\int_0^1 \frac{dt}{\sqrt{1 - t^2}} = \frac{\pi}{2}$$

and as $a \to 2_-$, the integral approaches

$$\int_0^1 \frac{dt}{1 - t^2} = +\infty.$$

Therefore, if $\lambda \leq (\pi^2/4l^2)$,

$$\frac{1}{\sqrt{\lambda}} \int_0^{\phi_0} \frac{d\phi}{\sqrt{2 \cos \phi - 2 \cos \phi_0}} > \frac{1}{\sqrt{\pi^2/4l^2}} \cdot \frac{\pi}{2} = l$$

for every $\phi_0 > 0$; thus no nontrivial equilibrium is possible. If, on the other hand, $\lambda > (\pi^2/4l^2)$, then there exists a unique ϕ_0, $0 < \phi_0 < \pi$, such that

$$\frac{1}{\sqrt{\lambda}} \int_0^{\phi_0} \frac{d\phi}{\sqrt{2 \cos \phi - 2 \cos \phi_0}} = l.$$

208

In practice, ϕ_0 could be found by means of a table of complete elliptic integrals. We note that as $\lambda \to \infty$, $\phi_0 \to \pi$. The picture of the column for increasing values of F (say it is made of piano wire so as to stand the stresses) is given in Figure 7.6.

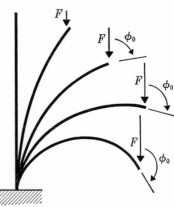

PROBLEMS

1. Show that if $\lambda > (9\pi^2/4l^2)$, there is a solution $\phi(s)$ of (7.25) such that $\phi(0) = 0$ and

$$\frac{1}{\sqrt{\lambda}} \int_0^{\phi_0} \frac{d\phi}{\sqrt{2\cos\phi - 2\cos\phi_0}} = \frac{l}{3}.$$

By the symmetry of the trajectories of (7.25), show that $\phi(s)$ is a solution of (7.27). Sketch the corresponding configuration of the column.

FIG. 7.6

2. If the column is built in at the top as well as at the base, the problem becomes

$$\phi'' + \lambda \sin\phi = 0$$
$$\phi(0) = \phi(l) = 0.$$

Show that the linearized problem has π^2/l^2 for its smallest characteristic value. Show that the nonlinear problem has a nontrivial solution if $\lambda > \pi^2/l^2$. Sketch the configurations of the column as λ increases.

3. Show that for the linear problem

$$\phi'' + \left[\frac{F}{EI} + \frac{\delta}{EI}(l-s) \right]\phi = 0$$
$$\phi(0) = \phi(l) = 0,$$

buckling will occur for some value of $F/EI = \lambda_0$ such that

$$\frac{\pi^2}{l^2} - \frac{\delta l}{EI} < \lambda_0 < \frac{\pi^2}{l^2}.$$

Employ the Sturm Comparison Theorem.

4. Let $y_1(x)$ be a solution of

$$y'' + q_1(x)y = 0$$
$$y(x_1) = 0$$

209

and let x_2 be the first zero of $y_1'(x)$ beyond x_1. If $q_2(x) \leq q_1(x)$ for $x_1 \leq x \leq x_2$, show that any solution of

$$y'' + q_2(x)y = 0$$

$$y(x_1) = 0$$

has no critical point on $[x_1, x_2]$. (This is a variant on the Sturm Comparison Theorem and the proof is entirely similar.)

5. With the result of Problem 4, show that for the linear problem

$$\phi'' + \left[\frac{F}{EI} + \frac{\delta}{EI}(l - s) \right] \phi = 0$$

$$\phi(0) = 0, \quad \phi'(l) = 0$$

buckling will occur for some value of $F/EI = \lambda_1$ such that

$$\frac{\pi^2}{4l^2} - \frac{\delta l}{EI} < \lambda_1 < \frac{\pi^2}{4l^2}.$$

▶ **7.3 ELECTRICAL NETWORKS**

A plane, connected electrical network can be represented schematically as N current-carrying branches connected at P vertices. Each branch has, in series, a resistor, a capacitor, an inductor, and an applied e.m.f., and we assume that all of these circuit elements are linear. They are lumped together in each branch shown in Figure 7.7, where, in all, there are six branches and four vertices. These N branches and P vertices generate F simple, closed loops, three in the case shown. We note that $3 - 6 + 4 = 1$, and in general it is true that

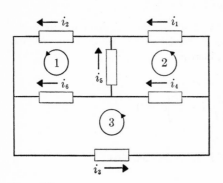

FIG. 7.7

$$F - N + P = 1.$$

This result is known as Euler's formula for plane polyhedra.

The equations governing the circuit are Kirchhoff's laws: For a fixed but arbitrary choice of directions of positive current in each branch and of orientation of each loop, the sum of the branch currents at each vertex is zero, and the voltage drop around each loop is zero. The current equa-

210

tions are algebraic and the loop equations are, in general, differential equations. This amounts to $F + P = N + 1$ equations in N unknowns, the branch currents. However, the P equations for the vertices are not independent. For example, these equations for the circuit shown are

$$i_2 - i_3 \qquad\qquad + i_6 = 0$$

$$i_4 - i_5 - i_6 = 0$$

$$-i_1 \qquad + i_3 - i_4 \qquad\qquad = 0$$

$$i_1 - i_2 \qquad\qquad + i_5 \qquad = 0,$$

and we see that the sum of any three equations is, to within a sign, the remaining one. This will always be true since we may write these equations so that each branch current enters into exactly two equations, once with coefficient $+1$ and once with coefficient -1. We may, therefore, drop any one, and the result is a system of N equations in N unknowns.

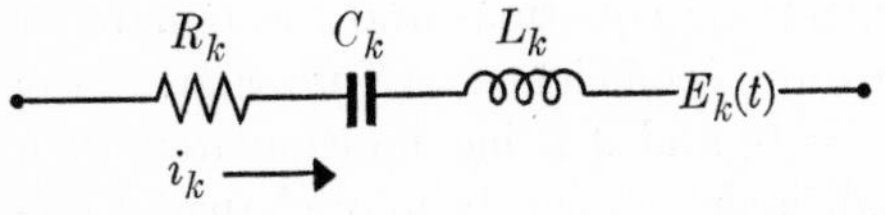

FIG. 7.8

As to the loops, we assume that the kth branch consists of R_k, C_k, L_k and $E_k(t)$ in series. The voltage drop corresponding to the direction of positive current is therefore

$$e_k = R_k i_k + \frac{1}{C_k} \int_{t_0}^{t} i_k(s)\, ds + L_k \frac{di_k}{dt} + E_k(t).$$

In one approach we write this as a second-order differential equation

$$e_k = R_k \frac{dq_k}{dt} + \frac{q_k}{C_k} + L_k \frac{d^2 q_k}{dt^2} + F_k(t),$$

where

$$q_k(t) = \frac{1}{C_k} \int_{t_0}^{t} i_k(s)\, ds$$

is the branch *charge*. A second approach is to write it as a pair of first-order equations by introducing v_k, the voltage drop across C_k, thus:

$$\frac{dv_k}{dt} = \frac{i_k}{C}$$

$$e_k = R_k i_k + v_k + L_k \frac{di_k}{dt} + E_k(t).$$

211

In either case, the loop equations become linear differential equations. For example, in the circuit shown in Figure 7.7, they are

$$e_2 + e_5 - e_6 = 0$$

$$e_1 - e_4 - e_5 = 0$$

$$e_3 + e_4 + e_6 = 0.$$

With the variables q_k, where

$$C_k \frac{dq_k}{dt} = i_k,$$

our system of N equations in the q_k become F second-order equations and $(P - 1)$ first-order equations. With the variables i_k and v_k, we have $2N$ equations, $(P - 1)$ of them linear algebraic equations and the remainder first-order linear equations with constant coefficients. (Note that, if the kth branch has no inductor, then $L_k = 0$, and if it has no capacitor, then $C_k = \infty$. Such a condition—or conditions—obviously may change a differential equation to an algebraic one, and/or eliminate some unknowns and equations.) The two problems posed by these approaches are, of course, equivalent, and each involves essentially the same computations in finding, or describing, solutions.

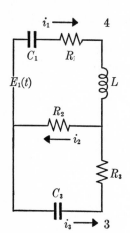

Consider the circuit shown in Figure 7.9. With the orientations indicated, we have

$$i_2 = i_1 + i_3$$

$$v_1 + R_1 i_1 + L_1 \frac{di_1}{dt} + R_2 i_2 + E_1(t) = 0$$

$$v_3 + R_3 i_3 + R_2 i_2 = 0$$

$$\frac{dv_1}{dt} = \frac{i_1}{C_1}$$

$$\frac{dv_3}{dt} = \frac{i_3}{C_3}$$

FIG. 7.9

as the system governing the circuit $(N = 3, F = 2, P = 2)$. If we first solve the two algebraic equations for i_1 and v_3 in terms of i_2 and i_3, we can write an equivalent system of three first-order equations in i_1, v_1, and v_3:

$$\frac{dv_1}{dt} = \frac{i_1}{C_1}$$

$$\frac{dv_3}{dt} = \frac{R_2}{C_3(R_2 + R_2)} i_1 - \frac{1}{C_3(R_2 + R_3)} v_3 \qquad (7.31)$$

$$\frac{di_1}{dt} = \frac{-(R_1 + R_2 R_3)i_1}{L_1(R_2 + R_3)} - \frac{v_1}{L_1} - \frac{R_2}{L_1(R_2 + R_3)} v_3 - E_1(t).$$

Recall now the solution methods of Section 5.5. Everything depends on the polynomial

$$p(s) = \begin{vmatrix} -s & 0 & \dfrac{1}{C_1} \\ 0 & \dfrac{-1}{C_3(R_2 + R_3)} - s & \dfrac{R_2}{C_3(R_2 + R_3)} \\ -\dfrac{1}{L} & \dfrac{R_2}{L(R_2 + R_3)} & \dfrac{-(R_1 + R_2 R_3)}{L(R_2 + R_3)} - s \end{vmatrix}.$$

For example, taking Laplace transforms and solving, we have

$$L[v_1(t)] = \frac{a_0 + a_1 s + a_2 s^2}{p(s)} + \frac{b_0 + b_1 s}{p(s)} L[E_1(t)],$$

and similarly for $L[v_3(t)]$ and $L[i_1(t)]$. The two terms here are the transforms of a transient—a solution of (7.31) when $E_1(t) = 0$—and of a solution of (7.31), respectively. The important physical property of transients going to zero as $t \to +\infty$ holds if, and only if, all the roots of $p(s) = 0$ have negative real parts. We see this from the decomposition of

$$\frac{a_0 + a_1 s + a_2 s^2}{p(s)}$$

into partial fractions, in any one of the following forms:

$$\frac{c_1}{s - r_1} + \frac{c_2}{s - r_2} + \frac{c_3}{s - r_3},$$

$$\frac{c_1}{s - r_1} + \frac{c_2}{(s - r_1)^2} + \frac{c_3}{s - r_2},$$

$$\frac{c_1}{s - r_1} + \frac{c_2}{(s - r_1)^2} + \frac{c_2}{(s - r_1)^3},$$

or

$$\frac{c_1}{s - r_1} + \frac{c_2 + c_3 s}{(s - \alpha)^2 + \beta^2}.$$

We argue that transients go to zero if and only if r_1, r_2, and r_3 are negative, or r_1 and α are negative, whichever applies.

If this is the case and if $E_1(t)$ is periodic, we may take the integral representation of solutions of (7.31) (see Section 5.5) and, in it, let $t_0 = -\infty$. It is easily shown that the result is the unique periodic solution of (7.31); moreover, it is a stable solution in the sense that all others approach it.

Finding necessary and sufficient conditions that all roots of a polynomial have negative real parts is purely an algebraic problem; however, on purely physical grounds we can argue that it must be the case for (7.31). In the undriven circuit there is no energy source, and energy is dissipated by the resistors; therefore, all currents and voltages must approach zero. We state the result for quadratic and cubic equations: all roots of

$$s^2 + as + b = 0$$

have negative real parts if, and only if, $a > 0$ and $b > 0$. This is easily proved by cases. All roots of

$$s^3 + as^2 + bs + c = 0$$

have negative real parts if, and only if, $a > 0$, $b > 0$, $c > 0$, and $ab > c$. This is proved by factoring the cubic $(s + \alpha)(s^2 + \beta s + \gamma)$, looking at the relations between a, b, and c and α, β, and γ, and seeing when and only when $\alpha > 0, \beta > 0$, and $\gamma > 0$.

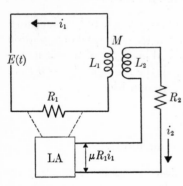

A circuit in which stability questions are not simply solved is shown in Figure 7.10, where there are really two circuits between which no current flows, but which introduce applied voltages to each other. One mechanism for this is the mutual inductance M between the inductors, and the other is the box labeled L.A. for linear amplifier. It takes the voltage across R_1, $R_1 i_1$, amplifies it to $\mu R_1 i_1$, and applies it to the feedback circuit. In the process, it draws no current from the first circuit. The equations of the circuit are

FIG. 7.10

$$L_1 \frac{di_1}{dt} + M \frac{di_2}{dt} + i_1 R_1 + E(t) = 0$$

$$L_2 \frac{di_2}{dt} + M \frac{di_1}{dt} + i_2 R_2 + \mu i_1 R_1 = 0. \tag{7.32}$$

214

Applying Laplace transforms we have

$$(sL_1 + R_1)L[i_1(t)] + MsL[i_2(t)] = -L[E(t)] + L_1i_1(0) + Mi_2(0)$$

$$(\mu R_1 + Ms)L[i_1(t)] + (R_2 + L_2s)L[i_2(t)] = L_2i_2(0) + Mi_1(0).$$

Determination of stability follows from

$$\begin{vmatrix} sL_1 + R_1 & Ms \\ \mu R_1 + Ms & R_2 + L_2s \end{vmatrix}$$

$$= (L_1L_2 - M^2)s^2 + (L_1R_2 + L_2R_1 - \mu MR_1)s + R_1R_2 = 0.$$

We first remark that if $\mu = 0$, i.e., no amplification, then the circuit is clearly dissipative and this argues that $L_1L_2 - M^2 \geq 0$ and, indeed, we must assume on physical grounds that $L_1L_2 - M^2 > 0$. Since $R_1R_2 > 0$, everything depends on the coefficient of s and we see that for sufficiently large amplification μ, unstable operation results.

It is clear that no linear amplifier can remain linear for all values of the applied voltage. It would have some nonlinear characteristic similar to, say, that of a vacuum tube. With this characteristic, $f(i_1R_1)$, in place of μi_1R_1 in (7.32), the system becomes a nonlinear, nonautonomous system. In practice, we might have unstable operation for small i_1R_1 and stable (i.e., dissipative) operation for large i_1R_1. By analogy with autonomous systems we can expect a cancellation effect, resulting in bounded solutions. At best we expect a periodic response to a periodic input $E(t)$. The ideas and techniques which can be brought to this problem are extremely difficult and we attempt no discussion of them.

PROBLEMS

1. Show that the circuit in Figure 7.11 is capable of unstable operation for sufficiently large μ. Show that for all $\mu \geq 0$ the transients of this circuit are non-oscillatory, i.e., real exponential.

2. Discuss the stability of the circuit in Figure 7.12 as a function of the amplification μ.

3. Find all solutions of the circuit shown in Figure 7.13, or at least show that all solutions are pure sinusoidal. (Assume $L_1L_2 > M^2$.)

4. Consider the point masses m_1 and m_2 constrained to move longitudinally by perfect springs of indicated constants. Let x_1 and x_2 be the displacements of

215

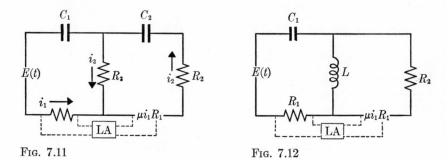

FIG. 7.11   FIG. 7.12

m_1 and m_2 from equilibrium and p_1 and p_2 their momenta. Show that the equations of motion are

$$\frac{dp_1}{dt} = -k_1 x_1 + k_2(x_2 - x_1)$$

$$\frac{dp_2}{dt} = -k_3 x_2 + k_2(x_1 - x_2)$$

$$\frac{dx_1}{dt} = \frac{p_1}{m_1}$$

$$\frac{dx_2}{dt} = \frac{p_2}{m_2}.$$

Show that these can be put in an equivalent form which makes the mechanism the mechanical analogue of the circuit of Figure 7.13.

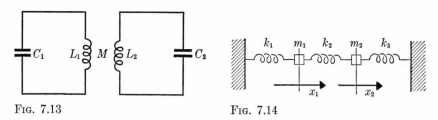

FIG. 7.13   FIG. 7.14

5. Write the equations of the circuit shown in Figure 7.15 so as to show that the circuit is also the electrical analogue of the mechanism in Figure 7.14.

6. For $R_1 > 0$ and $L_1 L_2 - M^2 > 0$, the circuit shown in Figure 7.16 is dissipative (hence stable) on physical grounds. The characteristic polynomial $p(s)$ is of fourth degree,

$$As^4 + Bs^3 + Cs^2 + Ds + E,$$

216

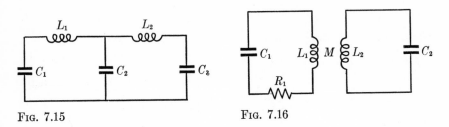

FIG. 7.15   FIG. 7.16

with all positive coefficients. Show that

$$BC > AD$$

and

$$BCD > B^2E - D^2A$$

hold only if $R_1 > 0$. Infer on physical grounds that if all coefficients of a quartic equation are positive, these inequalities are necessary conditions that all roots have negative real parts. Show that if a given quartic has positive coefficients which satisfy the above inequalities, then there are positive circuit constants C_1, C_2, L_1, L_2, M, and R_1 which yield the given polynomial. In other words, give a physical proof that the above inequalities are sufficient conditions that all roots of a quartic equation have negative real parts.

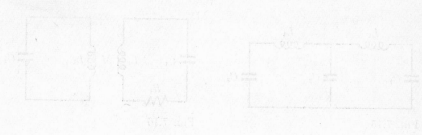

A BRIEF TABLE OF LAPLACE TRANSFORMS

1. $f(x) \equiv x^n e^{\alpha x}$, $L(f(x)) \equiv \dfrac{\Gamma(n+1)}{(s-\alpha)^{n+1}}$

2. $f(x) \equiv e^{\alpha x} \sin \omega x$, $L(f(x)) \equiv \dfrac{\omega}{(s-\alpha)^2 + \omega^2}$

3. $f(x) \equiv e^{\alpha x} \cos \omega x$, $L(f(x)) \equiv \dfrac{s-\alpha}{(s-\alpha)^2 + \omega^2}$

4. $f(x) \equiv x \sin \omega x$, $L(f(x)) \equiv \dfrac{2\omega s}{(s^2 + \omega^2)^2}$

5. $f(x) \equiv x \cos \omega x$, $L(f(x)) \equiv \dfrac{s^2 - \omega^2}{(s^2 + \omega^2)^2}$

6. $f(x) \equiv J_n(x)$, $L(f(x)) \equiv \dfrac{(\sqrt{s^2+1} - s)^n}{\sqrt{s^2+1}}$

7. $f(x) = \dfrac{\sin x}{x}$, $L(f(x)) \equiv \tan^{-1} \dfrac{1}{s}$

8. $f(x) \equiv \begin{cases} 1, & 0 \leq x < c \\ -1, & c \leq x < 2c, \end{cases}$ $L(f(x)) \equiv \dfrac{1}{s} \tanh \left(\dfrac{cs}{2} \right)$

$f(x + 2c) \equiv f(x), \quad -\infty < x < +\infty$

ANSWERS TO PROBLEMS

2. $a = 3$.
4. $n = 2$.
5. $y(x) \equiv 1$, $y(x) \equiv -1$.
6. $y(x) \equiv x^2$.
9. $v(t) \equiv v_0 - g(t - t_0)$.

1. $y(x) \equiv \tan\left(x + \dfrac{\pi}{4}\right).$

2. $y(x) \equiv x - 1$, $x > 0$.
3. $y(x) \equiv 1$.
4. $y(x) \equiv x$, $x > 0$.

5. $y(x) \equiv \dfrac{3 + e^{x^2}}{3 - e^{x^2}}$, $x^2 < \log 3$.

6. $y(x) \equiv -1$.

7. $y(x) \equiv -1$ if $y_0 = -1$.

$$y(x) \equiv -1 + \cfrac{1}{\cfrac{1}{y_0 + 1} + x_0 - x} \quad \text{for} \quad x < x_0 + \frac{1}{y_0 + 1} \quad \text{if} \quad y_0 > -1,$$

$$\text{or for} \quad x_0 > x_0 + \frac{1}{y_0 + 1} \quad \text{if} \quad y_0 < -1.$$

9. Solutions unique for $y_0 \neq 0$, not unique for $y_0 = 0$.
10. $\alpha \geq 1$, all proper problems have unique solutions.
$0 < \alpha < 1$, no uniqueness for $y_0 = 0$.
$\alpha \leq 0$, all proper problems have unique solutions.
11. All problems have unique solutions.
12. All problems have unique solutions.
13. All problems have unique solutions.
14. All problems have unique solutions.
15. $y' = \sqrt{y(1 - y)}$.

PAGE 14

1. $y(x) \equiv e^{x^2/2}$.

2. $y(x) \equiv e^{x^3/3} \displaystyle\int_0^x e^{-t^3/3}\, dt$.

3. $y(x) \equiv \frac{1}{2}(e^{3x - 2x_0} - e^x) + y_0 e^{3(x - x_0)}$.

4. $y(x) \equiv \dfrac{1}{2}\left(x + \dfrac{1}{x}\right), \quad x > 0$.

5. $y(x) = \frac{1}{2}e^{-x} + \frac{1}{2}(\cos x + \sin x)$.
6. $y(x) = \frac{1}{2}e^{x - x_0}(\cos x_0 - \sin x_0) + \frac{1}{2}(\sin x - \cos x)$.

7. $y(x) = \dfrac{2}{9}e^x + \dfrac{x}{3}e^x - \dfrac{13}{18}e^{-2x} + \dfrac{1}{2}$.

8. $\frac{1}{2}(\sin x - \cos x)$.

9. $\dfrac{e^{ax} - e^x}{a - 1}, \quad xe^x, \quad y' - y = e^x$.

PAGE 15

2. $-(\frac{1}{2}x^3 + \frac{3}{4}x^2 + \frac{5}{4}x + \frac{5}{8})$.
3. (Assume $a_2 \neq 0$), degree one if $a = -k$, degree two if $a \neq -k$.
4. $-(x^2 + 2x + 2)e^x$.
5. $\frac{1}{2}x^2 e^{-x}$.
6. $Q_m(x)e^{kx}$, where $Q_m(x)$ is a polynomial of degree m and $m = n$ if $a \neq -k$ and $m = n - 1$ if $a = -k$.

222

7. $\frac{1}{2}e^x$, xe^{-x}, $\frac{1}{2}e^x - xe^{-x}$.

9. $\frac{1}{4}(\cos 2x + \sin 2x)$.

10. $e^x(\frac{1}{2}x^2 - \cos x)$.

11. $e^{kx}[Q_n(x)\cos \omega x + R_n(x)\sin \omega x]$, where $Q_n(x)$ and $R_n(x)$ are polynomials of degree n.

12. $\dfrac{x}{17}(4\sin x - \cos x) + \dfrac{1}{289}(8\cos x - 15\sin x)$

$\quad + \dfrac{e^x}{13}\left[\dfrac{x^2}{2}(5\cos x + \sin x) - \dfrac{x}{13}(12\cos x + 5\sin x)\right.$

$\quad \left. - \dfrac{1}{26}(55\cos x + 37\sin x)\right].$

PAGE 19

2. $y_0(x) \equiv x^2 - x$.

5. $y(x) \equiv y_1(o) + \dfrac{1}{e^{-4\pi} - 1}\, e^{-2x}$ has the property that $y(o) = y(2\pi)$.

PAGE 24

1. $y(x) = 2(e^{-x} + x - 1)$.

2. $y(x) \equiv x + 1$, $u(x) \equiv 1$.

3. $y(x) \equiv 2xe^x$.

4. $y(x) \equiv \cosh x$, $u(x) \equiv \sinh x$.

5. $y(x) \equiv \frac{6}{5}e^x - \frac{1}{5}e^{-2x/3}$, $u(x) \equiv e^{-2x/3}$.

6. $\dfrac{1}{s(s+2)}(1 - e^{-s})$.

PAGE 29

1. Exact, $e^x \cos y - x = c$.

2. Exact, $2xy - \dfrac{1}{xy} = c$.

3. Not exact, rearrange into $\left(\tan^{-1}\dfrac{y}{x}\right)dx + d\left(\tan^{-1}\left(\dfrac{y}{x}\right)\right) = 0$.

4. Not exact, integrating factor $\dfrac{1}{x^2}$, whence $\dfrac{x^2}{2} + \dfrac{y}{x} + \dfrac{y^2}{2} = c$.

5. Not exact, rearrange to $y\,dx - x\,dy - xy\,dy = 0$,

then $\dfrac{y\,dx - x\,dy}{x^2} - \dfrac{y}{x}\,dy = d\left(\dfrac{y}{x}\right) - \left(\dfrac{y}{x}\right)dx = 0$.

Also, integrating factor: $\dfrac{1}{xy}$.

223

ANSWERS TO PROBLEMS

PAGE 31

2. $u' = \dfrac{1}{x}(f(x)g(ux) - u), \quad y' = \dfrac{1}{x}(f(x)g(xy) - y)$

3. $\dfrac{x^2}{2} + xy - \dfrac{y^2}{2} = c.$

4. $u' = xe^x.$

7. $u = y^{1-n}.$

8. (1.64) becomes $v' - xv = 1$ under $u = \dfrac{1}{v}.$

9. Any equation of the form $x^2 y' + 2xy = f(x)g(x^2y).$

PAGE 35

3. $\dfrac{dv}{du} + v = 0.$

4. $\dfrac{du}{dv} = \dfrac{u + v}{u - v}.$

6. $\dfrac{dy}{dx} = f(x, y), \quad$ where $\quad -f(-x, y) \equiv f(x, y).$

PAGE 42

7. $e^{x^2/2} \displaystyle\int_0^x e^{-t^2/2}\, dt - e^{x^2/2} \int_0^\infty e^{-t^2/2}\, dt \equiv -e^{x^2/2} \int_x^\infty e^{-t^2/2}\, dt$
is bounded.

PAGE 56

2. $M = 2, \quad K = 2, \quad \alpha = \frac{1}{2}, \quad \beta = -\frac{1}{2}.$

3. $y_n(x) \equiv a_n x^{p_n},$ where $\quad p_n = \dfrac{2^n - 1}{2^{n-1}} \quad$ and $\quad a_n = \dfrac{1}{p_n}\sqrt{a_{n-1}};$

$\lim\limits_{n\to\infty} p_n = 2 \quad$ and $\quad \lim\limits_{n\to\infty} a_n = \frac{1}{4} \quad$ follow.

4. $y_n(x) \equiv (-1)^n \dfrac{x^2}{4}.$

PAGE 69

1. $a_{2n} = \dfrac{1}{2^n n!}, \quad a_{2n+1} = 0; \quad r_0 = +\infty.$

2. $a_0 = 1, \quad a_n = \left((-1)^{n+1} \dfrac{1 \cdot 3 \cdot 5 \cdots (2n - 1)}{n!}\right), \quad n > 0; \quad r_0 = \dfrac{1}{2}.$

3. $a_0 = 1, \quad a_n = \dfrac{1 \cdot 3 \cdot 5 \cdots (2n - 1)}{n!}, \quad n > 0; \quad r_0 = \dfrac{1}{2}.$

224

4. $a_0 = 0$, $a_n = (-1)^{n+1}$, $n > 0$; $r_0 = 1$.

5. $a_0 = 0$, $a_{2n+1} = 0$, $a_{2n} = \dfrac{(-1)^n \, 1 \cdot 3 \cdot 5 \, \cdots \, (2n - 3)}{n! \, 2^n}$; $r_0 = 1$.

6. $a_0 = 1$, $a_n = (-1)^n (2^n + 2^{n-1})$, $r_0 = \frac{1}{2}$.

7. Majorant solution: $y(x) \equiv x + x^2 + x^3 + \cdots$.

8. A majorant equation is $y' = (y + 1)^3$, for which $r_0 = \frac{1}{2}$.

13. 12, since $1 - \dfrac{1}{e} > \log\left(\dfrac{3}{2}\right)$.

PAGE 76

2. $y_n = (1 + h)^n$.

3. $M = K = 2$, $\alpha = \frac{1}{2}$; in (2.53) we may assume $\epsilon = h$, hence
$$|y_n(x) - y(x)| \leq h(e - 1) \quad \text{for} \quad |x| \leq \frac{1}{2}.$$

PAGE 79

1. $x^2 + 2y^2 = c$.

2. $\dfrac{x^2}{1 - c^2} - \dfrac{y^2}{c^2} = 1$.

3. $y(x) \equiv \dfrac{c}{x}$.

4. Equation of trajectories (with $m = \tan\theta$): $y' = \dfrac{x + my}{mx - y}$;
Solutions: $x^2 + y^2 = ce^{m \tan^{-1}(y/x)}$.

7. $u(s) = e^{s^3/3} \displaystyle\int_s^\infty t e^{-t^3/3} \, dt$.

PAGE 84

1. $m(t) = m_0 2^{-t}$, t in years.

2. $m(t) = m_0 2^{t/5}$, t in hours.

3. $n(t) = n_0 e^{-k_2 t} + \dfrac{m_0 k_1}{k_1 + k_2} \left(e^{-k_2 t} - e^{-k_1 t}\right)$.

PAGE 92

1. $y(x) = \begin{cases} e^{x-1}, & x \geq 0 \\ e^{-x-1}, & x \leq 0. \end{cases}$

3.
$$ec(t) = \begin{cases} k_1 e^{-t/RC}, & t < 0 \\ (k_1 + RC)e^{-t/RC} + t - RC, & 0 \leq t \leq 1 \\ [(k_1 + RC)e^{-1/RC} + 1 - RC]e^{-t/RC}, & t > 1. \end{cases}$$

225

4. $ec(t) = \dfrac{e^{-t}}{1 - e^{-1}} + t - 1 \equiv g(t), \quad 0 \le t \le 1.$

$ec(t) \equiv g(t - n), \quad n \le t \le n + 1.$

PAGE 105

4. $y''' = 2y' + y.$

5. (a) $\dfrac{dx}{dt} = \dfrac{p}{m}$ (b) $\dfrac{dx_i}{dt} = \dfrac{p_i}{m_i}, \quad i = 1, 2$

$\dfrac{dp}{dt} = F(x, p, t).$ $\dfrac{dp_i}{dt} = F_i(x_1, x_2, p_1, p_2, t), \quad i = 1, 2$

6. $y(x) \equiv c_1 e^x + c_2 e^{-x}, \quad v(x) \equiv c_1 e^x - c_2 e^{-x}.$
7. $(y(x), u(x)) \equiv (c_1 e^{2x} + c_2 e^x, \quad c_2 e^x)$
$(y(x), v(x)) \equiv (c_1 e^{2x} + c_2 e^x, \quad 2c_1 e^{2x} + c_2 e^x).$
8. $y(x) \equiv e^t.$

PAGE 111

1. $(y(x), v(x) \equiv (e^x, e^x).$
2. $(y(x), v(x)) \equiv (\cos \sqrt{2}x, \; -\sqrt{2} \sin \sqrt{2}x).$
3. $(y(x), v(x)) \equiv (2e^{3t}, e^{3t}).$
4. $y(x) \equiv e^{-x}.$
5. $(y(x), v(x)) \equiv (-xe^x, \; e^x - xe^x).$
7. $y(x) \equiv y_0 \cos (x - x_0) + v_0 \sin (x - x_0).$
8. $(y(x)_1 v(x)_1 w(x)) \equiv (e^x, e^x, e^x).$
9. $y'' - 2y = 0.$
10. $y(x) \equiv \tan x.$
12. $xe^x.$

PAGE 118

1. $(y(x), v(x)) \equiv (e^x - 2xe^x, \; -e^x - 2xe^x).$
2. $y(x) \equiv e^x - 1.$
3. $y(x) \equiv \tan x.$
4. $y(x) \equiv \frac{1}{2}(\sinh x - 1).$

5. $y(x) \equiv 2 \log \left(\sec \dfrac{x}{\sqrt{2}} \right).$

7. $y^2 - v^2 = c.$

8. $v^2 + \dfrac{y^4}{2} = c^2.$

9. $v^2 - 2 \cos y = c.$
10. $y^2 + v^2 = ce^{\tan^{-1} (v/y)}.$

226

PAGE 124

1. $y(x) \equiv -e^{-2(x-1)} + e^{-(x-1)}$.

2. $y(x) \equiv e^{x/2}\left[\cos\dfrac{\sqrt{3}}{2}x - \dfrac{1}{\sqrt{3}}\sin\dfrac{\sqrt{3}}{2}x\right]$.

3. $y(x) \equiv (4x - 7)e^{-2(x-2)}$.

4. $y(x) = \dfrac{1}{3}\left[1 - e^{-3x/2}\left(\cos\dfrac{\sqrt{3}}{2}x + \sqrt{3}\sin\dfrac{\sqrt{3}}{2}x\right)\right]$.

5. $u = y + x + \tfrac{3}{2}$.

8. $L(y(x)) = \dfrac{11}{40}\left(\dfrac{1}{s-3}\right) - \dfrac{3}{8}\left(\dfrac{1}{s+1}\right) + \dfrac{\frac{1}{10}s - \frac{1}{5}}{s^2+1}$.

9. $L(\dot{y}(x)) = \dfrac{2}{9}\left(\dfrac{1}{s-1}\right) + \dfrac{1}{3}\left(\dfrac{1}{(s-1)^2}\right) - \dfrac{2}{9}\left(\dfrac{1}{s+2}\right)$.

10. $L(y(s)) = \dfrac{1}{(s+1)^3}$.

14. $b = \dfrac{1}{4}\left(1 + \dfrac{n^2\pi^2}{L^2}\right), \quad n = 1, 2, \cdots$.

PAGE 130

4. (a) $\sin x$ and $\sin(x + c)$, $c \neq n\pi$ are independent solutions of $y'' + y = 0$.

(b) e^x and e^{x+c} are dependent solutions of $y'' - y = 0$.

5. When $y(x)$ is not a pure exponential, e^{rx}.

10. $y(x) \equiv (2x^2 - 1)\displaystyle\int_{x_0}^{x}\dfrac{e^{t^3}}{(2t^2-1)^2}\,dt$.

11. $y(x) \equiv x\displaystyle\int_{x_0}^{x}\dfrac{e^{-t}}{t^2}\,dt, \quad \lim_{x\to 0}y(x) = -1$.

12. $y(x) \equiv x\log x$.

PAGE 137

1. $y(x) \equiv -\dfrac{x}{4} - \dfrac{7}{16} - \dfrac{9}{80}e^{-4(x-1)} + \dfrac{4}{5}e^{(x-1)}$.

2. $y(x) \equiv \dfrac{x}{2}\sinh x$.

3. $y(x) \equiv c_1\cos x + c_2\sin x - \cos x \ln(\sec x - \tan x)$.

227

5. (a) Independent solution: $y(x) = \dfrac{1}{\sqrt{x}} \cos x$.

(b) General solution: $\dfrac{1}{\sqrt{x}} (c_1 \sin x + c_2 \cos x + 1)$.

6. (b) None if $a = 0$ and $b = \omega^2$; otherwise,

$$y(x) \equiv \frac{1}{(b - \omega^2)^2 + a^2\omega^2} [a\omega \sin \omega t + (b - \omega^2) \cos \omega t].$$

PAGE 146

1. $y(x) = -\dfrac{1}{3} e^{-x} - \dfrac{2}{3} e^{x/2} \cos \dfrac{\sqrt{3}}{2} x + 1.$

2. One form is generated by $v(x) \equiv c_1 e^x + c_2 e^x + c_3 x^2 e^x$;
   $w(x) \equiv v'(x)$ and $y(x) \equiv w'(x) + 2v(x) - 3w(x)$.

3. Generate solution from

$$v(x) \equiv c_1 e^x + c_2 e^{(-1/2 + \sqrt{5}/2)x} + c_3 e^{(-1/2 - \sqrt{5}/2)x}.$$

4. $y(x) \equiv \frac{1}{2}(\sinh x - \sin t).$

5. $y(x) \equiv \frac{1}{2}(\cos x - \sin x).$

7. $y(0) = y'(0) = y''(0) = y'''(0) = 0.$

PAGE 151

2. $y(x) \equiv x + \displaystyle\sum_{n=1}^{\infty} \frac{x^{4n+1}}{4 \cdot 5 \cdot 8 \cdot 9 \cdots (4n)(4n + 1)}.$

3. $y(0) = 1, \quad y'(0) = 0; \quad y(x) \equiv 1 + \displaystyle\sum_{n=1}^{\infty} \frac{x^{4n}}{3 \cdot 4 \cdot 7 \cdot 8 \cdots (4n - 1)4n}.$

5. $x^\alpha \cos \beta \log x, \quad x^\alpha \sin \beta \log x.$

PAGE 157

5. $b_{2n} = \dfrac{(-1)^{n+1}}{2^{2n}(n!)^2} \left(1 + \dfrac{1}{2} + \dfrac{1}{3} + \cdots + \dfrac{1}{n}\right).$

8. $c_1 \displaystyle\sum_{n=0}^{\infty} \frac{(-1)^n}{(2n + 1)!} x^{-2n} + c_2 \displaystyle\sum_{n=0}^{\infty} \frac{(-1)^n}{(2n)!} x^{-2n+1}$

$\equiv c_1 x \sin \dfrac{1}{x} + c_2 x \cos \dfrac{1}{x}.$

PAGE 178

2. At $(y, v) = \left(\dfrac{\pi}{6} + 2n\pi, 0\right), \quad n = 0, \pm 1, \cdots$ linearized system is

$u' = w$

$$w' = -\frac{\sqrt{3}}{2}\,u;$$

at $(y, v) = \left(\frac{5\pi}{6} + 2n\pi, 0\right)$, $\quad n = 0, \pm1, \cdots$, linearized system is

$$u' = w$$

$$w' = \frac{\sqrt{3}}{2}\,u.$$

3.   (*i*) $a_{22}^{2} + 4a_{21} < 0,$
    (*ii*) $a_{21} > 0$
    (*iii*) $a_{22}^{2} + 4a_{21} > 0,$ $a_{21} < 0,$ $a_{22} < 0$
    (*iv*) $a_{22}^{2} + 4a_{21} > 0,$ $a_{21} < 0,$ $a_{22} > 0.$

13. At $(n\pi, m\pi) = (y, v)$
    $u' = (-1)^{n}w$
    $w' = (-1)^{m+1}u$
    vortex if $n + m$ is even, saddle if $n + m$ is odd.

14. $y' = v$
    $v' = -y - v.$

15. $y' = v$
    $v' = -y - 2v.$

PAGE 200

5.
$$y(t) \equiv \begin{cases} -\dfrac{1}{2\sinh\pi}\,e^{-t}\sin t, & 0 \le t \le \pi \\[2ex] \dfrac{e^{2\pi}}{2\sinh\pi}\,e^{-t}\sin(t - \pi), & \pi \le t \le 2\pi \end{cases}$$

REFERENCES

1. Coddington, E., and N. Levinson, *Theory of Ordinary Differential Equations* (New York: McGraw-Hill Book Co., 1955).
2. Cogan, E. J., and R. Z. Norman, *Handbook of Calculus, Difference and Differential Equations* (Englewood Cliffs, N. J.: Prentice-Hall, Inc., 1958).
3. Ford, L. R., *Differential Equations,* Second Edition (New York: McGraw-Hill Book Co., 1955).
4. Hurewicz, W., *Lectures on Ordinary Differential Equations* (Cambridge, Mass.: Technology Press of the Massachusetts Institute of Technology, 1958).
5. Kamke, E., *Differentialgleichungen, Lösungmethoden und Lösungen,* Vol. I (Leipzig: Akademische Verlagsgesellschaft, 1943).
6. Kaplan, W., *Ordinary Differential Equations* (Reading, Mass.: Addison-Wesley Publ. Co., Inc., 1958).
7. Leighton, W., *Introduction to the Theory of Differential Equations* (New York: McGraw-Hill Book Co., 1952).
8. Levinson, N., and O. K. Smith, "A General Equation for Relaxation Oscillations," *Duke Mathematical Journal,* Vol. 9, pp. 382–403, 1942.

231

REFERENCES

9. Milne, W. E., *Numerical Solution of Differential Equations* (New York: John Wiley & Sons, Inc., 1953).
10. Minorsky, N., *Introduction to Non-linear Mechanics* (Ann Arbor, Michigan: J. W. Edwards, Publ., Inc., 1947).
11. Murphy, G. M., *Ordinary Differential Equations and Their Solutions* (Princeton, N. J.: D. Van Nostrand Co., Inc., 1960).
12. Nemytskii, V. V., and V. V. Stepanov, *Qualitative Theory of Differential Equations* (Princeton, N. J.: Princeton Univ. Press, 1960).

232

INDEX